THE ROAD FROM CASTLEBARNAGH

THE ROAD FROM CASTLEBARNAGH

Growing Up in Irish Music, a Memoir

Paddy O'Brien

To Patty. With warm wishes,
Sláinte! Paddy O'Brien.

ORPEN PRESS

Published by
Orpen Press
Lonsdale House
Avoca Avenue
Blackrock
Co. Dublin
Ireland

e-mail: info@orpenpress.com
www.orpenpress.com

Paperback ISBN: 978-1-871305-69-2
ePub ISBN: 978-1-871305-92-0
Kindle ISBN: 978-1-871305-93-7

Printed and bound by CPI Group (UK) Ltd, Croydon, CR0 4YY

This book is dedicated to the memory of my parents, Christy and Molly O'Brien; to my sisters, Moira, Ann, Kathleen and Patricia; and to my wife, Erin.

Foreword

I've known Paddy O'Brien for many years and have known his music for even longer. He and I have spent many evenings in one other's company both playing music and talking 'til the small hours. Paddy is one of those rare musicians who love to talk about music almost as much as they like to play it. The philosophy, the history and the poetry of the music are second nature to him. Paddy has been a tremendous influence in my own musical life.

Paddy's life has been rich with musical experience and filled with a wealth of stories, memories and anecdotes that inform his musical vision. Coming of age as an Irish traditional musician as he did, in the last half of the twentieth century, has helped to give Paddy a clear and visceral understanding of our musical culture. He reveals a great depth of insight into the wisdom of folk culture and into the richness of a way of life that to some may have seemed ordinary or common-place. The characters he has come to know along the way and the insights gained have all made their way into his music and now into this book.

In this first book by Paddy, we are welcomed into his childhood life and mind in an engaging and entertaining manner. Music weaves its way all through the story, of course, and sheds light on a bygone way of life, but this story also details how the way of life at that time informed the music as well. Paddy is a great storyteller who knows his characters well; this book is full of the natural wit and humour that surrounded him and suffused his early years. He is passionate and poetic in his efforts to grasp the essential nature of the music, and of the many people who drew him in and nurtured his spirit as a young musician. Those kindnesses have never been forgotten and, throughout his musical career, Paddy has tried to honour the memory of those early influences by offering wisdom and encouragement to many younger players, myself among them, I am happy to say. May you find musical inspiration in these pages as well.

Martin Hayes

Preface

Three years ago, the idea of writing a memoir had never even entered my consciousness. Up to then, I suppose I looked upon authors as the possessors of a special kind of talent, a different class of people altogether. I had never considered chancing my arm at something like this, even though from time to time, some friend would say to me, 'Paddy, you have great stories. You should write a book.'

As a musician performing onstage, I had developed a fondness for telling stories about tunes and tune titles – I'm fascinated by the history and the lore that goes with the music. I think it was a fellow performer, Peter Yeates from Dublin (now living in Portland, Oregon), who was the first person to say to me, 'I know you have it in you, so when are you going to write a book?' Somehow, Peter's voice stayed in my memory, and it seemed that the longer I was living in the States (thirty-four years now), the more old memories of home began to emerge. Of course my father was a very good storyteller and had a large store of fireside material, as had many of the neighbours who rambled past our home during the 1950s and early 1960s. As a child, I would sit quietly in a corner beside our turf fire and listen for hours to the music and the chat with my sister Moira, never realising how much information we were absorbing.

I entered the world in 1945, the middle of the twentieth century, but my family's way of life had not changed substantially for more than a hundred years. The house where I was born was an old thatched cottage with no running water or electricity. The area around our house is still known as Castlebarnagh, which is a small townland near Daingean in northeast County Offaly, in the midlands of Ireland.

My childhood days were spent working around our farm and going to school, cutting turf and thatching the house with my father. I grew up immersed in Irish rural culture – storytelling, music and house dances that traced a long line back into the past, with characters, customs and ways of life now long gone. The characters who people these pages are my parents and sisters, friends and neighbours, schoolmates, fellow musicians, workmates – all ordinary folk from the Irish countryside, who worked and played and squabbled and endeavoured to keep themselves and their families afloat in hard times.

When money was scarce, as it always seemed to be when I was young, people had to entertain themselves with local stories and conversation with visiting friends and ramblers. Our house had its share of people who stopped in for a chat or a cup of tea, and I was raised on stories – of hard work and ruined harvests, of Gaelic sports, little people, ghost stories and hauntings. I began building up my own repertoire of stories as well: about the time my father got our first wireless, and when my mother bought my first musical instrument – a mouth organ – from a travelling peddler.

Three years ago, I started to experiment – writing down a few sentences, just to see what would happen, mainly to see if I could actually do it. Two hours later, I had written thirty pages, and as I continued, I noticed that the stories were pouring out of me. What had begun as an experiment became an obsession, and an experience like none other I've had. And on a regular diet of history and crime novels, I started to become more aware of the actual work of writing – I became particularly interested in word choices, fascinated by how writers were able to paint a whole world through descriptive language and dialogue, how they could actually shape a story.

So I continued writing as more stories came to mind from a time in Ireland when we lived without plumbing, running water, electricity or even a radio. Those were poor times, but I remember them better for all the happiness and enjoyment and all the local characters who are now scattered or gone to their happy rewards. All of them were part of our country landscape in the area around Castlebarnagh, Killoneen and Daingean in northeast County Offaly. I hope my book does them some measure of homage to their historical contribution to the 'Faithful County' of Offaly.

Writing down these memories was almost like getting to know my parents and younger sisters all over again, from a time when we were all so young and seemingly more innocent. All the characters of my childhood were suddenly alive again, and despite all the hardship, the easy social give-and-take of that time still envelops me like a warm handshake.

I also found that through and against all the stories of daily life runs the strong counter-melody of an awakening creative consciousness, a slow recognition of the one vital imperative in my life: playing Irish traditional music. The realisation of that imperative overtook me as a young child, so these are also the recollections of a young musician who had to learn tunes by ear from listening to the wireless – in those days my only source of inspiration. Without the aid of a tape recorder, my struggle to get to the heart of the music was an arduous journey, one of constant challenge and soul-grinding frustration.

And yet all of these things shaped me, the music and the stories by the fire, the hardships and the laughter. These stories are the reason you might hear the rasp of the corncrake or the howling curses of our neighbour Mick Hayes in the way I play a reel, or feel the cold wind blowing across the bog in the mournful melody of a slow air.

Paddy O'Brien

Acknowledgements

For their generous assistance during the writing of this book, I owe great thanks to Dan Donnelly, Tom and Juliet Clancy, Mary Bergin, Dáithí Sproule, Hughie Ryan, Alan and Conor O'Brien, Ethna McKiernan and Martin Hayes.

Table of Contents

The Visitor

One of my earliest memories is of a neighbour calling by our house and being invited in for a cup of tea. Inside, he sat in front of our open turf fire. As it turned out, he was a musician, and played a little on a new Hohner Black Dot accordion. He didn't have it with him, because it was early evening, and he was on his way home from work. As he was drinking the tea the conversation turned to songs that my father and mother sang and other songs that were being aired on Radio Éireann. He knew some of them, and sang one called 'Mockingbird Hill'. Shortly after that, he looked over towards me, to where I was sitting in a corner with my sister Moira. He said, 'Does Paddy sing?' and 'What about a little song?'

I was seven years old, my sister a year younger, and we were extremely shy. We usually said nothing when visitors called for a chat with my mother and father. As I was being pressed, my mother insisted that I should sing 'The Pub with No Beer'. Hearing this was like a hammer blow; I had often sung the song, but embarrassment overcame me and I quickly looked around, trying to find a hiding place.

It was as if the whole kitchen was saying, 'Come on, Paddy, give us a song.' I jumped up, ran across the kitchen floor and dived under the dinner table with its oilcloth cover hanging low. My sister came right after me and together we huddled beneath the table, sitting on one of its crossbeams. I still remember how uncomfortable it was, with the table timber pressing into our behinds, but we were two innocent children who were intimidated by any attention from outsiders. Our songs were part of our private world, for when we walked through fields or went picking daisies or cowslips. Finally, when the pleading for a song subsided everyone began to laugh, with my father saying, 'You'd want to hear him sing when there's no one here!'

At that time, our family lived in a townland called Castlebarnagh, which is outside Daingean in County Offaly. We had a small thatched house with two bedrooms and a kitchen. It had no electricity and no running water. We had to fetch all our water from a neighbour's well, a half-mile away. There was an extra room, with a tiled roof, attached to the back of our house, but it was too cold to sleep there during the winter.

One day when my sister and I were visiting our Aunt Mary in Daingean we heard her new radio for the first time and were amazed. My father was with us, and I remember my aunt saying to him, 'Christy, you should get one. There's mighty music on it on Monday nights, and it would be great for the kids. There's a programme called *Take the Floor*, and an auld fella on it, and he's a fierce jokester.'

'I've never heard of him,' said my father. 'What's his name?'

'His name is Din Joe, and he's a Corkman!' my aunt replied with a mischievous grin.

Of course, my father didn't care where Din Joe came from as long as he could tell a good joke. My sister and I were sitting on a small couch, sipping tea with a biscuit and listening to the conversation, and even then we had a curious feeling that our home in Castlebarnagh would soon have a radio.

It was about six or seven months later, during the winter of 1955, when Cavendish's delivery van arrived at our gate with a mahogany-coloured radio. I remember it as a very exciting evening for all the family. When tuning in to the various stations, our parents' first reaction was to stand back a little – 'just in case'.

'Just in case of what?' Aunt Mary shouted. She had come on a small visit a week later because my mother was unsure of where to tune in for *Take the Floor*.

'Just in case of what?' she shouted again. My father stood biting his lip as he did when he was stuck for words. 'It's not goin' to bite you!' my aunt continued, 'It's harmless.'

Then my mother cut in. 'Paddy thought he saw somethin' movin' inside of it.'

Aunt Mary laughed. 'Ho, ho, ho,' she roared. 'Don't let anyone outside ever hear a word of this. If the neighbours hear about ye, it'll be away to the quare place in a straitjacket for ye.'

In the end, it was all figured out and my mother became used to turning the couple of knobs to find her favourite programmes, especially dramatised radio plays, which were often aired on Sunday nights.

I remember one particular play, which was called *Murder in the Red Barn*. The play was advertised on radio throughout the week leading up to its presentation, which was the following Sunday evening at 8.00 p.m. When the time came the announcer told listeners to turn up the radio a little and to turn down our lights at home and make ourselves comfortable. My mother wasted no time in turning down our oil lamp and so we all listened in silence. A half-minute went by in almost total darkness except for the small turf fire on the hearth. All of a sudden an ear-piercing scream came from a woman's voice right out of the radio speaker. We all jumped in our chairs and I could feel myself trembling.

'Jesus Christ!' said my father.

'Holy Mother of God!' cried my mother, and then the play began in earnest.

Our radio was not the most constant of country luxuries because we didn't have electricity and so we had to recharge the radio battery every so often. In the beginning a recharged battery would last two weeks, but after about six months it would only last a week. Many people used radio batteries at that time, which meant that the local garage mechanic was inundated with requests to recharge them. As a result, lots of people (including ourselves) had to wait a week or more for their batteries to be ready, a huge inconvenience that caused us to miss many of our favourite programmes.

My love of the radio was especially inspired by the 5.30 p.m. children's programme that encouraged us to sketch and paint pictures of rural landscapes with crayons or watercolours. These suggestions were explained to us by Marion King, the presenter of the programme, who also read out the names of children who had won prizes. I had already begun to sketch and paint when I was seven years old, and felt very enthusiastic as I listened to Marion. My parents were very encouraging, as were many people who often rambled to our home. As a child, I felt extremely pleased about being referred to as an artist, and when I began to paint copies of holy pictures that hung on the kitchen wall some people saw it as the first step towards the priesthood. I could hear them say, 'Paddy is different from the rest of them around here,' or 'He has the face of a little saint.'

My mother noticed one of my paintings and said, 'We should send it to Marion King and maybe win a prize.' She posted it to Radio Éireann, and two weeks later my name was read out on the radio along with the names of other children who had also won prizes. My mother, who was getting ready to go shopping in Daingean when she heard my name read out, was excited and said we should celebrate when my father came home.

When she returned from the shopping trip she had two large bottles of lemonade. After supper we sat around the kitchen and drank some of it out of tea cups and mugs. My father drank from a bottle of porter and when he was halfway into it he raised the bottle and said, 'Here's to Paddy.' It was a toast to my name being read out on radio, and although I didn't understand what it meant, at the same time I felt he was proud of me. It also occurred to me that the black stuff called porter was a powerful drink and privately I liked the idea of trying it out. After all, it could be said that its effect was a good one, since it turned my father into a man filled with words of love and kindness.

In 1956 I was a nine-year-old country gossoon who played cowboys and Indians with my schoolmates. We were filled with ideas about good lads and bad lads as we ran around farmyards, ducking in and out of doorways, hiding behind haystacks or luring our friends, the bad lads, into amateur 'ambushes'. It was a great time in our lives but beneath it all were the sounds or portions of tunes that came and went, back and forth in my head. Small phrases of céilí tunes were teasing my memory and a very strong soulful feeling was beating in my chest. It was a long time before I understood it or could even speak of it. I also noticed that certain parts of tunes would remain in my head, especially if the tune had a name. From listening to the radio, I heard the name of a reel, 'The Boys of Ballisodare', and I became intrigued by where in God's name was this Ballisodare. My parents began to realise that I was very caught up with music when they heard me lilting and humming waltzes or parts of jigs, reels and well-known patriotic songs.

Late one Sunday night, a frosty night in December, my father returned from his usual few drinks in Watt Nolan's pub in Daingean. He had met a local lad there whose name was Joe Byrne, and Joe was 'well on it', as we used to say when a fellow had drunk too much. My father was a great believer in strong tea as a way to sober a man up, and because Joe's home was a mile past our house, he decided to accompany Joe and walk home with their bicycles.

When they arrived at our gate my father invited Joe inside and the kettle was quickly put over the fire and a couple of sandwiches made. Shortly after the tea, my father said, 'Joe, I heard you bought a new accordion.' Joe bowed his head a number of times.

My father spoke again. 'Joe, why don't you bring it in – it's not good for it to be outside in the cold.'

'Aww,' said Joe, 'it'll be all right.'

'Ah c'mon,' said my mother, 'we all love music here, especially Paddy – he eats and sleeps music.'

Finally, Joe went out to his bicycle, and when he returned he was carrying a small mesh shopping sack that contained his accordion. Sitting on his chair he bent down and took the accordion out of the sack. When he straightened up he put its shoulder straps on. I was watching all of this in quiet astonishment and when I saw the accordion – the very first musical instrument I had ever set eyes on – I became transfixed. Its sound was pure magic and the colour of its bellows was a warm pink, and I loved how Joe pulled it in and out as he played 'The Old Bog Road'. There were two rows of buttons on its right side, and two small rows of four buttons each on its left side. As I looked on I saw that Joe's short, fat fingers were pressing buttons on the middle part of the keyboard. I was so captivated that I immediately knew that I had to have an accordion, come hell or high water! Soon after, Joe went home and I went to bed, but the sight and sound of this little music box kept me awake for a long time.

A week later Joe's brother Tom came to visit. This time he had his accordion with him. He was the same fellow who had asked me to sing a song before I ran with my sister and hid under the table. To my relief, however, there was no mention of any songs. So after he had some tea, Tom played a few jigs, reels and waltzes. I can still remember their names, which were revealed to me in later years – reels like 'The Maid Behind the Bar', 'The Old High Reel' and 'The First House in Connacht'. A few jigs that come to mind were 'Gallagher's Frolics' and 'Saddle the Pony'. I was struck by Tom's fingers as he played because he would include a button on the inside row from time to time. He didn't know, and neither did I, that this is how a player accommodates the inclusion of a sharp or flat note.

Of course the radio was proving to be a big influence on me, particularly the popular *Take the Floor*, and *Céilí House*. On Sunday afternoons we tuned in at 2.30 for a half-hour programme of various céilí bands playing a variety of selections before the Gaelic games commentaries began. This was a wonderful prelude to the various matches that were broadcast live by the great Mícheál Ó hEithir. It's still true that radio stimulates the imagination with its many gifted personalities whom we grow to either love or hate. But no one had such a profound effect on the Gaelic sports world as the high and exciting voice of Mícheál Ó hEithir. His commentaries on the wonderful hurling clashes of the 1950s between Wexford, Cork, Kilkenny and Tipperary lifted people and spirited our imaginations to a point of delirious ecstasy that cannot be repeated in the world of today's mass media.

Hurling maestros like Cork's Christy Ring, the Rackard brothers of Wexford, Joe Salmon of Galway and Jimmy Smyth of Clare were names introduced by Mícheál, and his exciting descriptions of tussles in front of the goalmouth are still alive in my memory. When the ball landed in the square just in front of the goal line he would shout, 'There's a terrific shemozzle in the parallelogram!' or 'It's a goal! It's a goal!' It was a sound that shook our radio on summer Sundays as my father, with right ear between his head and the radio speaker, kept shouting a fusillade of *whishts*. 'Whisht! Whisht! Whisht!' he would hiss, as gushes of soluble air blew from his mouth. It was his way of preventing interruptions. On one occasion, our kettle came to boiling point and began whistling and my father, taken by surprise, found himself shouting at it.

Mícheál Ó hEithir was at his best during a do-or-die game. His wit and humour and lively descriptions set the scene. The colours of the teams, the referee, the wonderful Artane Boys' Band from Dublin, and the names of the fifteen players on each team – he brought it all into our humble country homes, and we loved him for it.

Hairpins and Combs

It was early spring in 1953 when I was sent outside in search of sticks – or 'firan', as my father would say. This was firewood that had to be gathered and brought home to our kitchen to dry by the fire. Much of it was small twigs, which were very useful for kindling and of enormous help in starting a fire. It was usually my job to keep my father supplied with enough of this 'firan' and any neglect of my duty meant an uncomfortable scolding.

One afternoon when returning with an armful of kindling I spotted a black donkey and cart outside our gate. The cart had no sideboards. A sackful of something lay near its tail-end, and several implements for farm work lay on the floor of the cart – pitchforks, spades, shovels and iron picks with their separate handles made of fresh ash. The man in charge was tying his donkey to our iron gate beside the road. Going back behind his cart, he unloaded a sackful of curios and hoisted it onto his shoulder. As I neared the door of our house I saw that he had beaten me to it and was already talking to my mother.

'Well, Jim,' she said, 'come in, and let's see what you have.'

I followed him inside and put my own load in the corner by the fire. He unloaded his sack onto the cement floor and, opening its neck, revealed a bunch of articles I recognised as mousetraps, spools of thread, and rat-traps. But when he turned his sack upside down I was astounded at the range of his other items: hairpins, brushes, combs, candles, Clarke's tin whistles, rings for ringing the snouts of pigs, rattles for small children, shoelaces and mouth organs. I ran to my mother when I saw the mouth organs. 'Mammy, Mammy, get me one, get me one!' I begged. And she did! For one shilling. And so began my musical career.

She bought a few other accoutrements as well, candles and St Patrick's Day badges. When the pedlar began his departure I saw that he was a tall, lanky man wearing a peaked cap and a long grey tweed topcoat. Some of its buttons were missing and it was held together at the waist by binding twine instead of a belt. He had a hooked nose and small dark eyes almost like an eel. His Adam's apple stuck out and his hands had very long fingernails, which my mother liked because this suggested he had an even temper: one of the many old wives' tales of which my mother had a store. She was later put on the defensive regarding the length of the pedlar's nails after he untied his donkey and climbed onto the front of the cart. With the reins in each hand, he gave them a short tug. 'Gid up there, Bosco,' he shouted at the donkey. The donkey stood motionless. The pedlar roared and shouted, 'Gid up! Gid up!' But Bosco the donkey stood still. Jim the pedlar reached behind him and grabbed a pick handle. 'Now,' he says, 'see what you think of this, you miserable bag of fuckin' glue!' He began beating the donkey's rump and was beginning to sweat himself into a frenzy when my mother came running up to the gate.

'Stop! Stop!' she yelled. 'Jim, I'm surprised at you. This is cruelty. Stop it!' She had a basin full of chopped turnips which she was preparing for dinner. 'Let me try a little bit of kindness; it goes a long way.' She stepped outside the gate and pushed the basin of turnips under the donkey's mouth.

I was standing nearby and began testing the mouth organ, hooting it and running it back and forth against my mouth. Bosco was probing at the turnips but then he turned his head in my direction and his ears stood to attention. In two seconds he plunged forward and, jerking the cart up the small hill, he started to run. The pedlar's cap tumbled from his head when he was suddenly pulled forward. I was still puffing at my mouth organ, a ten-year-old boy who didn't know that his 'music' had frightened a dumb animal out of its wits. I continued to blow into my instrument, and walking up onto the roadside I was just in time to see the donkey and cart disappear around a turn in the road. That was the last I ever saw of them. It was a story that was told over and over in front of many a hearth in our locality.

The following winter we hosted a house dance and invited two accordion players and a fiddler to provide some music. My father said he would beat his tambourine. It was on a Sunday night and we turned up our oil lamp and added a couple of candles to give extra light in the kitchen. Sandwiches were made with sardines and ham. Armfuls of turf were stuffed into a bin and an extra kettle was brought along by one of my aunts. A tall, dark man with a brown hat played a Hohner Black Dot accordion. His name was Paddy McGrath and he was noted as a good player. A second accordion, a red-coloured C#/D Paolo Soprani, was played by Mick Hayes. The fiddler was a friend of our family, a very generous, very shy man known to us children as Dinny. His last name was Doyle, and his place of abode was a half-mile north of our house beside the banks of the Grand Canal. I never heard him play by himself and didn't know until that evening that he had a fiddle. The three of them began playing together at about eight o'clock. I was sitting in my chosen spot in the corner by the fire. It was a good vantage point and I felt awfully happy as I waited for the proceedings to develop. My sister Moira was sitting near me and I could see her eyes open wider as the music was played. We had never heard musicians playing together like this and were convinced afterwards that it was better than the wireless. There were fourteen people, not counting my parents and the three musicians, and as the music was played four couples began waltzing around the floor. My sister and I were watching our aunts and their men laughing and joking. Moira and I thought they looked funny on account of not having seen them dance before. Soon other people took to the floor and in a short time the kitchen was crowded with people.

Later on in the evening, tea and sandwiches were provided; this gave the musicians a break but it didn't last very long. Soon they began again with another waltz and five couples took the floor while others were calling for a half set. Our kitchen was a small space and could only accommodate five or six couples at a time. However, everyone had a mighty time and the highlight of the evening was the half sets danced to reels or polkas. These were my favourites because of the tunes and the basket swinging, which meant a group of two fellows and two women, swinging with arms entwined about one another in a tight circle. Tom Byrne loved to basket swing, and he would propel the swing until it went out of time with the music and one or two people would become dizzy and disconnect from the circle and fall away against the wall. Tom himself lost his balance and fell against the dresser, almost knocking over a number of my mother's wedding plates. When the music stopped my father told everyone to keep calm and to desist from any unnecessary basket swinging during the sets. It was common in those days to remind dancers about unruly basket swinging because it ruined the continuity of the dance.

When it got out of hand women would scream and lose their footing on the floor and would be lifted and left hanging out of the bunch as it spun around and around. It reminded me of the swinging chairs at a visiting carnival, which also produced high-pitched screams from young ladies.

During a break, a few bottles of porter were produced from somewhere. The musicians were the ones to get the first round and it energised them greatly. Paddy McGrath removed his hat because he was sweating, and Mick Hayes followed suit. When Paddy reached over and gave me his hat it made me feel important, and as a kindly gesture I held it close to the fire to dry. More dancing continued with a highland fling and then another half set. I heard a lot of different tunes that I hadn't heard before, 'The Sally Gardens', 'The Salamanca Reel' and 'The Echo Hornpipe'. An all-time favourite of my father's was also played with all its four parts. It was a jig he drummed into my head for years afterwards. The name of 'The Lark in the Morning' made me cringe for at least twenty years, until I eventually realised that the tune was a nice piece of music and very well composed.

Our house dance lasted until midnight, when everyone began to leave and face the cold night on their bicycles. My sister and I had been escorted to bed an hour or so beforehand. I remember our mother tucking us in and reminding us to go to sleep. Meanwhile, the music carried on, and we could easily hear it through the wall between us and the kitchen. It was long after midnight when we finally fell asleep.

Turf Cutting

The following May my father and I walked with spade and *sleán* (a type of spade with an extra side wing used for cutting turf) the half-mile of a mucky pathway that led us to the bog. It was turf-cutting time and I was in charge of a short two-grained fork. My father had already prepared the turf bank during the previous weeks after he returned from work in the evenings. As we walked along the pathway, we passed old abandoned bogholes and I could see the high purple heather in the distance and furze bushes already in bloom with their luscious deep yellow flowers. The scent in the air was a breathing paradise, encouraged by a west wind that blew gently across the upper height of the bog. When we arrived at the freshly cleared bank, my father began by saying, 'In the name of God,' before pushing the *sleán* down and slicing the first damp sod. And then with a lift and a sweep he landed it in front of me. I dug my fork into it and, lifting it, placed it in a wheelbarrow that we had borrowed from a neighbour.

It was my first turf-cutting work with my father, and before noon I was beginning to tire. I was relieved when my father said we should take a break and make tea, which we had with buttered bread that we had brought from home. My father had a cigarette before he began again. Because I was tired, he told me to rest for a while. Working on the bog was hard, especially during the first couple of days. I was eleven years old, and tended to be frail. My mother was very aware of this, and as we left the house she reminded my father not to overwork me. As the day wore on I was given several 'rests', which allowed me to play a few tunes on the mouth organ. 'The High Level Hornpipe' was one I was keenly trying to learn, but I had to wait to hear it again on the radio. Later in the week with some help from a neighbour my father managed to spread at least seventy barrowfuls of turf in rows where the grass grew on the edge of the bogland. The rest of the grass area was used as a pasture, which measured something like three acres. Earlier in the day, several cows and calves had jumped an adjoining drain that ran between our fields and our neighbour's farm. The cattle were already grazing on our side, not far from the drain, and had probably been there a half-hour before we saw them. I was sitting on a blanket under a tree, deeply involved in playing my mouth organ, and didn't notice the cattle as they ambled towards the source of the music – which was me. Soon they were at the edge of where our turf lay across the grass, and two or three cows were beginning to trample the sods of turf. All of a sudden my father and his workmate began shouting: 'Paddy! PADDY! Stop the music!' I was taken by surprise and stunned by all the shouting. 'Hi, hi, hi! How, how!' came more shouts as the two men ran towards the cows. 'Hoo, howee! Hi, hi! Come on, whoosh. Whoosh!' It wasn't long before the cows were herded back across the field and eventually driven beyond the drain.

When the commotion ended, my father came over to me and said, 'Paddy, Paddy, don't play the mouth organ here again, wait 'til we get home. Those cows almost trampled over the turf.' I didn't know what he meant, but said nothing.

'Don't you know that cattle are attracted to music?' he said.

'No, Daddy, I didn't.'

'Well, now you know! Cattle love music. Cattle love music,' he kept saying as he walked over again to where his *sleán* stood deep in a fresh sod. I never forgot that experience with our neighbour's cows and somehow it gave me a new respect for these gentle creatures, whose behaviour told me something about the power of music.

A Job of Journeywork

Despite the ongoing inconsistencies of the radio, it still charmed our household. On Sunday afternoons we listened to programmes such as *Living with Lynch* and *Ranchhouse Revels*, comedy presentations that were a decent-enough cause for laughter. Joe Lynch was the host of *Living with Lynch*, or *Living with Himself* as we used to say, and my mother often remarked, 'He's a devil! How does he think so quickly? Oh, I'd love to meet him.'

My father stopped reading the *Sunday Press* and looked at her. 'Jaysus!' he said, 'this squawk-box of a wireless has you gone barmy!'

'Aw, Christy,' she replied, 'you're too serious! Have you no sense of humour?'

Of course my father had a tremendous sense of humour and a natural wit, which he put to good use when dealing with his friends and neighbours. When I was older I often marvelled at my father's tact and how he would console or encourage people. He often said that he was born to be in the right place at the right time in terms of assisting someone caught up in a tough situation. One true story that highlights his generosity concerns a Saturday night in Bill Brock's bar. Several pint drinkers were deep in conversation, huddled and spaced along the bar in private chatting. A few others were sitting near an old wrought-iron stove, which was burning its packed load of coal. As men talked in low tones, a loud bang split the interior of the bar. It was like a shotgun blast. Farmers, cattle drovers, shopkeepers, ploughmen, everyone who heard it was thunderstruck.

'What in God's name?' cried Bill Brock.

'Jaysus Christ Almighty!' exclaimed someone else.

'Holy mother of Jaysus and all the saints protect me!' roared Jim Wright, who was sitting in his wheelchair. He shouted to my father, 'Christy, will you come here? Quickly!'

My father lowered himself from his high wooden stool and walked over to where Jim sat. Jim looked frightened. 'There's an evil spirit workin' for the devil,' cried Jim, 'and it's here to punish me tonight!'

'It's all right, Jim,' my father said. 'It's all right. It's a simple thing that happened and nothin' to be worried about.'

'What? What?' said Jim impatiently.

'You've been sittin' too close to the stove. One of your back tyres exploded—' But before my father could finish, the second back tyre burst with another loud bang.

'Saints alive!' cried Jim as he felt his wheelchair shake. 'I never did a bad turn to anyone.'

'Would someone give me a hand?' my father shouted.

A couple of men joined him and pushed Jim in his wheelchair away from the stove. 'Holy mother in heaven!' roared Jim. 'What am I goin' to do now?'

'Take it easy, Jim. Take it easy. You'll be all right,' my father kept saying.

Bill Brock came out from behind the counter with a couple of freshly filled pints. 'Men,' he said, 'get these into you.'

'May every soul departed from the streets of Daingean bring you good luck and good health, Mr Brock,' cried Jim.

'Thanks for the pint,' my father said before lifting it to his lips, but in the back of his mind he wondered how Jim Wright would fare in his efforts to get home after the bar closed.

A few of the men had cars, but the wheelchair was too big to fit in any of them. I remember this wheelchair vividly. It had two back wheels about the size of bicycle wheels and two small wheels six inches apart in front. There was a T-shaped handle that jutted up from the front axle. Jim would push the handle back and forth, which in turn moved the vehicle forward.

My father was a great believer in the power of Arthur Guinness for inspiration and creativity, which may be why he thought of the idea of towing Jim all the way home.

'Anybody know where I could find a rope?' he shouted. As is often the case, a few men looked back and forth at each other, not knowing where, what, or how.

'Wait a minute, Christy,' Bill Brock said, 'I might have one.'

Bill topped up a few more pints and then went out the back door. In less than five minutes he was back again, carrying a twenty-foot length of hemp rope.

'Begod, Bill,' said my father, 'this'll do the job.'

When he tied the rope to the front chassis of the wheelchair, Jim Wright began to sense what my father was up to.

'Surely to Jaysus you're not goin' to—'

'I am,' said my father. 'It's only about a mile.'

'It's a mile and a half,' said Jim. 'Don't do it! You'll be worn out!'

'Don't worry, Jim, I'll get you home.'

Someone held the door of the bar open as my father, with the rope over his shoulder, pulled Jim and the wheelchair out onto the street. It was eleven o'clock. He kept pulling with the help of Jim's T-shaped handle, and after ten minutes they arrived at the top of the town and rested for a short while. Jim Wright looked back at the main street of Daingean, which is built in a hollow, and started muttering to himself. There was some illumination from the tall lampposts along each side of the street, and all the pubs still had their lights on. Jim began to pray, 'Hail Mary, full of grace—' and then started to shout, 'Where are you when a man is in need, you fuckin' hypocrites! Our father, who art in heaven—'

'Jim – Jim, keep your voice down.'

And so they continued on.

'Our father . . . who . . . Christy O'Brien, a born fuckin'. . . saint!'

My father found it tough to keep from laughing, and at the bottom of a second hill, close to my Aunt Mary's house, they stopped again for another rest. This time they had a cigarette together.

'O'Brien,' cried Jim, 'if you have all the luck and blessin's poured down on you from the depths of my heart, you'll never want for anythin'. Jesus was tested on the road to Calvary, and by God the road home tonight is another Calvary for the two of us poor mortals.'

Jim was feeling the effects of several pints as my father pulled the wheelchair up the hill that would take them past the new cemetery.

'Holy mother of orphans, give me the innocent mind of a child! Give me the strength to curse the town of Daingean and all of those recevin' tomorrow. Woe to those hoors who turned their backs on me this Saturday night!'

Just as they were passing the gates of the cemetery, Jim shouted at my father, 'Stop! Stop, Christy, stop! Let's pray for all the souls that are gone!'

Both of them removed their caps. After a minute of silence, Jim shrieked loudly, 'Jack, Jack, come back to life! We want a fuckin' song! Jack! Jack!'

Jack Walsh was a great local singer who had died sometime earlier in the year. His passing was a blow to everyone – especially my father. He and Jack were close friends, and would seek each other's counsel in times of trouble. My father removed his cap again and began to cry. In a minute it was over and he and Jim continued on. There was another half-mile to go.

'Mother of Jaysus . . . You're a walkin' saint . . . Lord preserve us from all harm.'

My father was trying to keep a straight face when he towed Jim to the door of his house. He was also beginning to tire.

'Come in, for Jaysus' sake, come on in and have a small one.'

My father thanked Jim for the offer but said he'd better be on his way. As he left, Jim pointed to a star in the sky. 'You're one of them, Christy,' he said. 'I'm a poor drunken invalid. I've never walked in me whole fuckin' life. I'll be sixty in a few m-m-months,' he stuttered. 'I-I don't know what it's like to walk.'

My father thought about what Jim had said as he walked back to the alleyway beside Bill Brock's bar. When he finally got there his bicycle was lying against the gable end of Brock's pub. He squeezed the tyres to check for air; they hadn't lost any pressure. He walked with his bike onto the empty street. It was very quiet. After about a hundred yards he stopped and topped his cigarette. With his left foot on the pedal he threw his right leg over the bicycle, and when he got to the top of the hill he turned east on the Edenderry Road. It was a mild night and as he cycled along the Mill Road his thoughts were of Jim Wright and what Jim had said to him about the star. He laughed to himself at the memory of Jim cursing and praying and all the blessings he'd showered upon him. When he reached our front gate he was still chuckling. I can still remember when he came into the kitchen. He said, 'Is the kettle on?' And then, 'You'll never believe what happened to me tonight.' My mother was unimpressed, that is until she heard the story.

The summer of 1956 was a turning point in my listening experience. It began when my sister and I were sent to Daingean to pick
up some groceries. My mother had directed us to visit Aunt Mary
and bring her a pound of sugar and some other groceries. When we
got there her husband Mick had just returned from work, and after
he had eaten he engaged us with light-hearted chat and mysterious
stories that he said came from the mouths of the little people. He
convinced us that he had met one or two of them when he was our
age. We were fascinated when he told us about what they were wearing and the magical powers they could use. He said they were very
fond of music, especially hornpipes and reels. Mick had a wonderful way with words – so much so that we all forgot about the time.
Meanwhile, my father had returned home from work and when he
asked my mother where we were she said we were probably at Aunt
Mary's. After an hour of waiting, both of them became worried, and
soon my father was wheeling his bicycle towards the road.

Mick was telling us a tall one about a ghost his father had seen
when my father knocked on the door. Aunt Mary let him in, and we
thought he looked a little upset.

'Sit down, Christy, and I'll make you a mug of tea,' said my aunt.

'Don't be too hard on the children, Christy,' Mick said. 'It's my
fault. We were talkin' and I forgot about the time.'

As my father looked at us, his expression softened. 'Paddy, you
and Moira should go on home,' he said. 'I'll catch up to you when I
finish the tea.'

'Before you go,' our aunt said, 'I want to tell Paddy somethin'. Have
you heard the new programme on the radio, Paddy?'

We hadn't listened to the radio in over two weeks as our battery
was at the garage. 'It's called *A Job of Journeywork*,' Aunt Mary continued with a gleeful look at me, 'and the fellow on it puts people on
from around the country. It's mighty!'

Mick got a little excited by the turn in the conversation. 'I've never
heard anythin' like it,' he said.

Aunt Mary, who was rubbing her hands, intervened with a shout,
'Fiddles! Whistles! Flutes and pipes, and he had on a wonderful
accordion player from Tipperary.' She came over to me and tapped
me gently on the back, and bending down to my ear she said, 'His
name is Paddy O'Brien, the same name as you!'

My father was curious. 'Who's the fellow that puts on this music?'

Aunt Mary was aglow. 'I can't think of his name offhand. It's an Irish sort of name, like "Matoona".'

'"Matoona",' said my father. 'I never heard of him. He wouldn't be from the Congo or one of those Balubas from there?' My father was always ready to make a bit of humour out of the simplest of conversations.

'Not at all,' said Mick. 'But I do remember that his first name is Ciarán.'

'Maybe he's half-Irish!' my father said. Everyone laughed. 'Children,' he continued, 'you'd better ramble off home, your mother will be worried. Go on now!'

Aunt Mary escorted us up the little pathway to the gate. She pressed a sweet and two pennies into each of our hands and said, 'Don't mind Mick, his stories about the little people are somethin' he made up!'

As we waved bye-bye, she shouted, 'Don't forget to turn on Ciarán Matoona on Tuesday nights!'

In less than half an hour we were home. We had been away most of the afternoon, and when our mother saw us she was very relieved and hugged us both. She had heated some canned oxtail soup for us with some bread. It was my favourite soup, with its little chunks of meat, and I loved its flavour. Moira said nothing as we sat at the table. Hers was a busy spoon. It spoke on her behalf as she lifted it up and down. 'Anythin' strange or unusual at Aunt Mary's?' our mother asked.

I couldn't wait to tell her about Ciarán Matoona and his new radio programme. My mother looked at me and said, 'Nobody has a name like that! Are you sure that's right?'

I insisted it was. 'Aunt Mary and Uncle Mick listen to it every Tuesday night, and the programme is called *A Job of Journeywork*. It has fiddles and accordions and whistles.' I was feeling proud of my memory with all this information I had for my mother. I told her more. 'He's had an accordion player from Tipperary and his name is the same as mine.'

'Another Paddy O'Brien!' cried my mother. 'Now we have three of yez!' (There was also a famous County Meath footballer of the same name.) 'God preserve us from all harm; three Paddy O'Briens,' my mother chuckled. 'The next thing we'll know, one of them will be elected to the Dáil. De Valera had better watch out!' She started to laugh and I didn't know why.

After a short while, we heard the sound of our gate; our father had returned from town. He had a charged battery with him, given as a loan from my Uncle Mick. When I saw it I was elated, and my appetite for music began to stir. My father wasted no time in hooking the battery to the radio. It was a Saturday night and in a short time we would hear *Ballad Maker's Corner*, which was presented by Arthur O'Sullivan. It was one of my parents' favourite programmes because it aired a lot of the great old-time songs that they had heard from their parents and grandparents. My mother had a pen and paper ready for trying to catch portions of the lyrics of songs that were repeated from time to time. She was especially fond of a new song called 'The Homes of Donegal'.

When I look back on it all I am struck by the humble imaginations and innocent attitudes of country people like my parents. Their lives were embodied by everyday values of give and take, the sharing of hardships, and by their children. Children of the neighbouring areas brought people together, confirmed friendships, and kept alive a spirit of goodwill among friends and neighbours. This was how it was.

Unknown to me, my mother had spoken to her sister about coming down to our house and had urged her to bring their father's gramophone. My grandfather had bought the gramophone some twenty years earlier and over a period of time had accumulated dozens of 78 rpm records. When our aunt finally came on a visit I saw her wheel her bicycle into our front yard with a box tied over its back wheel. It was the gramophone! My mother removed all the dishes from our kitchen table to make room for it. Aunt Maggie brought the gramophone in, placed it on the table and lifted its lid. There was a record already on the turntable and at its centre was a red label with something written on it. I was soon to learn it was a recording of uilleann piper Leo Rowsome. My aunt produced a handle from inside the lid and wound up the gramophone. We all waited in anticipation as the record began to spin, and as it did she lowered its arm with its slanted needle. The record started to play, with the introduction of a very long screaming pipe note within a cloud of other, deeper notes. Its sound pierced my ears, and our dog Rusty started barking. When my four-year-old sister began to cry my mother put her hand over her mouth and retreated towards the door. The first sound of Rowsome's pipes is a memory that has never left me. It was as if it was eating away at the core of my consciousness, and I felt a trembling inside my chest. I made a dash for the door and ran across the yard to our front field. I stayed there for quite a while and didn't return until my aunt convinced me that the record had been taken off the gramophone and wouldn't be played again. Of course, at the time we didn't know what uilleann pipes were, or that Leo Rowsome was a very well-known and celebrated piper.

When Tuesday night came, my mother tuned into *A Job of Journeywork*, and that soon-to-be familiar kindly voice came over the radio. It was slow and deliberate as he introduced the Tulla Céilí Band from County Clare. They played a great selection of reels, namely 'Tim Maloney' and 'Craig's Pipes'. This was a very different style of céilí music. The musicians were playing fiddles and flutes and had a pair of two-row accordions. I was immediately drawn to the kind of music this programme played. The presenter's name was Ciarán MacMathúna, and his radio presentation was to become very popular with lovers of Irish traditional music throughout Ireland. The programme introduced us to musicians from many parts of Ireland, and several became household names. On that very same night Ciarán gave us a taste of fiddler Paddy Canny, who played two powerful reels known as 'Lord MacDonald's' and 'The Ballinasloe Fair'. Canny was an instant hit, and letters poured in from fiddlers who wanted to hear more of him. Mrs Crotty was another musician who touched people's imaginations. She was, as my father used to say, 'a humdinger' on the concertina, and like Canny she was also from County Clare. She was in her late fifties when she was taped by Radio Éireann's mobile recording unit and she was also interviewed by Ciarán – he and his assistants travelled all the way from Dublin to her public house in Kilrush. Some people referred to her as the grandmother of the concertina. It was as a result of these radio presentations that County Clare developed a reputation as the home of traditional music: it had an array of great musicians whose feeling and interpretation gave genuine meaning and expression to Irish traditional instrumental music.

Ciarán MacMathúna played an under-appreciated role as a presenter during those early years of Irish radio. He introduced Ireland to its own music at a time when we knew little about local or regional styles. Up to then our music was played in small areas by musicians who were generally unknown or not recognised for their creative ability, but now, through radio, we were hearing a wider range of traditional music.

These programmes continued for as long as I can remember, with Ciarán's relaxed and comforting voice coming forth from the radio, purring in our ears. He introduced us to performers like Ann Mulqueen, whose unaccompanied songs inspired the singing of so many young women. Some of these singers caught the attention of other singers and collectors of songs in Ireland, and over time the groundwork for new radio presentations was developed with the inclusion of a variety of artists.

A Single-Row Accordion

During this time I was a young bystander, listening and learning as best I could. 'Mammy, I want an accordion!' I plagued my mother. 'I know I can play it!' I nagged so much that one day I heard her mention it to my father. This was a major breakthrough. At last they were taking me seriously. My mother picked out a single-row accordion that was advertised in the *Sunday Press* newspaper. It was a German make called a Hohner, a C-row. Tom and Joe Byrne also had a couple but they had double-row keyboards. We didn't know about keys, sharps, flats, or any kind of technique. Nevertheless, my mother sent a deposit of ten shillings to Cotts of Kilcock in County Kildare, which was a furniture store. The total cost of the accordion was ten pounds and ten shillings.

About three weeks later I was on my way home from the national school in Daingean when one of my schoolmates said, 'Paddy, here's yer Mammy!'

'Where?'

'Coming up the road,' said little Andy McCormack. And then I saw my mother cycling towards us on her way for groceries in Daingean and I remember she was wearing her maroon coat and white and blue headscarf.

'Paddy! Paddy!' she shouted. 'The accordion came! The accordion came! It arrived an hour ago.'

It was a huge surprise, because I didn't know she had ordered it. When she got off the bike she was a little out of breath. 'We could have told you, but we wanted it to be an early birthday present.'

I was stuck for words. 'Go on home,' she said. 'Your daddy is there mindin' your sisters Patricia and Kathleen.'

I began to run. I arrived home with my lungs hurting from the cold wind that blew eastward along the Mill Road. As I walked towards our door I could hear the sound of the accordion as my father played 'Believe Me If All Those Endearing Young Charms'.

I put my schoolbag away and sat by the fire. Moments later my father handed me the accordion and I immediately slid my right thumb into the thumb strap behind the keyboard. With my left hand inside the strap at the bass end of the instrument I began squeezing its bellows in and out. At the same time I began pressing my fingers nervously on the middle section of buttons along the keyboard. It was wonderful to hear all the different notes, and the excitement ran through me like a shot of ice-cold drinking water. I stopped and looked at my sisters and my father and I began to giggle. My sisters also giggled and my father stood up and reached for the empty kettle. A mug of tea was his way of relaxing. He filled the kettle and said, 'Paddy, why don't you play "Maggie in the Wood"?' I had often played it on the mouth organ, having learned it from my mother, but now I was put to the test of finding it somewhere on the ten buttons that made up the length of the keyboard. I pressed a couple of them and pulled the bellows back and forth and pressed more buttons as each note sounded with two notes for each button, depending on whether the bellows was pulled out or pushed in. An hour later my mother returned with her groceries with me beginning to find 'Maggie in the Wood'. She stood looking at me when I dribbled out the first part of the tune. 'Good lad,' she said. 'There's music in yer blood.'

In another hour I had all of it and was making headway with 'Saddle the Pony'. My mother was touched by this jig. 'Lord,' she said in a raised voice, 'your grandfather Johnny Dunne jigs that tune. It's one he's awfully fond of, along with "The Shaskeen Reel".'

After I put the accordion into its box I felt tired, my right thumb felt sore and my left hand also ached a little. I didn't try to play any more that night because I had chores to do and homework from school. I was exhausted when I went to bed and soon fell asleep. Waking up next morning I could recall a dream that came to me in the night. In the dream I saw several accordions being towed along the Mill Road. They were outfitted with rubber wheels and were gigantic in size, as big as the house we lived in. Several sturdy farm horses were hauling them along the road towards our home. There was a man in charge of the horses whom I didn't know. A neighbour of ours was also in the dream. As the giant accordions came closer he shouted, 'By God, look at him!'

'Who?' I said.

'It's . . . it's Ciarán MacMathúna,' my neighbour yelled, 'the man on the radio.'

With the new accordion, and the radio's presentation of *A Job of Journeywork*, I was beginning to sense that this traditional music was not as scarce as we first thought, and as I listened each Tuesday night I was intrigued to learn of a new organisation called Comhaltas Ceoltóirí Éireann (CCÉ) that was sponsoring music festivals and competitions in various counties, especially in the west of Ireland. These festivals or music gatherings were officially referred to as 'Fleadh Cheoils'. The very notion of hundreds of musicians in one town for three or four days was difficult for me to envision. The names of the towns where the All-Irelands had been held up to then were eventually introduced through the medium of Ciarán's weekly programmes. Some of them are still remembered in stories from Fleadh followers who reminisce about the great early days of mighty competitions and competitors who won or lost in Longford, Ennis, Loughrea, Dungarvan and Monaghan. During the 1950s it was a major honour to win a solo competition and winning an All-Ireland was regarded as the ultimate prize. There were programmes printed for these occasions with lists of competing performers on fiddles, flutes, uilleann pipes, accordions, etc. The céilí band competitions were usually the highlight of the weekend, and competitive rivalry was nurtured beforehand with weeks of practice. The Kilfenora and Tulla bands from County Clare were examples of the great spirit that prevailed. They played against each other in packed halls with adjudicators having to decide against one side or the other at a time when different bands and their supporters travelled far to claim the honour of victory.

Much of this had already occurred when we heard of it through the radio. Ciarán presented musicians from live recordings taped at prizewinners' concerts where the best of Ireland's amateur talent came together to play their best tunes and sing their finest songs. It was indeed a revival of Gaelic soul expression, and hearing it on the radio was magical and heart-warming.

An All-Ireland accordion champion was then the talk of the Midlands, and Offaly in particular. He was Ciarán Kelly from Shannonbridge in Offaly, and his box playing was all the rage. I first heard his music played on a Grundig reel-to-reel tape recorder when two brothers whose names were Mitchell stopped by our house. Their recorder was powered by a battery and when I saw and heard it I was astounded. They played a recording of Ciarán Kelly over and over for me, which they had taped off the radio. Ciarán was playing 'The Spike Island Lassies' and a companion reel that I can't recall. It was great stuff and hugely inspiring. I was almost twelve when my mother and father bought the single-row accordion for me, and from then on I was alone with it, to do with it whatever I could figure out by myself.

It was very common to learn music by ear because there were no accordion teachers around or even within cycling distance. Not many people, if any, knew or understood Irish traditional music and most people were unable to recognise the difference between a jig, a reel and a hornpipe. This was the musical climate in which I grew up, except for a few people here and there who enjoyed the music but did not really understand it. Many people in today's Ireland still don't understand our traditional music. But in all fairness, the same people are usually very sociable and accepting when they hear a tune in a pub or even at a wake.

As time came and went I struggled with the music and kept practising the accordion as best I could. The biggest problem was listening and learning a tune, and the need for further listening meant I'd have to hear it again on the radio. Sometimes a tune I was learning was played frequently on *Take the Floor*, *Céilí House*, or *A Job of Journeywork*, but very often I might have to wait several weeks for it to be played again. Learning music from the radio was a very tedious experience and very frustrating. It tested my patience.

One evening I was pleasantly surprised when Ciarán MacMathúna introduced the accordion player Paddy O'Brien, from Newtown near Nenagh, County Tipperary, who was then living in New York but was home that summer for a visit. 'And here he is,' announced Ciarán, 'with two reels, "Trim the Velvet", and "The King of the Clans".' O'Brien began with his controlled and steady flow, not too fast and not too slow. It was like a tonic; I can't explain the effect of his playing as it touched me and threw me into a musical quandary. The tunes were delicious; if only I could eat them! The structure of the melodies seemed to relay a profound message from the core of the tunes. And then he continued with a selection of jigs, 'The Lark on the Strand' and 'The Pipe on the Hob'. Lovely and steady again and well grounded. The tune choices were another strong point in Paddy's favour, and he had lots of them. It was a new experience to hear this man's music and how he was able to handle an accordion. As it turned out, he was a pioneer of the B/C accordion, and his influence was already established when I first heard him. And then hornpipes, also steady and solid and tailor-made for dancing. Two of them, 'The Flowing Tide' (an Ed Reavy composition) and 'The Cuckoo'. My God, I wondered, what kind of man is he? How does he play like that? There was no one to tell me anything. It was brutal and lonely. I felt exiled among the fields of Castlebarnagh and cut off from those who might give me some advice or encouragement.

By this time I had overcome my fear of my grandfather's gramophone and I would wind it up for playing from time to time. My aunt came to visit a lot, and each time she brought more records with her. One of the records had a couple of fiddle selections by the County Meath fiddler Frank O'Higgins. Frank played with piano accompaniment and this combination was also a new experience for me as I wasn't familiar with a lot of fiddle music. His tunes were jigs and reels, and one jig that moved me was 'The Maid at the Spinning Wheel', which had three parts.

There were also a couple of Michael Grogan's records, which I was very fond of because Michael was an old-time accordion player and I liked the sound and energy in his playing. As I listened to these recordings I struggled with the makeup and shape of the tunes, trying to figure out the sequence of the notes. My experience with hearing these recordings was limited and it would take a long time before I would truly appreciate what was involved. In the meantime, I'd have to do what I could with my minute amount of knowledge. Still, I was playing some jigs and reels but I wasn't able to play very fast, and much of it was riddled with stops and starts. And when I noticed that my instrument was not equipped with enough notes for many of the tunes, it bothered and irritated me, and I made my concern known to my parents.

'You should thank God for small mercies,' my mother confided. 'We are living in poor times.'

Of course she was right. The 1950s were a time of major economic problems for Ireland. My father was always employed as a labourer with Bord na Móna, a semi-state outfit that was in the process of developing the boglands in County Offaly. They were already mass-producing turf in the many bigger bogs throughout our area and my father, along with dozens of other family men, shovelled, dug, cleaned and helped drain thousands of acres of bogland. It was also a time of another development which went unnoticed, a cultural one of common understanding between the men of Offaly and many men who came from the western counties of Ireland. A language of the bog inspired their vocabulary – the names for various bog machines, nicknames for men and even some nicknames for wives or girl-friends. Everyone got to know a lot about each other and stories were formulated from experiences of adverse conditions or situations of camaraderie. I wasn't clear about what the purpose of all this activity was until my mother mentioned to my father that cutting and rearing turf in such large amounts didn't add up, especially when all of it was loaded onto small rail cars to be brought to the local power station, where it was used as fuel for generating electricity.

My mother couldn't reason with the logic of burning such massive amounts of turf. 'Paddy,' she said, 'play a few tunes. Maybe it'll help clear my head.' My father lit a cigarette and swallowed a mouthful of strong tea. I began with a march called 'Roddy McCorley', which my father and his fellow workers often sang in the pubs in Daingean. Their version of the song was 'Seán South of Garryowen', and it was new and immensely popular. It proved to be a song of enor-mous sympathy and one that guaranteed that the pledge of a young Limerick patriot would never be forgotten among Irish nationalists, wherever they might be. His name was Seán South, and he had died in action as an IRA volunteer during a raid and subsequent gun battle with the RUC in Northern Ireland. This episode had happened six months earlier, and in that time the song of Seán South awakened the consciousness of the Irish people and some individuals would listen to no other song. In any case, I played its melody a few times, and followed it with 'The Dawning of the Day'. My repertoire was now expanding with a small mixture of songs and tunes, not to mention a hornpipe or two.

Another slight turn of fortune entered my life with a visit one win-ter's night from an old melodeon player known to us from playing at house dances. The first time he came into our kitchen he was car-rying a new Paolo Soprani C#/D accordion. 'This is Mick Hayes,' my mother introduced the visitor, 'he's a great man on the accordion.'

Mick sat in front of the fire with me watching and waiting in my usual corner. He was a man who loved conversation and above all was in love with his own comfort. After a short while my father uncorked a bottle of porter and handed it to him, and my mother came with a glass. Mick poured and drank, and began pulling at the lobe of his right ear. 'Isn't it great to be a musician,' he remarked, 'and so much thought of us.' He looked at me and winked. I stared and waited.

I was beginning to get fed up when finally my mother asked him to play. 'Paddy would love to hear a tune, and so would I.' Mick reached for the accordion that was in his big black shopping bag. When he had it on his lap, he said, 'I'd better take off me topcoat,' and stood up. My patience was being tested by this sudden delay. When he had his coat off he began talking again about a funeral and a soul being lost somewhere on its way to heaven. He was really good at telling ghost stories, but I was wondering if he would ever get to playing. When he finished his story my father offered him another bottle of porter and Mick's face shone with sweat. 'Glory be to God,' he said. 'May all the relatives of the twelve apostles shower this house with graces and good luck for all eternity!'

There was little doubt about his sincerity and my father was impressed. 'You were always a good man, Mick.' Then he said, 'Molly! Why don't we put on the kettle and we'll make Mick a sandwich.'

'Don't bother,' said Mick. 'Don't go out of your way. I came here to help the young lad – where is he?'

I'm sitting in front of you, you amadán! I was saying this to myself when he once again lifted his accordion onto his lap.

'What would you like to hear?' he asked.

We couldn't think of anything. So he began with 'The Star of Donegal'.

'Good man, Mick,' said my father. 'You'll never, never die.'

It was good for Mick to hear this because he lived in dreadful fear of dying and going straight to hell. But then again he was also susceptible to praise and loved every word of it. 'You're too good to me,' he said. 'Too good. I don't deserve this.'

'Oh, you do,' said my mother. 'Everyone around here knows Mick Hayes. Your name and fame is everywhere.'

Mick became overwhelmed with emotion and began to sob. He pulled out his handkerchief and daubed at his eyes and nose. 'It's easy to get carried away,' he whispered. 'It's times like this that put me in mind of me mother. She had a heart of gold, and if ever there was a saint, she was one—'

'Molly, is the kettle boiled yet?' my father intervened.

My mother dried the teapot and my father set about cutting slices of loaf bread. Soon we were all drinking tea and eating bread and jam. Mick ignored the loaf bread and was eating my mother's bread-baking, which was wheaten bread with a tasty crust. When we were finished, Mick enquired of me, 'Are you playing the basses yet?'

Before I could say anything, my mother said, 'We were hopin', Mick, that you'd show him a little about how to do it.'

'Well,' says Mick, 'it's not too hard. It just takes a little bit of getting used to. Watch me play a march,' which he did, and then he played a jig. He said, 'Get your accordion out.' I had it close by, and immediately set it on my own lap. 'Now,' said Mick, 'follow me.' He played the march again, one-two, one-two and one-two as his fingers crossed over on the top two inside basses. Then he played a waltz with the basses one-two-two, one-two-two. He was playing 'Under the Bridges of Paris'. I'll always remember him for this, and for playing extra tunes the same night. After an hour he got up, moved his chair away from the fire and put his accordion out of reach. 'God,' he said, 'it's very warm.'

My mother opened the door to let in some cool air. We could see some brown sweat trickling down the sides of Mick's forehead, and I was curious to know what it could be. I was later told that Mick used brown shoe polish to colour his hair and used a little Vaseline to keep his hair in place for when he had his cap off at Mass. This was the kind of behaviour that some people enjoyed. If you were a little odd or eccentric, my father would make friends with you. It was common for people to make funny remarks about each other and laugh at one another's point of view. When I heard about Mick and the shoe polish I came to his defence by saying that I didn't care what colour his hair was. Needless to say, Mick wasn't around when someone talked about this, and my father and mother later consoled me by saying he was a good neighbour and musician and that they thought highly of him and respected him a lot. I was now reassured and asked when he'd be back again. It was a month later when he called, but I was disappointed when I saw that he hadn't the accordion with him.

I was aware that Mick loved my mother's bread-baking; he couldn't resist asking for some when tea was made. He once remarked, 'What do you put in it?' and when she told him he said, 'I make mine with the same mix and it doesn't come even halfway as good as yours. I'd love to get to the bottom of it.' He looked at my father. 'Christy,' he said, 'is it possible that different kinds of turf might cause a cake to bake better or worse?' My father looked at him in search of something rational but could find no glimmer of an answer. He wasn't sure what to say, but to try and conclude Mick's nonsense, he said, 'I suppose anything is possible.'

'Christy,' said Mick, 'you never said a truer word.' He and my father continued talking and as I listened I heard them discussing the big tree that grew beside Jimmy Mac's house.

'I remember the evenin' well,' said my father.

'That's right,' said Mick. 'You were there when it began to rain in bucketfuls. It was like a deluge and lasted almost an hour.'

"Twas a fierce downpour,' said my father. 'And when it stopped, we still had two tons of beet to load on to Jimmy's trailer. We were all under the tree. The lorry, the beet, and ourselves. Everythin'! Jaysus, it was hard work tryin' to fill the trailer in time for the boat in Daingean. We were sweatin' like pigs and I had to take off me shirt.'

My father went on to say that they were making good headway with their beet forks, when all of a sudden Mick began to curse. He looked at Mick and said, 'Meself and Jimmy Mac stopped to listen. You had your cap in your hand and you were shoutin'. "What's wrong with Mick?" Jimmy enquired. "By God, I think I know,"' I said. 'Jimmy Mac began to laugh when I told him, "It's the drops of water fallin' from the leaves in the tree . . . The breeze is knockin' them down the back of Mick's neck."

'I can still see you, Mick, standin' there . . . cursin' and shoutin' at the tree and you roared out a litany of curses. You said from that day forward its seed and breed, its limbs and its leaves would forever rot and would stand there in that very spot as a reminder to everyone of the penance it put you through. And Mick, I remember before you put your cap back on your head you shouted up at the tree again. "You hoor's melt," you said, "may every devil torment you and the devil's nature destroy every root that ties you to the ground!"'

My father looked at all of us. 'That was three years ago, and the same tree hasn't sprouted as much as one leaf! It still stands there today and its branches are rotten and fallin' off its trunk. Mick,' he said, 'you're a fierce man. How did you do it?'

Mick looked over at me. 'Paddy, give me your accordion. Sometimes a man's patience is tried to the limits of normal understanding,' he said, and then he began to play 'The Trip to the Cottage'.

6

Long Tom

I could tell that my father was in the humour for telling a story when he said, 'Mick, you don't happen to know Long Tom Galligan?'

'I don't know him too well.'

'I know him very well, a very reliable man and awfully sincere, or maybe too sincere. Talkin' about the straw and the thatchin' reminds me of the time he had eleven acres of barley, wheat and rye. Anyway, when the time came he cut it and put it into stacks for to let it ripen and settle into itself. Long Tom was very satisfied and was lookin' forward to a good yield. He and his father and a few neighbours began haulin' the stooks home to the haggard and buildin' large stacks each side so as the thrashin' machine could be pulled in between. It took them two days to get it in and ready, and Long Tom was very thankful to God and said a few prayers as he stood between the stacks when everyone was gone home. Then he made arrangements with the owner of a travellin' mill (or thrashing machine) to thrash his corn on the Saturday of the followin' week. Now, you should all know somethin' about Long Tom.'

'What's that?' said Mick.

'He is the best in the world when everythin' is goin' well and is a great workman,' said my father, 'but if anythin' went wrong, or if he was disappointed, or if someone stood on his toes . . . well, woe be with them. He had an uncontrollable temper. He would froth out of the mouth and curse everythin' and anythin' that was born.'

Mick was looking down at the floor as he listened to my father, who said: 'Everythin' was ready and in place for the thrashin'; it was only a matter of waitin'.'

When Friday evening came, Jim Tracey and his tractor could be heard as it laboured on a hill where the boreen wound its way near Long Tom's home. The tractor looked small in front of the huge mill as it gently moved along on its four large wheels. My father said it was like a fish pulling a whale.

The tractor belched black smoke and coughed and stuttered but finally arrived on the top of the hill and then began turning right into Long Tom's haggard. When Jim Tracey had pulled the mill between the stacks, he unhooked his tractor from the mill and made a rounda-bout circle for home. He would return next morning at eight o'clock. When he was gone, Long Tom said he was relieved that the tractor didn't stall on the hill or get bogged down.

'It's at times like this that anythin' could happen,' said my father. 'And what's more . . . Long Tom is a God-fearin' man and a bit super-stitious. The following Saturday mornin' was the beginnin' of a glorious day of sunshine and Long Tom had risen early. People began arrivin' at nine o'clock, one after the other, and Jim Tracey had his tractor warmin' up. A small wheel from the gearbox of the tractor was linked with a long canvas belt that went all the way to a fly-wheel on the side of the mill. Long Tom had a lengthy ladder that lay against a stack, and was climbin' to its top when a large raindrop hit him on the forehead. He stopped to look up at the sky and couldn't believe what he saw. A massive raincloud was gatherin' momentum and spreadin'. Drops of rain followed. Nobody noticed it comin' and the men were taken by surprise. Long Tom began retreatin' down the ladder. Within moments, everyone had scattered and taken shelter in a hayshed. Long Tom and his father were runnin' to the farmhouse. A half-hour later it was pourin' steadily and the sky was a dark grey as Long Tom stood inside the door of his home lookin' out in disbelief. An hour went by and the rain was still fallin' with no sign of light in the sky. Another hour later the men in the hayshed had given up but it was rainin' too hard for them to leave the hayshed. In the meantime, Long Tom lost his patience and began cursin'. His father shouted at him to stop it and reminded him that he didn't want him cursin' inside the house or in front of his mother. But it didn't stop him, he was livid with rage and mad with disappointment. "The thrashin' is destroyed," he shouted. "It's ruined, and it's all His fault!" as he pointed his finger at the ceilin'. The rain didn't ease until two o'clock in the afternoon, and a half-hour later everyone had left for home. It was four o'clock in the evenin' when the rain stopped.'

My father struck a match and lit a fresh cigarette. 'That's the worst bad luck any farmer could face,' said Mick. 'Jesus Christ, he lost almost all of his harvest.'

'That's the truth, Mick,' said my mother.

'I haven't finished yet,' my father said, anxious to continue.

'What?' said Mick.

My father reminded us again that Long Tom's anger was something that had to be seen and heard. He was about to explain when we were shocked by three loud knocks on the door. My father jumped from his chair. 'If it isn't Dinny Doyle himself!'

Dinny stepped into the kitchen. 'Hello missus, and Mick, hello girls and Paddy, how's the music?'

Before Dinny sat he had greeted us all. My mother said, 'It's time to make a pot of tea.'

'I hope I haven't interrupted anythin',' said Dinny.

'Christy was tellin' us a story about Long Tom Galligan,' said Mick.

'I can finish it now,' my father said. 'Late in the evenin', after supper, Long Tom went out into the haggard and stood between the rain-soaked stacks. He looked up at the heavens and removed his cap and began to scream, "You louse, you fuckin' lousy bastard," he screamed. "Three fuckin' nails weren't good enough for you. Three nails," he cried. "Three nails weren't good enough."'

'Oh my God,' said my mother. 'What an awful thing to say.'

'It's hard to blame him,' said Mick.

My father didn't say any more about Long Tom.

As we all drank our tea and ate bread, butter and jam, Dinny mentioned about the tea being a great tonic and that the Chinese were not appreciated enough for giving it to us. We all looked at Dinny and laughed a little. He was an unusual man and very charitable, and I always felt he knew what he was talking about.

7

Going Astray

Our social life was very much centred on our fireside, where a multitude of problems were discussed or argued. At times we would be irritable or cranky and it was rare for everyone to be in a good mood at the same time. Sometimes the radio was not in keeping with our taste or expectations, and my efforts at playing music were often criticised or complained about, and my practising was sometimes relegated to the cold interior of the bedroom with the light of a feeble candle for company. In winter time I would intermittently come from the room and heat myself by the fire. When it was time for my sisters to retire to bed I usually got a reprieve from my mother, who shouted to me to come to the kitchen and warm myself. This also meant that I could resume playing my accordion by the fire.

On one of those winter evenings my father came home from town, where he had intended to have his hair cut. Daingean town never had a barber and sometimes men made appointments with some known handyman who could use a clippers, a shears, or a scissors. One such man lived alone in the townland of Riverlyons, which was two miles from our house. My father met him in the back room of a pub just as he had finished cutting another man's hair. Paddy McEvoy was in no mind for another haircut and my father thought it a better approach to invite him for a pint. 'I don't mind if I do,' was Paddy's reply.

The two of them had a few drinks, which is how this socially accepted encounter is referred to. My father waited until they were well into their second pint before he asked Paddy about the best time for him to give another haircut. 'Next week,' was Paddy's reply. 'Come to think of it, I'll be comin' from Daingean next Thursday night, and I can stop at your house on my way home.'

The following Thursday night Paddy did indeed stop at our house amid the noisy barking of Shep, who snarled at him when he opened the gate. What followed was a well-directed boot that greeted Shep on the ribs. The dog retreated, howling and whimpering, with no appetite left for further adventures.

Paddy McEvoy was a very down-to-earth and honest individual. He was probably in his early sixties, with a week's beard and thick sideburns. His complexion was pinkish and he was tall and sturdy and his face weather-beaten. My mother invited him to sit on a chair by the fire, but instead he pulled the chair to the centre of the kitchen and sat down. He was asked if he would like a cup of tea, to which he said he would. He was a wonderful man at telling stories, which he did with great sincerity and profound assurances. When he had finished his tea he took out a brown paper bag from inside his jacket. He removed its contents – a small shears, a scissors and a device that could cut hair very close to one's scalp. 'Begod, Paddy,' my father said, 'you came well prepared!'

'Missus,' Paddy asked my mother, 'do you have a sheet or a towel handy? I want somethin' to wrap around Christy's neck.' My mother went to her bedroom and came back with a white sheet. My father was sitting in Paddy's chair and looked very reconciled and passive. Paddy put the sheet around his shoulders and tucked it in around his neck.

He began with the shears while behind him my mother blessed herself anxiously with her eyes looking upwards. Within a short while my father's dark hair was scattered on the floor beside the chair as Paddy and him chatted about football and how frost delayed the growth of potatoes. Paddy was working around my father's ears when he mentioned that he had a mysterious experience while taking a shortcut home one summer's night four or five years ago. Without moving his head, my father said, 'What happened?'

'I'm not sure what happened,' said Paddy, adding, 'Let me finish this small patch here and I'll tell yeh.'

When he was finished with my father he reached for a small mirror that hung on our back wall. 'Now,' he says, 'have a look, Christy.'

My father looked into the mirror. 'Holy Jaysus, it's younger I'm gettin', Paddy,' he says. 'A great job. You're a born magician.'

'Christy, get Paddy a bottle of stout,' my mother said. You won't refuse a bottle of porter, will you, Paddy?'

'Never in my life,' said Paddy.

My father uncorked two bottles. 'Paddy, tell us about what happened on your way home.'

'Well,' he said, 'it was a few years ago and I was walkin' home from Daingean after cuttin' hair. It was a nice moonlit night, and 'twas during the month of July. When I got to Riverlyons, I decided to take a shortcut through the fields because I know that area from huntin' or sometimes helpin' men savin' hay or cuttin' oats. Anyway, I was walkin' along with not a worry in me head when I came to a hayfield. Just then I saw a small little broken-down wall almost covered by bushes, but 'twas enough for me to climb. When I got across the wall I started for the far side of the field, and I remember thinkin' that this would save me at least ten minutes of a walk.'

Paddy was holding his bottle of stout in his right hand with its bottom resting on his thigh. He had forgotten to take a swig when my father said, 'Paddy, take a mouthful of porter.'

Paddy lifted the bottle and put it to his mouth. I could see the movements in the glands of his neck as he swallowed. Then he put the bottle on the floor beside his chair and began searching his pockets for cigarettes. My father offered him a Woodbine.

'No, thanks, Christy, I'd rather stay with these.' He was pulling from his inside pocket a small packet of Craven A's. Paddy went over to the fire and grabbed the tongs and used it to lift a small coal. In this way he lit my father's cigarette and then his own. He began to talk again to my father and mother in a more direct way. 'You all know me. I'm a no-nonsense kind of man,' he said. 'I've never believed in ghosts or fairies or the supernatural. A lot of people around here are full of pishrogues and the like and I've never met anyone or anythin' worse than myself.'

My father could tell that Paddy was clearing the way for the rest of his story. 'So you crossed the stone wall and you were in the field. What happened after that?'

'Well,' said Paddy, 'I kept walkin' until I came to the other end of the field.'

Meanwhile, I was sitting in my favourite corner and in my own mind I wasn't very impressed with Paddy's story until he said, 'When I got there, I couldn't find any openin' in the ditch! I saw an old drain and on the other side of it was a hedge with briars and blackthorn bushes but I couldn't for the life of me see any way I could get out.

Well,' he said, 'that was all right, or so I thought. I remember saying to myself that the best thing to do was to double back to where I climbed over the stone wall and forget about the shortcut. So I began walkin' back – it wasn't too far, since the field was somewhere in the two-acre size, but when I got to the other end I couldn't find the stone wall. I walked along slowly, lookin' for a gap in the bushes until I was sure I missed nothin' and to my surprise I could not find an openin', nor could I see any sign of the stone wall. It had disappeared!'

'The cross of Jaysus,' said my father. 'I've never heard of anythin' like it.'

'You won't believe the rest of it,' said Paddy. 'It was then I began to panic a bit and with the moon shinin' its bit of light I decided to try lookin' for holes in the sides of the field. I tried the first one up and down and up and down, but to no avail. I walked over to the far side and walked back and forth several times but could see no openin' in the ditch. I went back again to where I thought the stone wall might be hidden in the bushes, but nowhere was it to be seen. I started to feel trapped and all sorts of strange ideas were playin' hide and seek in my mind. It's a very hopeless feelin', Christy.' He went on to explain how he searched every side of the field for as long as he could stand it. He said he turned his jacket inside out and put it back on (this was a remedy that was supposed to break the spell) until finally he was worn out and had to lie down against a haystack. 'After a while, I fell asleep. I must have slept for six or seven hours because when I woke up it was early mornin' and the sun was shinin'. When I realised where I was I stood up and began walkin' again to where I thought the stone wall might be. When I got there I was shocked to see the little broken wall as plain as my eyes could see. It was impossible to miss it, but somehow my eyes deceived me on the night before. As a sort of comparison I walked to the opposite end of the field for another look and what I saw was very frightenin'. There were several gaps in the hedge and I couldn't see any sign of the drain. The openings in the ditch were caused by cattle breakin' in and out and 'twas easy for me to walk through to the next field. It was eight o'clock in the mornin' when I got home and I remember that all of a sudden I felt very hungry and tired. Without eatin' I went to bed and fell asleep. I didn't wake 'til about three in the afternoon. Now,' he said, 'what do you think of that'?

My mother looked at Paddy. 'I heard of somethin' from the old people about someone bein' kidnapped by the little people,' she said. 'I think that's what happened to you, Paddy. It's the only explanation.'

I was still sitting in the corner listening to this strange story. While he was telling it, I thought he was a little nervous or perhaps it was my imagination. We had little doubt that something of a very unusual nature had stranded him in the hayfield and that somehow he was humbled by the whole experience.

It was the strangest thing that could happen to anyone, and as he was leaving for home he told us he never tried the same shortcut again, not, he said, 'for all the money in the world'. When he was gone we all had a lot to talk about. My mother was the first to speak. 'That man gives me the shivers,' she said.

My father, however, was sympathetic. 'Sure it wasn't his fault. All he was doin' was tryin' to take a shortcut.'

But my mother wasn't convinced. 'He must have done somethin' wrong if the fairies had it in for him.'

'Holy Christ,' said my father. 'Now we're talkin' about fairies!'

8

A Ghostly Confrontation

Storytelling was a pastime we all enjoyed and most stories were regarded as the God's truth, as my mother would say, and if someone told a story it was often preceded by 'May God strike me dead if I'm not tellin' the truth.'

My father told us a ghost story one evening when Jim McDonald, a boatsman friend of his, was present. Jim was from Ballycommon, three miles west of Daingean, and the two of them went to national school together. My mother relied on Jim's ability to spot a weakness in a story, especially since Jim had known my father over thirty years. It was while we were all drinking tea and sitting around the fire that my father began.

'Jim,' he said, 'do you remember the two brothers who inherited the old slated cottage on the way to Tullamore?'

'I think I do – was it Malachy and Martin Coyne?'

'The very ones,' said my father. 'Did you know the cottage is haunted?'

'No,' said Jim, 'indeed I didn't.'

'Neither did the two lads, at least not until Martin lived there,' said my father. 'Anyway, on the first night he went to bed early. He was well worn out from movin' heavy furniture and cyclin' back and forth to Ballycommon. He said afterwards that he fell asleep about ten o'clock, but suddenly woke up about one o'clock. He thought he heard somethin' like a groan or a moan and sittin' up in bed he noticed it was a bright moonlit night. He could see the whole bedroom, even the wallpaper. As he was about to lie down on his pillow he noticed the door movin' inwards . . . and then he saw it. 'Twas a tall shadowy shape that came forward. Martin was petrified. "What do you want?" he asked. "Leave and leave now," a voice said. Martin tried again. "What can I do to help you?" The ghost spoke again. "Those yet to be born are destined to take away my burden." It then began shakin' Martin's bed and said in a low voice, "Leave, leave, leave!"'

My mother looked at my father. She was visibly shaken. 'Will you stop, Christy. You'll frighten the children, especially the little girls.' Jim McDonald said nothing and was looking at the floor.

'Well,' my father said, 'I suppose I'll have to finish it some other time.'

'What?' said my mother. 'You don't mean to tell me there's more of it?'

'My dear woman, I've only just begun,' my father chuckled.

'Well,' said my mother, 'in that case I'll put the girls to bed. Moira, Ann, Patricia, Kathleen, come on!'

Moira and Ann wanted to hear the rest of the story. 'Mammy, Mammy, we don't want to go. We don't—'

My father lifted his voice. 'Not another word.'

Jim McDonald took a swallow of his tea. 'Well, Christy, what happened next?'

My father was about to say something when my mother shouted from the bedroom door. 'Wait! Wait! I'll be back in a minute.'

'I thought you didn't want any more of it!' my father shouted back.

During this time I was thinking about what the auld ghost said to Martin Coyne about those who were yet to be born. Thinking about it a little more, I concluded that I was lucky to be already born!

When my mother came back she refilled the kettle and my father lit a cigarette. 'You don't smoke, Jim?' he asked.

'No, said Jim, 'I gave them up five years ago.'

My father resumed the story. 'I suppose I don't have to tell you that Martin Coyne left the cottage that very night. He put on his clothes when he got outside the door and skedaddled home to Ballycommon. When he got there he told his brother about what had happened. His brother stood looking at him for a few seconds and then began to laugh. "Who put you up to this?" he asked, "Or are you losin' all of your senses? You must think I'm a thunderin' jackass, or worse! Listen, I've heard enough. You must be tired and so am I." The next morning after breakfast, Martin said, "What happened last night is the God's honest truth, and what's more, I'm never goin' back there again!" "Well," said his brother, "the best thing I can do is to go over there tonight and see what this is about. There's no fuckin' ghost ever goin' to evict me from my own house."'

My father took a few more pulls from his cigarette. We were all staring at him. 'Christy,' my mother said, 'you're an awful man for draggin' out a story. Isn't he, Jim?'

But before Jim could say anything my father said, 'Any sign of the tea?'

'Here it is,' said my mother. He hadn't noticed her pouring it, nor had he seen the plate of sandwiches she had prepared.

'In any case,' he continued, 'this is what happened. Malachy, of course, didn't believe in ghosts. So the followin' night he walked all the way out to the cottage and prepared for bed. He told the story himself about bein' sound asleep and awakened by the bedroom door openin' and shuttin' with a bang. And then he saw the shadow of the ghost, which he said wore a long black cape and tall hat. The shadow moved near his bed, and Malachy got up. He had his clothes on in readiness, and as he confronted the ghost he still thought it to be someone tryin' to frighten him. "You dirty rotten fiend," he shouted at the ghost, who backed away into one corner of the bedroom. "Jaysus Christ," Malachy shouted. He tried to corner the ghost and tried in vain to hit it with his fists. He swung again and the ghost ducked and shoved him against a cabinet. He tried kickin' and punchin' but each time he hit the wall or the end of the bed. The ghost lifted him up and threw him against the door. After half an hour of fightin', Malachy was broken in body and spirit. When he didn't return home next mornin' Martin became worried, so he decided to cycle over to the cottage. He found Malachy in the bedroom lyin' on the floor, and he wasn't able to stand up. Martin pulled his brother up against the wall and made him as comfortable as he could. He said he was goin' for help and in an hour an ambulance came.'

Apparently Malachy was badly hurt, somethin' to do with his spine. My father didn't like the story to have such a sad ending, and finished in a low voice. 'Poor fellow. He ended up in a wheelchair for the rest of his life.'

Jim McDonald took off his cap and rubbed his forehead with the sleeve of his coat. 'By God,' he said, 'what a story! And did anyone ever live in the house?'

'No one, as far as I know. It's still there near the side of the road, an old abandoned house, and no one will ever live in it.'

It was a sad ending for a hale and hearty man. 'I've heard rumours about the fellow in the wheelchair,' Jim said to my father. 'His younger brother blamed himself for what happened; he felt very guilty about it.'

The two of them continued talking, and I picked up the single-row and laid it on my lap. All of a sudden we could hear Shep barking outside and the gate shaking and then the dog was yelping like he was burned. A voice shouted, 'You dirty, rotten, slimy fuckin' snake!' And again the gate was slammed against the pillar and Shep was silent. In a minute a knock came to the door. *Tot! Tot! Tot!*

My father opened the door. 'Mick,' he said, 'it's you!'

'Christy,' said Mick, 'I'm goin' to shoot that fuckin' dog!'

'Paddy,' my mother said, 'it's Mick Hayes.'

Mick had his accordion with him. 'I want to leave the box with Paddy for a while,' he said. 'He might like to try it out.'

'I'll mind it,' I told him, 'and make sure no one else touches it.'

'I hope I didn't interrupt anythin',' Mick laughed.

'Not at all, Mick,' said Jim, Christy just finished a mighty ghost story.'

Mick looked at Jim. 'I'd rather hear one of those when the sun is up.'

I started to finger my accordion and was anxious to play something.

'That's right,' said Mick. 'Play us a tune.'

I tried a new one I had learned but got stuck after a few bars.

'Try it again,' said Jim. So I began again, but lost my memory of the tune as I tried to play it. Everybody was looking at me and waiting, and I could feel myself blushing. My mother rescued me. 'It's the ghost story has him unsettled,' she said. 'Twould frighten anyone, isn't that right, Jim?'

Jim was looking into the fire. 'You don't have to tell me, missus. I couldn't agree with you more.'

9

Croghan Feis

Mick Hayes left his accordion with me for five weeks. It had nine couplers that provided various tones when pressed individually. There were at least four of them that I couldn't quite make my mind up on, and so I would use them depending on the sound of a particular tune. I would often play Mick's accordion for a couple of hours, trying out this and that until finally my hands began to ache, especially the heels. A revelation to me was the existence of several tiny muscles in my hands and wrists that pained me for weeks before I got used to the instrument. A long slot or indentation on the side of Mick's keyboard meant that I needed to keep my thumb pressed against the slot while playing, and this was another difficult task. The accordion was also heavy and too big, which was more of a problem than I first imagined. During other times of practice I would use my single-row box and this helped me to rest my hands somewhat. About the same time, I had gotten over the shock of hearing Leo Rowsome's uilleann pipes and had made some progress with listening to my grandfather's gramophone. I also learned Rowsome's rendition of 'Rodney's Glory', which he had recorded on one of his 78 rpms.

The sound of this tune always took me back to when I was five years old and how my mother lifted me onto the back of her bicycle and put me sitting on its back carrier. She had already folded a small blanket several times and tied it to the carrier so as to make the seat soft for my backside. And then off we went to the feis. It was St Patrick's Day 1951, and many people had travelled to Croghan Hill where they would climb to its summit and pay their respects to the saint.

In local folklore, it is said that Patrick walked across north Offaly on his way to Tara in County Meath. When he came to Croghan Hill he decided to climb it, and with his followers he put out a message that he would speak. He had his harpers on the hilltop strum their harps together. Their collective sound was carried by the wind for miles around and next day Patrick spoke to a huge crowd of curious listeners who gathered to hear his message of Christianity.

My mother cycled the four miles from our house with me sitting behind her on the carrier. Now and again she would look back and say, 'Paddy, are you all right?' We arrived at the feis during the early afternoon and everything was in full swing, with a football match on the far side of the field. I could see white canvas tents that were steadied by stout ropes tied to wooden pegs pounded into the ground. Men, women and children were everywhere, strolling around or watching a performance on one of the stages. On one particular stage was a man playing a set of uilleann pipes, and my mother lifted me up so I could see him. 'That's Leo Rowsome,' she said. 'He's supposed to be the king of the pipers.' He was playing for four young girls who were step dancing and they were wearing green skirts with all types of Celtic designs in golden colours. They were also wearing black polished shoes with silver buckles and black stockings that contrasted with the green skirts of their uniforms. I could see shiny medals attached to their white blouses and these glittered in the sunshine as they hopped up and down to the rhythm of the piper's music. After we had watched for a while my mother said, 'Paddy, would you like an ice cream?'

'Oh, yeah!' I replied.

Within minutes we were licking two penny ice creams pressed between two wafers. As we were passing by a tent that sold holy pictures and crucifixes we saw bottles of orange juice for sale. My mother bought me one and took a few swigs for herself before giving it to me. We walked some more and arrived at more canvas tents. We could hear sounds of groaning and cursing, and also the sound of belching! 'In God's name, what's goin' on?' my mother said. Then as we rounded a corner we saw it: a tug-of-war contest, with seven men on each side pulling and slipping on the grass. The long rope was the thickest I'd ever seen and there was a ribbon tied to its middle section. This defined the rope boundary between each team and two sticks, two feet apart, were stuck in the ground. When the ribbon was between the sticks the rope was in neutral territory, which is when the pulling began. The men of each side had one foot pushed forward and dug into the ground, and they were all lined up at a slanted angle. Some of their hands were overlapping a little, depending on the rope's movement. Some had undone their shirts, which were hanging loosely. One fellow, who was a team captain and led the pulling in front of his team, was stocky and had a round stomach that I learned many years later was a prime example of a well-developed porter belly. His face looked red and puffed up. Suddenly he blasted a tirade of farts that sounded like a ton of small stones rolling down from an upended cart! The man behind him lost his concentration and skidded on the grass. Another man behind him shouted, 'Hold tight! Hold tight!' But it was too late. The opposing team were gaining momentum while the losing team were slipping and the rope lost its steady-handed control. The match was lost within a minute. Both teams walked among each other and shook hands. Someone said, 'The best team won!'

'Let's go and see the balloons,' my mother said, laughing. The balloons were tied on a board and were spaced small distances apart. For a penny you were given a small ball and if you hit a balloon you won a prize. While we were watching, a little girl won a doll which was presented to her on the spot. Everyone cheered as she held the doll and showed it to another little girl. After some more wandering we began to feel tired, but didn't see any chairs so we sat on the grass for a while. My mother remarked about how we might have a nice suntan after the outing at the feis. Before we knew it it was evening and time to return home. As we walked, I looked up at Croghan Hill and was amazed at how steep it was, especially on its southern side. Just below it were some level fields which facilitated the feis area; on the side of the hill were bunches of furze bushes that were burning and smoke was twisting its way upwards and then drifting towards the east.

It was an exciting sight with the flames jumping out of the burning furze, and the smell of the smoke mixing through the fresh air was intoxicating. We continued walking until we came to a narrow lane where my mother's bicycle was under a shady tree. She had to remove three other bicycles in order to free her own, and once we were on the side of the road my mother lifted me again onto the carrier. When she was seated on the bicycle she began pedalling alongside other cyclists who were also on their way home. The road was crowded with people walking towards Croghan village, and in a short time we could hear the sound of pipers in the distance. We soon caught up to the source of the music and my mother told me it was Saint

Colmcille's Pipe Band from Tullamore. Then we saw three lines of kilted pipers, drummers, and a pipe major out in front who was wearing a huge Glengarry hat! My mother had to pedal slowly behind the band, which had taken over the full width of the road. It was a deafening sound as they played 'Scotland the Brave'.

I was amazed by the sight of the band's scarlet and black uniforms, with tassels that hung from the pipes, and by the heavy thuds of the bass drums. Just as we all arrived at the crossroads in Croghan, the pipes ceased playing while the snare drums continued to beat out the final *tit-tat, tit-tat* in time with the marching of feet on the old tarred road.

As we passed them by at the village, the band was breaking up and I saw some of them lighting cigarettes. Others were coughing up smoke or removing their caps, while more were unbuttoning their tunics. It was a warm March evening, and the sun was still shining when my mother and I arrived home. The experience of the feis has stayed with me ever since, and when I learned the set dance 'Rodney's Glory' from Leo Rowsome's piping I could have sworn it was the same tune I had heard seven years earlier when Leo played for the four young girls who danced at the feis in Croghan.

10

National School

Before I joined the boys-only national school in Daingean I did two years in the girls' school, which also accommodated young boys in what was known as low infants and then a year in high infants. I still remember the first day when my mother brought me into the low infants' room and told me my teacher was Mrs O'Neill.

Mrs O'Neill stood looking down at me with a pretentious smile and I could see a wooden one-foot rule in her right hand. She was a small, stout woman in her mid-forties, and she wore a blue costume with a skirt and buttoned jacket and blouse. She was my very first teacher of Christian doctrine, sums or maths, English and Irish reading. When my mother was gone I began to cry, as did other children in the classroom. We were all separated from our parents and a feeling of being lost to the unknown overcame us. It may have been an hour before I tired of crying, at which point I began making chalk marks on a black slate. This amused me and I was enjoying myself when I heard Mrs O'Neill raising her voice. 'Now, now,' she said. 'This won't do. It won't do at all.' She was looking towards a sobbing child who sat at another desk. He hadn't stopped crying. He was sitting on the other side of the classroom and was lying face down on his desk. I looked up at the teacher and said, 'I'm not like him. I wouldn't cry like that.' The teacher grinned and pointed her finger at me. It was a subtle warning, but I didn't know it.

At midday we had a half-hour break for lunch. We all clambered outside to the school yard and sat on the grass. Some of us had schoolboy satchels and others had biscuit tins. My mother had given me two sardine sandwiches with a small bottle of milk, but I wasn't very hungry and only ate half a sandwich. I drank almost all of the milk, though, just in time to hear the school bell ringing. It was time to return to the classroom! I spent the next two hours scribbling on my slate. The boy on the far side of the room had stopped crying and was playing with crayons on a piece of white paper. Our teacher spent most of her time asking us our names and where we lived and if we believed in Santa Claus. This was her way of reminding us that Santa was very nice to good children, and that he'd be rewarding us for paying attention in school.

We were all dismissed from class at 2.30 and when I came out the front door I saw my mother waiting for me at the school gate. She carried me home on the carrier of her bicycle with my legs hanging down each side. I would be six years old in less than two weeks, and my little head was alive with images of the teacher, the chalk and the slates, and the little boy who was crying became one of my earliest memories. When we arrived home my mother heated chicken soup and I ate that along with some buttered bread. I answered lots of questions from my mother and my eldest sister, Moira. Later on, when my father came home, he too wanted to hear how I had got on. I went to bed early as I was tired of the attention and craved the quietness of the bedroom. Before I fell asleep I heard my parents say my name in the kitchen. As I lay there I felt very secure, but I knew tomorrow would be another day, because I heard my father say, 'A good sleep and Paddy should feel better tomorrow.'

Over the next few days I became more confident, until one day I was caught looking behind me and Mrs O'Neill with her wooden rule stung my forefinger where my hand was resting on the desk. This woke me up to the reality of what kind of a person she was, and as the months passed I was shocked by some of her treatment of other children. Vicious slaps on the hands were prevalent, and hard, open-hand slaps to the sides of our faces turned normal children into resentful little rogues. If the children didn't remember something she would pull their hair, especially the little girls. She was more forgiving of the town children and looked down her nose at children who came from poorer families. Whether country children were favoured depended on the financial status of their parents. We weren't aware of how much class discrimination touched our lives and our parents knew little about it either.

A large percentage of Irish children who are now grown up have their own stories of schoolroom neglect by teachers who ignored them in their belief that some children were incapable of learning. This was a situation that was never addressed by the clergy, teaching authorities, or the school principal. Teachers were never properly trained in communication techniques or how to coax or give children some sense of accomplishment. Instead, our years at national school were times of extreme intimidation and fear and a lot of us have never fully recovered from the experience. Many of the teachers had secured employment because they spoke Irish, but were totally inadequate at teaching us how to put together (in Irish) the words necessary to form ordinary comments on the weather, how to get from here to there or to describe what a cowboy did in a film. I suppose it's easy to be critical and yet the very idea of a method for teaching children was never considered, never mind as a means to an end.

The tragedy of it all was that we grew to dislike the Irish language because we associated it with the grim faces of our teachers who beat us, called us names and generally made us feel worthless. Particular pupils were also singled out and humiliated in front of an entire class of twenty to thirty children. It was a devastating time in our young lives.

Slowly but surely, we all settled into our low infants class until one day we were told that we were being moved to another row of seats that gave us the honour of becoming high infants. Mrs O'Neill made it her business to warn us that a better standard was expected, and she would remind us several times what it meant. She would walk up and down between our seats, looking over our shoulders as we wrote short essays. If we spilled ink or blotted our pages we were dealt an unexpected slap on the back of our heads. We were all seven years old and this woman was overseeing us like a prison guard. The result was poor concentration, nervous tension, and some children developed stammers or stutters when she questioned what they had written in their copy books.

About this time I became friends with a few other boys who would talk about cowboys and Indians. I had never heard about Indians and had never seen the pictures that were being shown in the new courthouse, which also served as cinema and dance hall. My friends spoke of the Durango Kid and Roy Rogers. I was fascinated and wanted to know more.

'What are Indians?' I enquired.

Seamus Carr was only too glad to inform me. 'I saw them,' he said. 'They wear very little clothes, just a bit of a towel around here.' He pointed to his crotch. 'Yeah,' he said, 'and they have horses and they circle wagon trains.'

'They have bows and arrows,' said Willy Smith, who had joined us. 'Yeah,' he said, 'I've made some. Bows and arrows. What—'

The door was opening; she was back. The whole class went silent. 'Now,' she said, 'let's begin again.' Then all of a sudden she addressed my friend Seamus. 'Carr! What were you talking about when I opened the door?'

Carr lifted his English book to his face and was hiding behind it.

'O'Brien,' she shouted, 'what was Carr talking to you about?'

'Nothin' ma'am,' was my answer.

She said, 'If I see you two talking again, I'll brand your ears for ye.' Willy Smith had disappeared under our desk and then reappeared behind us at his own desk. Mrs O'Neill shouted, 'Smith! Where were you? What are you doing, you little ferret?'

'I found my pencil, ma'am. It was on the floor.'

Mrs O'Neill had put on a fresh colour of lipstick. It was a darker blend of red. It made her look very stern and bossy, and for the rest of the afternoon we were as quiet as lambs in a manger.

Mrs O'Neill prepared us for our first Holy Communion and brought us all to the church in preparation for the big event. She played the role of the priest in the confession box and each one of us would go inside and wait until she pulled the sliding door of the hatch open.

Willy Smith was first. 'Bless me, Mrs O'Neill, for I have sinned—'

'You little nincompoop!' she yelled. 'You half-baked dummy. It's "Bless me *Father*, for I have sinned." Now,' she said, 'I'm closing the door and when I slide it open you are to say, "Bless me Father, for I have sinned. It's my first time at confession."'

They began again, and the second time Willy had his lines right until he came to his list of sins. She shouted, 'Don't tell the priest any such thing or he'll send you away!'

Finally, Willy came out. His face was white as he turned and walked slowly to the back of the church. Soon it was my turn, and in I went. She pulled back the sliding door of the hatch.

'Bless me Father, for I have sinned. I have never been to confession—'

'Just say it's your first confession,' she urged. Then she said, 'Tell me your sins.'

'I stole such-and-such—'

She interrupted me, saying very slowly, 'You . . . must . . . say . . . WHAT IT IS YOU STOLE!'

I began to understand and said I stole sugar from my mother, and that I stole socks from my father.

'Stop,' she said. 'You are forgiven. And for your penance, say three Hail Marys.'

I blessed myself and opened the door. When I stepped outside I was sweating from the heat of the confessional and I could feel the cold air in the church.

When we returned to the schoolroom Mrs O'Neill removed her headscarf. Then we saw she had her hair permed and it looked shorter. A couple of the girls giggled.

'What are you giggling at, Miss Hickey?' Marie Hickey blushed. 'And Greta Hanlon – what's so funny?' Greta lowered her head and said nothing. 'Lift your head and look at me,' shouted Mrs O'Neill. 'My sly little damsel, it's your prayers you should be saying. Don't you know your parents expect you to be a nun?' The little girl was embarrassed, and began to cry. 'Someone give the pet a hankie,' teased Mrs O'Neill.

First communion was a big occasion for us children and an expensive one for our parents, who had to buy us boys first communion suits, with new shoes and stockings and a new shirt and tie. My mother and father were in a quandary about the cost. 'Where are we going to get the money for this?' my mother was saying.

'My father might be able to help,' said my own father. 'I'll go to Ballycommon and ask him.'

A few weeks later we were confirmed, with a large turnout of spectators at the church. There was a group photo taken and my aunts gave me half-crowns, and our neighbours were also generous with ten-shilling notes and coinage of varying kinds.

'Look at him,' said a friend of my mother's. 'Isn't he the purest little angel, and not as much as one little stain on his soul. Imagine,' she said, 'if he died now, he'd go straight to heaven.' This made me feel uneasy, and I began wishing she'd go away and leave me alone; and besides, I wasn't ready to go to heaven any time soon!

After church we all went home and my Aunt Maggie came with me and stayed at our house until late in the evening. She was very proud of me and gave me several hugs, then held me out at arm's length so she could see me and she would cry a little and then laugh in the middle of her tears. It was her way of expressing her kindness and affection. I would never forget her demonstrations of how she felt for me on that particular night.

I didn't get to see Roy Rogers at the pictures for some time, but I remember hearing him sing on one of my grandfather's records. On the label was written 'Roy Rogers and the Sons of the Pioneers'. From talking with Seamus Carr I knew that Roy Rogers was a cowboy and that Seamus had seen him in the pictures. 'What is it this fellow does?' I asked Seamus.

'He's a great gunfighter, and his horse is Trigger and he rides all over the West.'

Upon hearing this, my curiosity knew no limits. On the other hand, I wasn't so sure about how much Seamus knew about Roy and his horse.

Seamus was a fair-haired boy whom I sat beside in the girls' school. He had a nasty habit of eating his nails and picking his nose. He also liked to eat the bottom ends of his school books. I remember his English and Irish books having been eaten in a half-moon shape through all of their pages and the widest part of the half-circle being at least two inches. His books were damp from his saliva, and I could see him biting little bits of wet paper and very often he would pick small pieces with his thumb and forefinger and roll them into a tiny ball before transferring it to his teeth for more squeezing and chewing.

It was on rare occasions that Mrs O'Neill said a word of chastisement to Seamus. On one occasion, when he got bogged down in his reading, she walked down the little aisle in the classroom and asked him for his English book. When she looked at it she yelled, 'No wonder you couldn't finish reading your book – it's because you've eaten it!'

We always looked forward to lunch break and began devising ways to shorten our meals so as we'd have more time for playing on the grass or running around the two huge oak trees that stood in the playground. Our games included tig and blind man's bluff, but when the weather was sunny we loved to push and wrestle with each other. We were having a delightful time rolling in the grass when a stout little boy came running at me with a wide grin on his face. I pushed him away and he fell. As soon as he did he began to cry and bawl so loudly we thought he was hurt. He created such an outburst that some of the older girls gathered around him. I thought I'd done something terribly wrong, and without thinking I ran across the school yard to the wall by the road, jumped over it and ran and walked as fast as I could, and in less than fifteen minutes I was home.

Sitting in the kitchen, I told my mother what had happened when I pushed Martin Lynch in the school yard. When she asked if he was hurt I said I didn't know. The following morning my mother spoke with the headmistress. Martin was fine, but the teachers were keen on making me pay for pushing another child and, more than that, for leaving school during school hours. My mother was guaranteed leniency for me, however, when the headmistress considered how my father had given the school a load of free turf the previous winter. My mother came home and brought me back to school and as soon as she was gone I was confronted by Mrs Phelan, the headmistress.

'You are a bad little boy,' she said. 'Now hold out your hand.'

She hit my palm five times. 'Hold out the other hand.' And then five more painful slaps. I was crying a little as I walked down the hall to my room. I remember hearing Kitty Pilkington say to another girl, 'The poor little devil.' Later on it became common knowledge that Martin Lynch was in fact a crier and would burst into tears if someone looked at him without a smile. It was so common that many of the other children avoided him during play time and teachers were careful not to cause him any upset. Indeed it was a very sensitive issue.

One of my favourite schoolmates was Vincent Cuskelly, who was the same age as myself, and then there was Seamus Carr, Willy Smith and Jimmy Quinn. We loved to play cowboys and Indians and hide-and-seek. Willy Smith on occasions came to school wearing a belt, holster and cap gun. As soon as our new teacher saw him she said, 'Come here, you. Yes, you,' as she pointed her finger. Willy marched up to her desk. She said, 'Who told you to bring those to school?'

Willy didn't answer. 'Take them off and I'll return them to you after school.' Near the end of the class she told us she had something to tell us and to wait for five minutes. We all watched as she removed Willy's belt, holster and cap gun from her desk and laid them on a chair under the blackboard. Then she began.

'Listen, everyone. I have been told by Father Doran that he and the other priests are organising a fancy dress parade and that all the children in the boys' and girls' schools are invited to take part. In other words, you can all dress up in your funny clothes and walk in the fancy dress parade, which will be from the top of the town all the way down the street until you get to the square outside the courthouse. There will also be judges who will decide who the winners are, and prizes for first, second, third and fourth. By the way,' she added, 'the parade will be held on the second Sunday of next month, which is September. Any questions?'

Several children raised their hands. She looked around and said, 'You!'

'Can I be a cowboy?'

Another said, 'Can I be Robin Hood?'

A little girl asked, 'Can I be Saint Teresa?'

There were lots of questions, but instead of answering she told us all to hush. 'I know many of you boys will want to be cowboys or Indians, so let me say that the parade committee wants you all to dress in different clothes, and to have new ideas, like dressing up as a clown or a scarecrow. One of you could be a beggarman. Little girls could dress as angels or one could be a queen from the Hill of Tara.'

Seamus Carr gave me an elbow. 'I know what I'm goin' to be.'

'What?'

'A leprechaun.'

'What's a leprechaun?'

'It's a fairy chief,' said Seamus. 'And they have magic.'

I hadn't heard anything like this before, but had to wait until another time before asking Seamus more about it.

In the meantime, our school day was finished and we all headed home. At this time I was walking back and forth to the school by myself and occasionally I would be treated with a lift from a neighbour. On one such evening Richard Daley's father Dick called at the school to collect his twin sons Paddy and little Richard and take them home. The boys were in the same class as me and I knew them as neighbours and schoolmates. When their father came he had a horse and cart that he'd used earlier in the day for carrying pigs to the fair in Daingean. The cart was empty as we climbed onto it, but the smell of pig manure was still very strong. Dick Senior had sold his pigs, but had neglected to sweep the bottom of the cart. All four of us stood near the front, looking down on the horse's back as it trotted along up the side road, and then up the main street of Daingean. Dick Senior reined in the horse off the street to an alleyway and we all climbed down.

After he tied his horse to a gate, young Richard enquired, 'Where are we goin', Daddy? Where are we goin'?'

Dick Senior pointed to a side door. 'In here,' he said. 'Come on.'

We all walked in and I looked around. It was a public house and men were sitting or standing at the bar counter drinking and talking. I had never been in a pub before and everyone looked so tall, and the counter was too high to see over it. Dick Senior looked down at me and his sons. 'What would ye like to drink?'

We didn't know. We heard him order something for all of us, and when I saw what it was I was puzzled by its colour. It was in a tall glass, and as I looked at the two Daleys they were already drinking it, and so I took a sip. By God! It was gorgeous, the nicest drink I ever had, and when I swallowed, it had a beautiful smell of some sort of fruit. I later learned that it was raspberry juice. Dick Senior himself was drinking a half pint of porter that seemed to disappear with a couple of swallows. Then he said, 'Come on,' and we quickly finished our raspberries and followed him out the door. We had been in the pub less than ten minutes. The thrill of the horse and cart ride has stayed with me for many years. I had never been so high off the road before, and the rapid speed of the horse, the sound of the cart wheels and the excitement of looking out over the high creels of the cart gave me a feeling of wild adventure that I really enjoyed. After a mile Dick Senior pulled up outside our gate. My father was sweeping the yard and when he saw us he began walking towards the gate just as I was descending from the cart.

'Dick, thanks for minding Paddy,' he shouted. 'The Lord leave you your health!'

'Not a bother, Christy, not a bother,' Dick replied. Then he shouted at the horse, 'Get up there, get up!' and away home they went.

11

The Fancy Dress Parade

Our teacher returned and said she had been talking about the upcoming fancy dress parade to Father Cronin. She said anyone who wanted to enter the competition would have to write their name and the name of their entry on a card. She held up a pack of pink cards. 'Here are the cards and I will leave them over on the table next to the door. You must return them no later than Friday after class and they are only for those who will take part in the competition.'

At home my mother was saying that everyone around was very excited about the parade. 'It's the talk of the town,' she said. She told my father that women in the post office and grocery shops were all looking forward to the day of the parade.

For the next couple of weeks the town was alive with talk about who was competing in the fancy dress competition. There were posters everywhere and an amusements carnival arrived and set up its business near the side wall of the courthouse square. There was a dance in the town hall on the Saturday night before the parade with music by the Ballinamere Céilí Band. I was too young to be taken to the dance but heard one of my cousins talking about how great the band were.

The next day a large crowd of people gathered at the top of the town, which had a Y-shaped crossroads. The parade began slowly with a children's fife and drum marching band, dressed in green and white. It was a boys' band and they looked very organised as they marched along three lines abreast. Then they were followed by the parade. As it began, my mother, sister Moira and myself ran down a back lane so we could see the parade as it came towards the town square. Soon we had a good vantage point and saw that some adults had joined the parade and were dressed in clowns' attire. I saw another dressed as a cowboy and he was riding a white horse and wore a vizard on his face. The girls and boys of our school were well represented with a wide variety of colours; some were dressed as queens, witches or vampires, with capes covering their shoulders, while one little lad had a full cowboy outfit which was black with silver buttons and a studded belt and holsters with cap guns with white handles. He looked very impressive as he waved his black hat and fired a couple of shots.

The parade moved along slowly, and then there was a small break. My mother said, 'Look! Look!' She lowered her voice and said to me, 'Will you look at him! Paddy, don't you see who it is?' I wasn't sure who she was talking about. 'Look, look,' she said again. 'Look at the goat!' And then I saw him. It was Vincent Cuskelly! He was from my class and he had a sheet wrapped around him, hanging from one shoulder. He was also wearing sandals and his face, shoulders, arms, hands, and legs were painted brown. His hair was also shaven close to his scalp, and in one hand he held a short rope that was attached to the neck of a small goat. As he passed by we saw a placard on his back with clearly written block letters that read: 'GANDHI AND HIS GOAT'. Vincent was ambling along almost as though he was sleepwalking, with his small goat following him in the middle of the street. People were clapping and cheering him on and it was a supreme moment of magic for everyone. The little lad from the townland of 'The Little Island' was the hero of the afternoon.

Father Doran came through a side door and walked onto the dance floor. Then came our headmistress and one of the teachers from the boys' school. They all stood at a microphone that was clipped to a stand in front of the stage. Father Doran welcomed everyone and praised the parade. The fourth prize was given to a little girl for dressing as an old crone. The third was for the 'Florence Nightingale' entry by another little girl. The second prize was for the lad from the boys' school who wore the black cowboy suit. And first prize went to Gandhi and His Goat! Vincent Cuskelly came out of the shadows to receive his prize. He was still wearing the white bedsheet and his goat followed him as he walked onto the dance floor. Father Doran said he was proud to present Vincent with the first prize for his excellent portrayal of Gandhi.

Everyone stood in their seats and wild cheers and applause shook the hall. We all whistled, shouted and clapped when Vincent and his goat came walking up the steps between the seats. My mother got up and we followed her to the entrance area as Vincent was going towards the front door. 'Well done, Gandhi,' she shouted. 'You're a great little lad.' Vincent's sister appeared with an ice cream for her brother. She was much older than Vincent and my mother was glad she was there to help the little fellow and usher him through the crowded square. Shortly after they were gone we also headed off and took the shortcut home by way of the back road.

It was many years before I was to learn about the significance of what Vincent Cuskelly's prizewinning entry meant to so many people, and why the result of the competition was so popular. During the 1950s nationalism was an emotive issue in Irish politics, and the story of India's independence, and Mahatma Gandhi's passive resistance movement, was very much alive in the Irish consciousness. The very idea of this little man taking on the might of the British Empire stood well with Irish people who had seen him on the newsreel reports shown before the main attraction in their local cinema. Remembering that time, I also think of Vincent Cuskelly himself, who was my classmate and playmate when we ran and hid and shot our cap guns as cowboys and rustlers. Like Mahatma Gandhi, Vincent too was a very passive young fella. In school he was shy, humble and somewhat private. He was a scholar and avid reader of cowboy comics. He was the lad who introduced me to stories of the Old West with tales of Billy the Kid and the James Boys of Missouri.

12

The Sure-Sures

We had an old grey horse that my father used for carting stones when he worked for Offaly County Council. It was 1955 and I was ten years old, and my sister Moira was nine, when one day we heard him talking to our mother about the horse, saying he was going to get rid of him. He said the horse had become wicked and had nearly bitten him earlier in the day while he was unharnessing him from the cart. 'It's dangerous for Paddy and Moira to be near him,' he said. He showed our mother the sleeve of his coat, which was torn where the horse had tried to bite him. 'I'll tell yeh, he's become a bad bastard and the sooner we sell him the better.'

A few days later I was playing with Moira and was taking a short-cut between the back of the hen house and the hedge behind it. It was a narrow passage and when I was almost at the end of it the horse's head rounded the corner of the shed. It was as if he was waiting for me. I saw him stripping his teeth and can remember their brown colour with bits of juicy green grass stuck between some of them. I'm glad to say that I was too fast for the old horse. I made a quick retreat back behind the hen house as the animal tried to force his way in after me, but the space was too narrow. I waited a long time before he rambled away. My sister didn't notice anything unusual, otherwise she would have told our mother. When I came through the door of the kitchen my mother saw my hands shaking and asked me if I was all right. I told her about my lucky escape and she put her arms around me and held me close. Within a week my father had traded the horse for a two-year-old that had to be broken in. My mother was unhappy about the choice, saying the horse was too flighty to be around children.

Meanwhile we put the new pony to graze in a field next to the road. This caught the attention of some of the travellers who had an eye for good horse flesh. A couple of weeks later the Mullowney brothers came knocking at our door. 'Is the boss at home?'

'He should be home any minute,' my mother answered. It was very cold outside and the two men looked like they needed something hot. My mother said, 'Come in and sit by the fire.'

'Sure, sure,' said the elder brother, 'sure, sure.' My mother closed the door to keep the wind out of the kitchen and the two brothers pulled their chairs close to the fire. They were wearing heavy brown topcoats with high collars, and wore nothing on their heads. Our mother gave them some hot chicken soup and they held the warm mugs gratefully with both hands, and sipped. In a little while they began to praise the young horse, asking if it was for sale. My mother said she didn't know and that they should ask the man of the house, repeating that he should be home shortly. However, the two brothers were impatient and after they finished their soup stood up to leave. The younger one said, 'Sure is a fine little horse.' Then they thanked my mother for the soup and were gone. They had their own horse and trap waiting for them outside our gate. I ran onto the road to look after them as they sped away. It wasn't the last I saw of them.

My father was amused when my mother told him about the two travellers. He said, 'Those fellows are goin' to plague me from now on.' He was right. They returned on their way back from Edenderry with two horses tied to the back of their trap. My mother again invited them to sit by the fire and made tea and buttered bread and then pasted it with jam. They immediately asked, 'Is the boss home?' My mother said she was sorry that he wasn't but he would definitely be home in half an hour. They drank tea and ate a slice of bread and asked who played the whistle that was on a nearby chair. My mother looked at me but I remained silent. The elder man asked, 'Can I see it?'

'Of course', my mother said, and he lifted the slotted end to his mouth and blew. He ran his fingers back and forth along its six holes, playing a scale before breaking into a slow jig. It was wonderful to hear the whistle being played by someone who knew how. My father came in and the music stopped.

'Good day, boss,' said the whistler.

'Hello, men,' said my father.

'These are the Mullowneys who want to talk to you about sellin' the pony,' my mother told him.

My father looked at each one of the brothers and said, 'I never said I would sell her.'

'We have a good workhorse outside and he's only six years old,' the younger brother said. 'What about makin' a swap?' My father distrusted the offer and said he was training our two-year-old to plough and would try her out with a breaking harness next week. The two brothers rose from their chairs and said they would be back in a couple of weeks. After they were gone my father said he had little doubt they would return to see if he'd changed his mind.

The following week the breaking harness was put on the little horse, who appeared jittery and nervous. My father used a long rein to drive her around the bog pasture. It went very well until he yoked the horse to a plough. As soon as he said 'giddy up' the horse took off, dragging the plough after her with my father pulling hard on the reins. The horse stopped when she ran blindly into the corner of the field. My father coaxed the horse, patting her gently, and removed the harness. In a few days the Mullowneys returned. My father and mother were dropping potatoes and moulding the furrows for closing the drills in the field behind the garden. When I saw the Mullowneys at the gate I ran out from the yard, around the back of our house and into the garden and began shouting at my parents, 'The Sure-Sures are here! The Sure-Sures are here!' This was our nickname for the travellers, who used the two words after nearly everything they said.

My father came around to the front of the house and told them he'd sold the horse and bought an old black one from the McCormacks who lived outside Daingean. The Sure-Sures were clearly disappointed and walked away in silence. In minutes they had disappeared in their horse and trap. We never saw them again.

13

Long Trousers

Mick Hayes arrived on a night when we were expecting little of any kind of human company. He was in a foul mood. Shep had made another charge as he came through the gate and had barely missed Mick's right leg; instead the dog had torn the bottom leg end of Mick's trousers. We could see Mick's white leg when he walked into the kitchen. My mother put her hand over her mouth to shield her giggling as Mick cursed. He looked at my father and said, 'Where in the name of our Holy Mother did you find that vicious fucker, that poorly bred fiend that you call a dog?'

My father told him to sit down. 'Let me have a look. Did he bite yeh?'

'No,' shouted Mick, 'but not for want of tryin'!'

My father gave Mick a bottle of stout, which transformed his mood. He lifted his glass and said, 'Here's to the power of music, there's nothin' like it for puttin' a man in good form, not to mention the man himself, Arthur Guinness.' My father knew exactly what he meant and lifted his mug of tea and clinked it against Mick's glass. 'Happy Christmas,' he said.

My mother looked at my father. 'You must be losin' all yer wits,' she said. 'Don't you know that Christmas is four months away?'

Mick laughed. 'There's nothin' wrong with lookin' forward to it. By the way, did Christy tell you we are goin' out with the wren this year?' My mother looked astonished. 'We're hopin' to bring Tom Brewer with us,' Mick continued. When my mother laughed heartily at the mention of the name my sister Moira asked, 'Who is Tom Brewer?'

My father intervened. 'He's the one-man band! He plays the mouth organ and beats the tambourine and the foot drum, all at the same time. He's goin' to be on the radio in a couple of weeks.'

'That's right,' said Mick. 'He's goin' to be on *Céilí House* on Saturday night week.'

My mother was curious. 'How did he manage it?' she asked.

'He went to Dublin a few months ago,' Mick told her, 'and did some sort of test for the radio.'

'Nobody tells me anythin'!' my mother complained.

'I just found out, the same as you,' my father said in solidarity, 'and Mick heard the news as late as last night. Brewer would be a great attraction if we had him with us on Saint Stephen's Day.'

Mick could understand the logic of the choice. 'I'm goin' to Daingean tomorrow night,' he said, 'and I'll drop by his house and ask him. We also need a couple more to make up the batch. What do you think, Christy?'

'Well,' said my father, 'what about Tom and Paddy Brien from Clonadd?'

'The very fellows I was thinkin' of,' said Mick. 'We should run into them next Sunday after Mass.'

'One of them goes to first Mass and the other goes to last Mass.'

'There's no need for both of them to be together,' said Mick confidently. 'One of them will be enough, when we see him.'

It was a typical night at our house when Mick stopped in. There were a few more tunes, more tea with my mother's bread, and Mick pulling at the lobes of his ears. When he was leaving he took his accordion with him. I was sorry to see it go, and so I was left with my own box to fare away with. As Mick was on his way he asked my father to see him to the gate, just in case Shep came at him in the darkness. He was takin' no chances, he said, with such a vicious little bastard!

When Saturday night came we were very excited about Tom Brewer being a guest on Seán Ó Murchú's *Céilí House*. The featured band for the programme was Joe Delaney's Céilí Band, who were based in the Rhode/Croghan area of northeast Offaly. Seán Ó Murchú introduced Tom Brewer of Daingean as the first and only one-man band he ever heard. Tom played two marches on his mouth organ and whacked away on his tambourine with his foot drum beating a strong *thud, thud, thud*. We were very proud of Tom, and Seán Ó Murchú said he was one of Daingean's truest heroes. Later he played two more selections, which were jigs and hornpipes. On the same night my father was in Daingean and met Tom Brewer himself on the street, and when he returned home my mother told him about Tom playing on *Céilí House*.

'Woman, you must be dreamin',' my father said. 'Didn't I talk with Tom a little over an hour ago?' He couldn't be in two places at the

one time.' My parents jokingly argued about Tom's radio performance for over a week, until the next time my father went to town
for his Saturday-night drink. The next morning I heard him say to my
mother, 'I found out last night about Tom Brewer.'

'What did you find out?' my mother asked.

'*Céilí House* was recorded a month before it went on the radio and
they played the recordin' on the night you heard him. That's the way
they do it nowadays with the radio, and if anyone makes a mistake,
they can always re-do the recordin'.'

When my mother heard this she said no more, and neither did my
father. And so it was time to talk about something else.

In the coming months I tried my luck with my mother's bicycle,
but its saddle was a little too high. Another difficulty was staying on
as it moved while trying to steady it and keep it balanced. An idea of
putting my right foot on the right pedal came to mind and soon I was
allowing the bicycle to take me down a small incline in front of our
house. I practised this routine of riding down the small hill with my
left foot hanging close to the ground as a precaution. All went well
until I tried pedalling with both feet and then I lost control and rode
into the doorway of a shed. I hit my forehead against a crossbeam
and fell sideways, with the bicycle running from under me. The initial
shock and throbbing ache in my head unsettled me, and I didn't even
look at the bicycle for almost two weeks. In any event my determina-
tion returned, and in a matter of months I was able to cycle back and
forth to Aunt Mary's or take our battery to Daingean for charging.
There was a great demand for my services as a messenger and delivery boy.

When I was approaching my thirteenth birthday my parents spoke
of buying me long trousers and when the day came for trying them
on I was thrilled at how they concealed my skinny legs and how easy
it was for me to adjust to my new image. One Saturday evening my
mother asked if I would cycle to Aunt Mary's and bring her a dozen
eggs. Our hens were over-producing and my aunt would appreciate
a few extra eggs. I asked if I should take my accordion with me and
play her a few tunes. 'Of course,' she said. 'She would love to hear
you! Don't forget to play "The Kid on the Mountain". It's one she's
fond of.' And so off I went along the Mill Road to Daingean.

When I leaned the bicycle against the gable end of my aunt's house
I removed the accordion from where it hung in a sack on the left

handlebar. The eggs were also in the sack. I was about to knock on the back door, when it opened suddenly and I saw my aunt standing there with a look of surprise. She said, 'Pat,' and then yelled, 'Hooee! Hooee! When did you start wearin' the long trousers?'

'About a month or so ago,' I replied.

'Come in, come in, and I see you have the accordion with you. Hooee! Hooee!' 'Aunt Mary,' I said, 'my mother gave me eggs to give you.'

'Oh, lovely, lovely. Your mammy has a heart of gold, and you are a great lad for bringin' them to me. Sit down here next to the range and I'll boil the kettle.'

My aunt was all alone and her children were away on various errands or playing somewhere with other children. Her husband Mick was at work in charge of a bagger on Clonsast bog. Clonsast was another developed bog area that mass-produced bricks of turf for Bord na Móna. At that time Mick was working three eight-hour shifts. He was working the four-to-midnight shift when I visited my aunt. 'We have the house all to ourselves,' she said, 'and when we have a sup of tea I'd love to hear a tune.'

Before I finished my tea I reached for the accordion and began playing 'The Kid on the Mountain'.

'Oh, ho!' she said, 'it's better yer gettin'.' I started on a reel and she shouted again, 'Oh, ho ho! I can't sit still! Oh ho!' And then she began to dance and pulled her dress up over her knees. 'Yow! Yow! Yow!' she yelled. I could feel myself begin to sweat from the hot tea but didn't stop while she hopped and glided around her tiny kitchen. She was the liveliest woman I ever met and dancing was her favourite form of expression. I played many more tunes for her while sometimes she sat quietly looking at my fingers or smoking half a cigarette. In between when she caught her breath she would shout and dance more, depending on what I played. She also liked waltzes and would waltz with a broom when I played one. She told me to take a rest while she opened a drawer in a cabinet and took out a biscuit tin. She put some biscuits on a plate and said, 'Pat, if ever a lad deserved a biscuit, it's you!' When I heard this I felt very gratified. She always made me feel like this, and would invariably include me in a little small talk when adults were gathered. Suddenly she said, 'Did you hear the Gallowglass Céilí Band is comin' to Daingean at the end of the month and are due to play at a dance in the courthouse?' I hadn't heard. 'You should tell your Mammy,' she said. She had surprised me and I could see that she was delighted to be the first to tell me the news.

As twilight approached I began to feel edgy and said to my aunt, 'I want to head home before darkness.' I was nervous about cycling alone on the Mill Road because of the ghost stories I had heard. My aunt was very sympathetic. 'If you leave now, you should have enough light to get home.' So once again she saw me to the front gate and as I cycled away I turned and waved goodbye. I was home in twenty minutes with news about the Gallowglass Céilí Band.

The Gallowglass

It was the end of August when the dance was scheduled to be held in Daingean and many people were looking forward to hearing the Gallowglass Céilí Band. My mother talked to my father about both of them going but he insisted that she take me so I could hear the music and watch the accordion players. Like most bands in those days, the Gallowglass had two accordions, one fiddle, a saxophone, piano, drums and a bass fiddle.

On the night of the dance we cycled to Daingean and leaned our bicycles against the side of the courthouse, which, as well as serving as cinema, dance hall and courthouse, had other rooms for official town business. In front was the town square which was appropriated as a car park, but on occasions was an ideal spot for travelling carnivals or amusement exhibitions.

We bought our tickets and moved towards the inside door of the hall, but all the cinema seats were taken and the dance floor was thronged with people sitting along the side walls while others were dancing. My mother beckoned me towards a stairway in the foyer area and we climbed to the top. I saw two rows of seats beside the front section and two of them were empty. It was our chance to get a full balcony view of the band. The front wall of the balcony was high enough for me to rest my arms on while sitting on the edge of my seat. I could see my mother was sitting in the same way, and once in a while she would sit back in her seat and listen to the music. The band were all dressed in black suits and white shirts with dickey bows. My mother had bought a programme, a four-page booklet with photos of the band and the names of its members. The band was from Naas, County Kildare and its leader was Pat McGarr, who played a piano accordion. Pat's sister Kathleen was playing a fiddle and a young red-haired fellow was playing a three-row accordion.

I read in the programme that he was Tony O'Dowd from County Cavan. We had a great view of the dancers and saw many people that we knew. I had never seen such a spectacle of enjoyment and the sound of the music had my full attention. There were waltzes, haymakers' jigs, military two-steps, barn dances, 'The Siege of Ennis', 'The Waves of Tory'. The band played a strict-tempo style of music which was how they communicated with the dancers. They also had a girl singer who wore a flowery dress and white cardigan draped across her shoulders; she also had on a white necklace. She removed her cardigan when her time came to perform. Some of her songs were in waltz time and she stood in front of a microphone with her hands behind her back. All the other musicians were sitting on chairs except for the man playing the bass fiddle. Pat McGarr introduced all the various dances and would finish by saying, 'For your next dance, please!'

Rumour had it that a local girl singer had joined the band and would be singing at the dance. We all knew her as Teresa Duffy, whose family lived in the town. She was known to be a very fine singer, and we were looking forward to hearing her perform. However, she wasn't to be seen anywhere and later we heard that she'd been stricken suddenly with a head cold with chills. My mother was disappointed. 'There's always somethin',' she said.

As I continued to look down I was impressed by the energy of the dancers and in particular the many girls who were dancing with each other. They were in no mood for abiding by the usual protocol of waiting to be escorted to the floor by some Prince Charming. These were no-nonsense ladies who wanted a dance one way or the other and as I watched I was impressed by the natural rhythm of their feet. Many of the younger men rambled into the céilí when the pubs had closed, having fortified their courage with porter. Dancing didn't come naturally to some and a few individuals had an abundance of movement around their shoulders while dragging their feet to the rhythm of a slow waltz. There were examples of some funny styles of footwork during the haymakers' jig – a few dancers almost missed their turns for connecting with their partners between a clapping gauntlet of other dancers.

A couple of hours later I had a severe urge to find a lavatory – which was on the ground floor. My mother informed me that the men's was downstairs beside the dance floor, but the prospect of having to walk through spectators and dancers was frightening and made me nervous so I postponed nature's call, at least for a while. My mother was concerned, however. 'It's bad for you to be holdin' it in like that. We should head home.'

I didn't want to leave, but had no choice. When we got outside I found a dark alley near the side of the building. My mother waited for me in the darkness. 'Did you enjoy the music?' she asked.

I didn't answer, so she said, 'Paddy, are you all right?'

I was beginning to feel a wonderful sensation of relief and said, 'The music was great, it was fuckin' great!'

'Keep your voice down,' my mother said, 'and don't be cursin', I'll tell your father on you!'

I didn't say any more. We found our bicycles, and on the way home my mother spoke of all the people she had seen at the dance, of the style of them, and their not-a-care-in-the-world attitude of let's live and enjoy. I wasn't able to engage her with any interest, because my mind was teeming with fragments of tunes from the dance hall.

As the following weeks became months I was kept busy helping my father with sowing sugar beet, dropping – or planting – potatoes, cutting black and white turf on the bog, and saving hay. Most of the time my mind was busy trying to piece together sections of a reel or hornpipe, and a particular waltz was causing me a lot of unrest. Mick Hayes had given me its name, 'The Valetta Waltz'. It was sentimental, romantic and a little sad, and its note structure was a challenge. It nagged at me for weeks. I would be alone in the drills ploughed for sowing with a praskeen of seed potatoes, bending and placing each one on droppings of cow manure, while inside in my chest this dreary waltz flowed and teased me and persecuted my emotions. It was the same sense of endurance that enslaved and tied me to other tunes like 'Haste to the Wedding' and another reel from the radio called 'I'm Waiting For You'.

I've come to the conclusion that trying to explain or verbalise the extent of one's emotional servitude while grappling with music is well-nigh impossible. The condition of half-knowing a reel or hornpipe is a combination of frustration, loneliness and anxiety. I suppose much of it was the result of listening to the radio with its abundance of new tunes and the challenge of trying to learn them. It was an emotional time, of music, hard work, and obedience to my father, who was struggling to make a living, and my mother, whose concerns were outward appearances and how her daughters were coping in national school.

The radio was our main entertainment, with Ciarán MacMathúna presenting the music of Johnny Pickering's Céilí Band from the North of Ireland and fiddler Denis Murphy with his sister Julia from Gneeveguilla in County Kerry. Both of them played the fiddle together, with selections of slides, polkas and more polkas. We didn't know what to make of the Kerry music, since we weren't used to it. Later I learned that it was essentially a dance style of music played in small parts of County Kerry and that the way it was played was an old traditional interpretation and not easy to emulate. It was easier for us to relate to accordion players like Martin Mulhaire from County Galway or Paddy O'Brien of Tipperary or the Bridge Céilí Band from Newtown in Tipperary. The Tulla and Kilfenora céilí bands of County Clare were always welcome in our kitchen and Ciarán was always ready to give any of them a warm introduction. My interest was always aroused when I heard the names of particular box players, fiddlers or flute players. I was able to somehow perceive their physical appearance by the sound of their names or the sound of their music. This imagery and personal imagination began to influence my creative sensitivities, and it helped consolidate my feeling and appetite for practising.

15

The Drowning of Shep

My mother usually stayed at home, except for Mass on Sundays or shopping for groceries. Sundays were a busy day on our main road, or the Mill Road as it was known to us. People would walk or cycle to either the eight o'clock Mass or the later one, which was at eleven. Some families travelled together on traps pulled by donkeys or horses. During this time Shep kept himself busy barking at anyone who passed by. My mother remarked to my father that he should put the dog in the cowhouse as a way to shut him up. My father said, 'It's ten to eleven; nearly everyone goin' to the chapel is either gone or almost gone.'

In the meantime I went outside and began calling Shep. The dog turned around and walked slowly towards me. We were pals and I was teaching him to lie down on his back and die for Ireland. 'Go and lie down! Go and lie down!' I shouted. Shep was trotting towards the cowhouse when suddenly he stopped and turned. We could both hear it, it was a bicycle. I shouted, 'Shep! Shep!' but he was already running in a low crouch, and out he went through a small hole in the hedge beside the gate's pillar. He wasn't barking and the woman on the bicycle was taken unawares. Shep zipped out to the far side of the road and sunk his teeth into the calf of her right leg. She let out a loud scream and fell on the grassy edge of the road. A few other people were behind her when it happened, and their immediate reaction was to stop and help. Shep was already in retreat and, watching him, I sensed that he knew he had done something very bad. My father and mother heard the scream and were running towards the gate. Someone was shouting, 'Get a towel! Get a towel!' My mother rushed back and went into the kitchen. She returned quickly to where the woman was lying on the verge. There was a lot of blood. My mother wrapped the towel around the woman's leg and a man removed his tie and wound it around the towel. It was just enough to help her up and my father and another man, Tom Canton, helped her as she limped off the road. It was a relief that she was able to limp the rest of the way as we slowly walked her to the door and sat her on a chair in our kitchen. My mother heated hot water and found a scissors to cut the nylon stocking from her leg.

'My God, missus, what happened?'

''Twas the dog. He bit her.'

My father was horrified. 'Mother of Divine Jaysus, I'll have to drown him. There's no two ways about it. I'll go get him and bring him to the boghole.' He looked at me and said, 'The sneaky little bastard.'

My mother was very embarrassed and kept saying, 'You poor woman! You poor woman!' When she saw the wound after she had bathed it with disinfectant she was aghast. 'Oh my God, missus, the fecker left a big gash and it's still bleeding badly. I don't know what to do except bandage it.'

'Mrs O'Brien,' the woman said, 'don't fuss over me. I'll be all right, please don't fuss . . . maybe you'd make me a cup of tea.'

'Paddy, fill the kettle and put it on the fire,' my mother said to me before tearing part of a white bedsheet into three-inch strips and wrapping them around the woman's wound. She then tied the end of one by splitting it in two and tying it around the leg. She said, 'Aren't you Mrs Dolan?'

'I am indeed.'

'Lord God, Mrs Dolan, I am heartily sorry for what happened. How are you feelin'?'

'I think I'll be okay . . . after a cup of tea I should be able to cycle home. I'm awfully grateful to you, Mister Canton,' she said.

'I'm sorry, Tom,' said my mother. 'I forgot to offer you tea.'

'That's all right, ma'am,' said Tom.

My father had been quiet all this time. He was very relieved that the bandage had stopped the blood flowing, and was about to say something when my mother looked at him. 'Christy, you'll have to do away with that dog. I won't sleep tonight if he isn't done away with.'

'Don't anyone worry about that, I'm puttin' him into a sack and it's off to the boghole for him. Paddy,' he said to me, 'would you go outside and look for a sack? One of the potato sacks will do.'

After everyone had had tea, Mrs Dolan stood up. 'I'd better be on my way before everyone comes back from Mass.'

My mother was very concerned as Mrs Dolan and Tom Canton began to leave. 'I hope you are all right on the way home.'

'Don't worry, missus,' said Tom, 'We'll be all right.'

'Paddy, did you get the sack?' my father asked.

I already had it folded and tucked under my arm. After my father grabbed a four-grained fork by the cowhouse he said, 'Where's Shep?' I said he was in the shed by the dairy. When we opened the door of the shed Shep was cowering in the corner. His mouth was trembling as he growled and snarled. My father had the sack in one hand and the fork in the other as he closed in on Shep. He pulled him with the fork and shoved the opened end of the bag over the struggling animal. It was the last time I saw Shep. We tied the neck of the sack and my father hoisted it onto his shoulder and back. I carried the fork and we headed for the bog. We found a fresh boghole filled with water, and, standing by its edge, my father lowered the sack from his back. There was no sound from Shep. Then he lifted the sack with both hands and swung it into the water. He took the fork from me and used it to hold Shep and the sack underneath. The dog was struggling inside the sack and I knew he was fighting for his life. My father was also struggling to keep the sack submerged and there were bubbles beginning to form on the water's surface. Our dog made a final lunge inside the sack, but my father's fork kept shoving him below the water's surface until groups of miniature bubbles were clouding the swirling water. And then the water settled and became calm and my father withdrew the fork. We stood in silence, waiting, listening, but the only sound we heard was a curlew somewhere on the heather. I was feeling very sad and shocked. A confused mixture of compassion, forgiveness and sorrow was churning around inside me. It was also a feeling of frustration because Shep was dead. He died because of a flaw in his temperament that wasn't his fault, nor was it something that humans were ready to comprehend. As we walked back from the bog we held a long silence, until I heard my father say, 'I hope I never have to drown another dog.'

16

Thatching the House

My father and mother had many responsibilities that my sisters and I weren't capable of understanding because of our youth, and our love of novelty and excitement. We loved the game of hide and seek and were always scouting out hiding places and making plans for outwitting each other. One evening I heard my father talking to an old neighbour who was my mother's uncle. He was a good friend and would pass our house when he drove his cows home for milking. Mick Dunne was someone who was wise in his years and was always ready and reliable with advice. My father would talk to him about his usual concerns, which were related to crops, cows, weather conditions or personal health.

One evening as I was hiding in the hedge by the road I overheard him talking to Mick Dunne about thatching our house. Mick was saying, 'Why don't you do it yourself?'

'Mick,', my father replied, 'I've never thatched a house in my life!'

'You're lookin' at a man who thatched his own house without any experience,' Mick replied. 'Christy, you can do it. All you need is a long ladder and a load of oaten straw.'

I was fascinated by what they were saying, but I wasn't able to hear any more of their conversation because my sister Kathleen surprised me and I had to run.

As the summer evenings continued, my father had many chats with Mick when he stopped at our gate so his cows could graze by the roadside.

One evening I was standing close by when my father said to Mick, 'You know, I've been thinkin' about what you said about the thatchin', and maybe you're right. Maybe I'll have a shot at it.'

'And Paddy here can tend to you when you're on the roof,' Mick said.

'Do you think he can do it?'

'Do it?' said Mick. 'Of course he can do it! Hasn't he eyes and ears and hands like the rest of us?'

This was the advice that convinced my father to go ahead with his first attempt at thatching. It also gave me a great sense of being included and I was thrilled at the prospect of how this undertaking would unfold during the coming weeks. A few days later I heard my father telling my mother that he was going to cycle over to Riverlyons and talk to Jimmy Mac about buying a load of oaten straw and to see if he could borrow one of Jimmy's ladders.

'Jimmy Mac is a great neighbour and a true Christian,' my mother said, 'and he'll always have good luck in his life.'

'I think I'll bike it over there now,' my father continued. 'He'll just be after finishin' his supper.'

A couple of days later Jimmy arrived with a huge load of oaten straw on a trailer towed behind his Massey Ferguson tractor. As it passed the door and window of our house the inside of our kitchen darkened almost as if it was night-time. Jimmy's trailer had a small hydraulic system that lifted its front end upwards, and the load of straw fell over into a huge pile at the north end of our house. It turned out to be an excellent playground for me and my sisters: we marvelled at its width and elevation, and the straw was wonderful for hiding in or falling on. We shouted and screamed and pushed each other into the soft bed of straw until twilight came.

After three days of games in the straw, my father began building a straw reek in the adjoining haggard. This was where we kept our straw and hay. We helped him carry the straw as best we could. In the evening it was finished, and looking up at the tall reek we felt a great sense of achievement. We were also eager and ready for a nice supper of boiled eggs with bread, butter and jam – and, of course, plenty of tea.

Next day I helped my father push Jimmy's ladder up onto the roof. It reached well beyond the ridge and I stood at the bottom end, holding it as my father climbed onto each rung. His first job was to check where the old straw was leaking or was rotten and needed to be replaced. The first days of preparation were important and it was my job to hand-pull lots of barley straw and tie it into small bunches. These were used as packing or fillers on the roof where the original straw or thatch had rotted all the way to the rafters. Pulling the straw was tedious work and when I finished my father told me to pull the oaten straw from the reek and lay it out in larger bunches. We already had many sizes of hazel rods that he had cut the week before. He had kept them for drying in the kitchen because we needed to twist and bend them and sharpen the ends and cut them into various lengths, or into U-shaped spikes for holding down the new thatch. Several other hazels would be laid on the fresh thatch and then pinned down by some of the U-shaped spikes. A number of small tools were used for this particular work, such as a fork with two prongs of steel that tapered into a wooden handle with a round polished end. This was used to plug and push bunches of straw into the old thatch. It was the most important tool next to the wooden mallet.

The first line of thatch was usually stuffed into the old thatch from the eave (alongside the wooden ladder) all the way up to the crest or ridge of the roof. This line or layer was about nine inches wide, and when the thatcher finished at the ridge he would climb back down to the ground and move the ladder forward another nine inches and the plugging and stuffing was repeated.

When all was ready my father climbed the ladder with a bundle of straw under his left arm. His two-grained fork was stuck into the old thatch at a right angle to the slanted roof and this was where he placed his bundle of straw, which was between the roof and the fork handle. As he worked his way upwards he would remove the fork and stick it in again at a higher location. It was a slow process and when quitting time came we saw that the total advance for the day was a three-foot-wide layer of straw from the ridge to the bottom end. Before we finished for the night we had to carry five or six bucket-fuls of water for splashing on the new thatch. When I had filled the bucket, my father waited above as I moved slowly upwards, step by step, moving the bucket from rung to rung. My father threw the water down onto the new thatch to flatten it, and then he'd beat it over and over with a short, round pole. During the night it would settle into its intended slant, or 'lay' as it was known.

On the third day we made a ridge cover of twisted straw pulled down onto an upright hazel rod stuck into the ground. The rod could accommodate forty twisted straw lengths that were criss-crossed, with half their length pulled to one side and the other half on the opposite side. It was very impressive to see the final capping when rod and straw as one unit was placed on the ridge. This procedure lasted a few hours before we began pulling more of the oaten straw for the next layer of thatch.

My father always wore a peaked cap and an old Local Defence Forces (LDF) overcoat. (He had been in the LDF, the volunteer army reserve, for a brief time during the Second World War.) I never saw him wearing gloves except when frosty weather greeted the winter mornings before he set out to cycle the ten miles to his work. I often admired his perseverance and how hard he worked. Thinking of him and watching how he continued on as a father and breadwinner, I tried to compare myself with him. But every time I thought about it I was forced to conclude that I would never measure up to his particular standard. His was an older generation of hard work and hardcore honesty and simple values that I had yet to understand.

Each of us was on our knees, pulling from the reek long lengths of yellow straw, length after length, that we neatly laid out as a bundle to be carried to the roof. Sometimes my father would talk to the straw, or say something like, 'You stubborn bastard, I'll best yeh yet!' or 'Aha, now I have yeh!' This was his way of announcing his victory when he pulled out a huge amount in one tug. Sometimes I thought he was trying to entertain me as a subtle gesture of appreciation for my help.

17

The Banshee

We hadn't seen Mick Hayes for over three months. This was unusual, so we wondered if perhaps he was sick or had an accident, but one Saturday morning my mother met him on the main street in Daingean. She asked him how he was and he said he had been in Tullamore Hospital with pneumonia. My mother apologised for not visiting him and he said it had happened very quickly and that many people didn't know about it. She told him we hadn't heard a word of him being sick and said, 'You know, Mick, a person could be dead around here and not a soul would know. How did it happen?'

Mick explained that an old man near where he lived had died and on the same night it was pouring rain outside. Mick was at home sitting by the fire reading a newspaper when he heard a horrible wail in the wind. It got louder and he felt the hair standing on his head. 'It was a high-pitched crying sound and there was something about it that drew me towards it, so I went outside to see what direction it came from. It was still raining, but had eased a little and like a fool I stood there listening, and that's how I got the pneumonia.'

My mother said, 'Mick, don't you know what you heard?'

'I think I do,' Mick replied.

'Yes,' said my mother, ''twas the Banshee.'

'Curse of God on her,' said Mick. 'She frightened the bejaysus out of me, and then I got the feckin' pneumonia and was six weeks in the hospital. Bad cess to her!'

'When are you comin' for a ramble again?' my mother asked. 'I've started makin' scones on the griddle, I still have more than enough.'

'Next week,' said Mick. 'Next Wednesday night.'

As my mother wheeled her bike to the towpath, she shouted back to Mick, 'Don't forget to bring the box. Paddy would like to hear you.'

When she got to Mooney's in the terrace she knocked on the door. She knocked a couple of times and then the door opened slowly. Standing there was a small boy of about six and he was holding his pet puppy. My mother asked him if his mother and father were at home. The little fellow disappeared and after a minute Joe Mooney himself came out. 'Well, hello, missus,' he said. 'Come in and sit down. I think I know why you're here. Are you lookin' for a dog?'

'I am, Mr Mooney. Do you have any?'

'I might have one,' said Joe. 'It's a little terrier, a kind of a Kerry blue.'

'How much do you want for it?'

'Nothin' at all,' Joe laughed. 'We've had a total of fifteen pups over the last several months. I don't know how they came to be here. I suppose my wife and the young lads bring home their mothers and bed them down outside in the shed, and then all of a sudden there's pups, pups and more pups everywhere. We've been givin' them away to people like yourself, people who have children. And the children,' he added, 'love to cuddle them and have them for pets. Wait a minute, missus, and I'll go outside and get you the little fella.'

My mother said she'd go outside to her bike and bring in a basket that she left on the carrier, and when she came back inside Joe was already in the kitchen with the little animal. My mother looked at the tiny pup. 'God,' she said, 'our Kathleen will be over the moon with it, she'll want to bring it to bed with her!'

When my mother came home with the pup she put the basket on the table, and we all gathered around looking at the new addition to our home.

'What are we goin' to call him?' my father asked. Nobody had a name until our mother said, 'Paddy, what's the name of the cowboy you've been readin' about? It's the fellow with the light brown horse.'

'Rex Allen,' I replied. Our mother had her mind made up. 'That's what we're goin' to call him. Rex.' Then she leaned into the basket and whispered, 'Rex, Rex, Rex.'

The following Wednesday evening around nine o'clock a knock came to the door. I was told to answer it like I was the only person qualified. It was Mick, and he had his accordion with him. I was thrilled. 'Mick, it's yourself,' I said, 'and we're just makin' tea.'

'Where's the dog?' asked Mick. 'I don't hear him barkin'.'

'Well,' said my father, 'we had to drown him.'

'Drown him,' he said. 'Well, isn't that somethin'? My prayers have been answered. Well, I don't need these any more,' he added, as he pulled four stones from his pocket and threw them out the door into the night. 'What a relief,' he said. 'What happened?'

'The fecker bit Mrs Dolan on the leg,' my mother was saying, and my father said, 'What else could we do?'

I could see that Mick was relieved. Sitting on a chair, he said, 'There was something wrong with that dog because it's not often a collie bites anyone, or could be so sneaky and wicked.'

My mother was knitting a small cardigan for our youngest sister, Patricia. 'I'll make tea in a minute,' she said. 'I've just a few more stitches to do.'

My father offered Mick a cigarette. 'No thanks, Christy,' he said. 'I only smoke now and again.'

When she had finished her row of knitting my mother boiled the kettle on the fire and, as was so often the case, Mick and my father continued talking about what had transpired since the last time they'd seen each other.

'Well now, Mick,' said my father, 'anythin' strange?'

'Not too much,' said Mick, 'except I found out the name of the aul' fucker that died at the time I got the wettin'.'

'Who was it?' my father asked.

'Dick Allader,' said Mick. He was convinced that this old fellow was related to a landlord of bygone days and was adamant that this man would never see the light of heaven.

'Was he that bad?' my mother asked.

'He belonged to the same people that evicted innocent families and left them destitute on the byways of this country,' Mick said. 'Fuck him! He's no fuckin' loss! And I heard he left thousands to relatives in England. I suppose they'll know what to do with it, or probably piss it against some foreign wall.'

My father was curious about Mick being laid low. 'Molly was tellin' us you were in hospital. Are you feelin' all right since you came home?'

'Yes,' said Mick. 'I think I am. They told me my lungs are cleared up, and my energy is better.'

My father was still curious, however. 'She told us you heard the Banshee.'

Mick looked at my father and then at the floor. 'Christy,' he said, 'I definitely heard somethin' from the hereafter. It was the most frightenin' cry, inhuman it was, the wounded cry of a soul in exile. Drops of sweat fell from me forehead and I felt a terrible fear crawlin' down the small of me back. I'm not the better of it yet.'

'It was the Banshee – it follows some families,' my mother said. 'I heard her cryin' on the night my uncle was dyin' here in the room behind the fireplace. I was only seventeen and I was sittin' where Paddy is now sittin', in the corner.'

I could feel a little bit of sweat when my mother mentioned where she sat. 'My second cousin Jack Dunne,' she continued, 'also heard the same fearsome wail as he was cyclin' by on his way to Daingean. He had to get down off his bike because the cryin' had such an effect on him; he felt a weakness in his legs. I wouldn't believe in such a thing if I hadn't heard it and the fact that other people heard her cryin' on the same night is enough proof for me or anyone else.'

Mick was also convinced. 'I hope I never hear it again because it's the strangest wail of torment that any human ear could ever endure.'

I was amazed at such a story. It had a ring of truth about it that confused and bewildered me and I felt a little bit afraid. My sisters were listening quietly and were wide-eyed with wonder. My father told us not to worry. 'The Banshee,' he said, 'never cries around here and won't be here again. She never cries again where she has been before, isn't that right, Mick?'

'That's the truth,' said Mick. 'You children can sleep like babies tonight. There's no Banshee within an ass's roar of Castlebarnagh, so there's nothin' to be afraid of.'

'Mick knows more about this than any of us,' my mother joined in. 'Anyway, the house is blessed, and nothin' can get near yez.'

My father lit another cigarette. 'Mick,', he said, 'what about playin' the accordion?'

Oh God, I was so relieved. And when Mick grabbed his box I sensed he too was happy to change the subject of the Banshee. When he had finished his tea he started to play. It was a jig I didn't know and I had never heard him play it before. He played it over a few times, so I could get a feel for its shape and melody. I believe I learned it that same night because it came back into my mind during the days that followed. Mick played for about half an hour and then asked me to have a go. I played it for a while but soon got tired. Mick's accordion was too much for me because of its size.

My mother wasn't finished. 'Mick,' she said, 'if you don't mind, I have a question for you.'

'Go ahead missus, I don't mind at all.'

'Have you heard of somethin' called ringworm?'

'Indeed I have, missus. Don't tell me you have it!'

'I might have it,' she said. 'Bridgie Rourke had a look at my leg and said she thought it was definitely ringworm. It started very small, smaller than a sixpence, and now it's bigger, maybe bigger now than a penny. Here,' she said, 'it's on my right leg on the inside, just down here below my knee.'

Mick could see it, a red spot the size of a penny, and it was weeping a little. 'Missus,' he said, 'I'm afraid that's what it is.'

'Is there any cure for it?' my father asked.

'There is,' said Mick. 'That is, if you believe in quacks.'

My mother was looking hopefully at Mick. 'Do you know anyone that has the cure?'

'I know a man,' said Mick, 'by the name of Jim Bromagem who lives way down beyond Mountlucas. He has a cure that was handed down to him by his grandmother. I saw him at last Mass on Sunday. You might see him cyclin' past the house here.'

My father was in a hurry about getting the cure, and said to my mother that he'd cycle down to Bromagem's house the next evening.

'You're a great man, Mick,' my mother told him. 'You have an answer for everythin'. Here's another scone.'

Mick was pulling at the lobe of his right ear. It was a sign that he felt appreciated. The tea and scones, he said, were made by a woman who had 'a special way of mixin' bakin' soda with flour and buttermilk'. He looked at me and my sisters. 'You've got a great mother – don't ever forget it!'

After the tea was drunk we drifted into more chat about everything and anything until my father remembered to ask Mick a question that he kept forgetting about.

'What is that?' said Mick.

My father asked him if he remembered to ask Tom Brewer about going out with the wren next Saint Stephen's Day.

'I did ask him, Christy,' Mick replied, 'and he said he would. In fact, he was delighted to be invited. Now I've a couple of questions for you, Christy,' Mick added. 'Were you able to talk to any of the two Briens?'

'I did,' said my father, 'I talked to one of them, and he was to talk to his brother Tommy. I think they'll be all for it.'

'What should we do about a car?' Mick asked.

'I haven't thought about it yet,' said my father.

My mother was pouring more tea. 'What about Gilbert McCormack?' she asked.

'By God,' said Mick, 'the very man. He's reliable, and doesn't drink.'

My father was in agreement. 'Well, that's what we'll do,' he said. 'I'll have another chat with Paddy Brien and I'll drop up to Tom Brewer and remind him.'

'It should be a great bit of sport,' Mick said.

My father changed the conversation by asking Mick about his thatching, or if he'd seen it.

'I did,' replied Mick. 'Where did you learn the trade, Christy?'

My father was curious as to what Mick would say when he told him. 'I never did it before and anythin' I know about it I got from Mick Dunne.'

'Well, the mother of the livin' Jaysus,' Mick exclaimed. 'It's not possible or else you have some sort of an angel guidin' your hands, because it's a perfect example of tradesmanship and I say that because I know you still have a lot of thatchin' left to do.'

'Oh,' said my father, 'Oh, it's a big undertakin', but I have Paddy here to help me.'

Mick saw me in the corner. 'It'll be hard on your hands,' he said. 'Not much music will be played.' I didn't mind. I was tired and preferred listening to everyone talking.

I went to bed a little early while Mick and my father and mother were still chatting. Lying awake, I could hear the three of them talking about me and the music. Hearing some of the conversation, I realised that Mick was saying how great I was with the accordion. I felt a twinge of excitement and I tried holding my breath so I could hear more. My father and mother were also saying good things about me, and I soon fell asleep.

18

The Power of the Cure

Jim Bromagem called at our house on the second Sunday after my father visited him at his home. Jim was a gentle sort of man, with a grey moustache that was tainted with tobacco juice. He wore a brown hat, brown suit, brown topcoat and brown shoes. My mother offered him tea but he refused it, saying he didn't have a lot of time.

'Missus,' he said, 'let me see the affected area.'

My mother showed him the spot on her right leg. 'Yes, yes, you have it, it's the ringworm, no doubt about it. Well, let's see,' he added as he reached into his inside pocket he pulled out a small purple box. Opening it, he removed a small gold ring that was tied to a brown scapular. He took off his hat and put it on a chair. Reaching down to the spot on my mother's leg, he made a circle around it three times. Then he made the sign of the cross over it three times and with his head bowed he whispered some words that were his private prayers. In less than a minute he was finished. He said to my mother, 'I'll have to do this three times and I'll be back next Sunday.'

My mother was very thankful. 'Mr Bromagem, what do we owe you for this?'

'Missus,' he said, 'I don't take any money. The cure was given to me on condition that I wouldn't charge anythin'. If I did, I'd lose the power of the cure.'

My mother was undaunted. 'But surely you don't expect me to give you nothin'.'

Jim saw her concern. 'Missus, I don't usually take small gifts, but some people buy me a half pound of tea or a bit of tobacco. I never take both.'

'All right,' said my mother, 'and thanks very much . . . Are you sure you wouldn't have a cup of tea?'

'I think I'll change my mind,' Jim replied, 'and have a quick cup.'

My mother was delighted to be able to give the man something for his trouble. Jim was a chatty kind of man who spoke of his wife and paid us compliments, saying we were very well-behaved children. My mother pretended to protest, saying, 'You'd want to see them when you're not here!'

In moments, Jim had drunk his tea and was gone. 'I'll see you in a week,' were his words as he walked to the gate.

'Now there goes a great gentleman,' my mother said. 'It's no wonder he has the cure. I hope he can get rid of this rotten thing on my leg, I'm fed up with it.'

Towards the end of the week we noticed that the penny-sized blotch on my mother's leg was slightly smaller. And the following Sunday Jim came and did another 'rub', as he called it.

It was the same routine as the first time. He was sure the ringworm had gotten smaller but said he'd need to 'rub it' one more time. He said he'd be back again in two weeks to finish off the cure, then wished us all the best of luck and was gone. My sisters and I were getting a great charge out of watching our mother's leg. All of us, including our parents, were busy with different chores and somehow forgot to look at the size of the spot. Then on the Saturday morning after breakfast my mother yelled to my father, 'Look! Look! It's almost gone!'

My father was stunned. 'Holy Christ,' he said. 'I've never seen anythin' like it.' And my mother blessed herself.

The next morning Jim was back again. After he looked at her leg he took out the little gold ring for the third time and said, 'This'll be the final rub.' Once again he made three circles around the spot and then the sign of the cross three times and finished with his silent prayer.

My mother gave Jim a gift of a pound of tea and thanked him again. I thought he looked a little embarrassed – like a man who wasn't comfortable with being fussed over.

As he was about to leave, my mother said she had a sort of embarrassing question to ask him.

'Go ahead,' said Jim. 'It's what makes us human.'

'Do you know of anyone that has a cure for worms?' my mother asked. 'Because I think the children here might be carryin' some. I'm not totally sure, but I heard that some of the school children have been infected, so I'm worried about whether or not it's catchin'.'

'Indeed it is,' said Jim. 'And it so happens I do know of an old man that lives near Croghan, and he has a definite cure for it. His name is Thomas Pender, and anyone in the vicinity will tell you where he lives. His daughter and her husband and children live with him and some say his daughter will inherit the cure.'

My mother was greatly impressed with Jim's answer. 'Well, she said, 'I know I've said this many times, but I want to thank you again and again and again.'

'Don't mention it, missus,' he said. 'It was my pleasure.' And then he was on his way, cycling towards Mountlucas.

My mother made an appointment with Gilbert McCormack to pick us up at our gate on Sunday afternoon. McCormack was a very reliable man and as punctual as the sun on a summer's morning. His car pulled up slowly outside the gate and all six of us climbed in. Gilbert knew the road that would take us to Thomas Pender's house. It was a four-mile journey to where we turned left into a laneway that brought us through a marshy area of bogland and small pastures. A few lone trees dotted a landscape of heather, bogholes and broken black soil that lay in flattened ridges used to grow potatoes and turnips. Furze bushes grew in abundance along the lane, and small blackthorn bushes still carried their berries. That they had escaped the attention of the bird population was seen as a sign of a mild winter to come.

When we arrived at the front door of the house we all jumped out of the car. My mother told Gilbert that she hoped he wouldn't mind waiting in the car while we went inside. 'It's all right, take your time,' was Gilbert's reply.

Tom Pender's daughter met us at the door and politely ushered us inside. Tom was sitting at the fire while his grandchildren played blind man's bluff. The children were told to go to their room and stay quiet. Tom stood up and asked my mother, 'What can I do for you?'

My mother explained her concerns about us children being affected with stomach worms.

'Hmmm,' said Tom. 'We'll soon find out.'

He took a mug from the dresser and filled it with raw porridge. He packed it tightly and with a wooden rule he levelled the porridge with the rim of the mug. Next he took a clean white handkerchief from a drawer in the table and covered the mug and its contents tightly with one hand. He held the handkerchief around the mug and said, 'Who's first?'

Moira volunteered. He told her to open the buttons on the front of her dress. With her skin exposed, he placed the top of the mug tightly against her tummy with the handkerchief between the mug and her stomach. He held it there for a minute while he closed his eyes and whispered words that we could not hear. In a moment he removed the mug from my sister's stomach and took the handkerchief away from the top of the mug. We were flabbergasted at what we saw.

The porridge in the mug looked a lot like a rat had eaten it. It was incredible! Nearly half the raw porridge was gone! It had disappeared!

My mother and sisters were astounded. Where had the porridge gone? my mother asked Tom.

Tom's reply was to the point. 'Missus,' he said, 'it's the power of the cure.' Then he looked around and said, 'Who's next?' Ann was waiting and had her clothes unbuttoned. Tom filled the mug with fresh porridge, covered it with the handkerchief and pressed it tightly against her stomach. When he removed the mug and then the handkerchief, we saw that several tablespoonfuls of the raw porridge was missing, but not as much as the first mug.

Tom told my mother that both girls were in a bad way with the worms and would have to return to him again. This was how the healing process worked. We all had some porridge missing from the refilled mugs. When he pressed a full mug against me I could feel the softness of the handkerchief and didn't notice anything unusual. At least a third of the porridge disappeared, and I had to return for a second session with everyone else.

Tom wouldn't take any payment, but on our last visit we gave him and his grandchildren some tea, sweets and biscuits. Returning home, we all had something to say, but had no idea how the porridge had vanished. My mother was a little superstitious, but gave up trying to understand the mystery of the cure. My father was far more practical, saying that we should believe in the cure instead of questioning it. In a matter of days we started to feel a sensation of extra energy and our appetites improved, and so we concluded that the cure was doing its job. When we went over to Tom's house for the second visit we saw that Moira's mug was almost full. Tom told us that she need not return, that she'd be fully recovered in a week. In fact, all of us were on the way to full recovery with a couple of mugs showing no missing porridge. I've never forgotten this particular experience with what some people refer to as quacks.

19

Mysterious Travellers

I always had the urge to practise the accordion, especially after a long day of work, and as time went by I developed a special feeling about Saturday night. To me it was a night of conclusion when I would wash, go to confession, play my accordion and hopefully hear some good band on Seán Ó Murchú's *Céilí House*. On some Saturday nights we would hear a knock on the door, and would be surprised by someone we hadn't seen in a long time.

It was a couple of weeks after we finished thatching the roof and the evenings were getting dark earlier when we were surprised by the sound of scraping on the outside of our door. It was like a rasp being pulled slowly over the paint on its surface, and on hearing it we all looked at each other for support or a possible explanation. My mother was the first to speak. 'Christy, why don't you see what it is?'

'Oh it's probably a cat caught between the half door and the big door,' he replied, before getting up from his chair and opening the door. It was then he saw the little man with a hat and a white clay pipe sticking out the side of his mouth. 'Good night to ye all,' the little man said. 'I'm Tom Carey and I'm doin' a bit of work for Phil Rourke on Killoneen Hill. I was wonderin' if I could come in and warm me shanks at the fire.'

'Come on in, Tom,' said my father. My mother knew the fellow as soon as he walked into the kitchen and remembered that she was a teenager when she last saw him.

'Well,' she said, 'if it isn't Tom Carey! The dead arose and appeared to many. Where in the name of God have you been all these years?'

He said he had been working for a big farmer near Edenderry. My father had never seen Tom before and was watching him closely. I sensed he was amused by Tom's way of saying things. For example, as Tom finished a sentence he would exude a coo of a laugh that sounded like air escaping from a bicycle tube. Tom was about five feet tall and wore old wellington boots with the tops turned down. He continued to keep the short clay pipe stuck in his mouth and a constant dribble of saliva came over his bottom lip. My sisters were disgusted at how careless he was, and cringed every time he spat into the ashes by the fire. My mother was a little impatient but polite, and in a while she began filling the teapot. She asked him if he'd like a drop of tea, and he said he would. After the tea went around he was talking with extra fervour and appeared more at ease with what he was saying. As he continued he started to smirk, and his eyes were moving from side to side in search of approval. The hot tea was making his nose drip, which in turn made him sniff and cough and forced him to remove the pipe from his mouth. This gave him the liberty to use the sleeve of his coat for wiping his nose and mouth back and forth. When he raised his voice he produced a cackling sound, and when he got excited by the tone of his story he would wheeze and coo like a wood pigeon.

He spoke about seeing a man in a field where there were several sheep. The man seemed to be counting the sheep, he said, and then he swore to us that this man turned into a sheep right in front of his eyes!

'That's impossible! I don't believe a word of it!' said my mother. Her remarks went unnoticed by him, or else he pretended not to hear.

My father was pulling on a cigarette when he said, 'Tom, you must have seen some fierce things in your day.'

'Oh God,' said Tom, 'to be sure I did.' Then he began with another story about the road from Larry Farrell's well that went all the way past the big house in Mountlucas. This was the same road that went past our house.

'It's haunted,' wheezed Tom, and this led to another little cackle of a laugh.

'How do you know?' asked my father.

'I know,' he said, 'because I was on the same road one moonlit night. It was October a couple of years ago. All of a sudden I met a dark coach, with four black horses pullin' it. I jumped out of the way, and as it passed me by I saw the driver with a whip. I got a terrible fright when I looked at him.'

'What was wrong?' my father asked.

Tom spat a big one into the ashes. 'I'll tell you what was wrong with him. He'd no feckin' head.'

'Jaysus Christ,' said my father.

Then my mother said she had heard something about a ghost coach from the old people. It was said that the coach would be seen on a particular night of the year and was supposed to carry the body of a cruel landlord for burial. The old people believed that the driver couldn't find the cemetery without his head and that the coach was cursed by the matriarch of an evicted family.

Tom Carey left for home at midnight. His visit left us with our own impressions of this strange little man. My mother was glad he was gone, and my eldest sisters Ann and Moira both agreed he should be sleeping with the pigs in the shed. One of them was convinced he hadn't washed himself in a year. I was also a little relieved when he was gone, but I wasn't sure what it was that made me distrust him. My father was adamant that Mr Carey 'would drown eels', meaning that he was as crafty as a ferret and wily as a fox. We didn't see him again or hear anything about him working anywhere around our locality. Phil Rourke said later that he didn't know him at all when my father mentioned that Tom worked on his farm.

My father continued to cycle ten miles to work each morning and would be gone from 6.30 a.m. until 6.30 p.m. One late afternoon in August my mother came rushing from the bedroom next to the road. In a hushed voice she said, 'Paddy, quick, lock the door.'

'What's wrong?' I said.

'Lock the door,' she repeated.

When it was locked she whispered, 'There's a strange man at the gate and he's whistlin' a long, sad whistle.' There was a window in the bedroom that gave us a clear view of our gate and when I went into the room to have a look I could hear a long, wailing whistle. My mother pulled aside a lace curtain in an attempt to get a better look at the man, who was standing outside our gate with his arm resting on its pillar.

'Who is he?' I asked my mother.

'I don't know, but I wish your father was here. Whoever he is, he might be dangerous or he might be a madman that escaped from Portlaoise Asylum. Listen to the way he's whistlin' and tell me who in his right mind would whistle like that.' She was right – I couldn't make any sense of it either. It was a long whistle that may have had two or three tapered notes, and he seemed to be repeating it over and over. A strong east wind was blowing directly towards the front of our house, which was why our door was closed. The sound of the wind and the long, wailing whistle was making my mother very nervous. She was on the brink of crying. 'Don't worry, Mammy, he'll be gone soon,' I said reassuringly, 'because it's beginning to rain. Let me have a better look.' I crept closer and peered through the window again, and this time I saw a young man with a peaked cap, long grey overcoat, and wellingtons. There was a slash across the big toe of one of his wellingtons and I could see a couple of toes. I concluded that he wore no socks and was probably a poor man. The remarkable thing that held my attention was how he was still whistling after half an hour. We could still hear him blow his lonely tune even though it had begun to rain. After what seemed like an hour the whistling suddenly stopped and when we ran to the window we saw no one at the gate.

'Thanks be to God,' said my mother, 'I think he's gone.'

We were very relieved, and my mother was confounded by the thought that a man displaying such bizarre behaviour could succeed in frightening her out of her wits. When she was sure he had gone on his way she became angry with herself for not running out to the gate and giving him a good telling-off. I suppose we both had mixed feelings about the experience. Shortly after, as my mother was preparing dinner for my father, we could hear several loud claps of thunder and the lightning outside had the effect of lighting up our kitchen. The rain, which was making a steady rhythmic clatter on the corrugated roof of the cowhouse, had developed into a downpour.

'That'll teach him,' yelled my mother. 'I hope the fucker drowns in a ditch by the side of the road, it would serve him right!' I had never seen my mother so frightened, nor had I ever heard her cursing before.

On their way home my father and the men with him had to stop and take shelter under a couple of trees and were delayed for the best part of an hour. When he eventually arrived home my father was tired and soaking wet. He changed into his dry Sunday clothes before eating. My mother and I waited until he had finished his dinner, and while he was drinking a mug of tea she said, 'Christy, a strange man came to the gate today.' And so she told him what happened.

When she was finished, my father started to laugh. 'Jaysus,' he said, 'I'm surprised you didn't know him. Sure that was Davy Mallon – he's got the mind of a child. He's a harmless wretch, suffers from the "eating diabetes". He's like that when he's hungry for potatoes, and he has all the houses down the road plagued to death with the beggin' sound of his whistle. You poor woman,' said my father. 'Davy – you need not have been afraid, because he himself is afraid of his own shadow.'

My mother was embarrassed and looked at me. 'Aren't we the right country yobs? Good God, I feel like a fool that lost her way in the world.'

'Oh, don't let it worry you,' my father countered. 'You're not the first to be afraid of Davy, and in any case he's just out of Portlaoise for a holiday. They'll be takin' him back there this week.'

'God help him,' my mother said, 'it's a poor way to be.'

20

The County Final

It was a couple of weeks later on the Saturday night before the Offaly county football final and my father was worried. He hadn't seen Jimmy Mac in weeks. 'I hope he's in town tonight,' he said, 'because I want to be sure about the match tomorrow.' Even though I was practising my accordion, I was also listening to what was being said. In truth, I wasn't sure if I was going to the football game because no one had mentioned it to me in weeks. My mother saw that I was anxious and said to my father, 'Don't forget that you promised Paddy that you'd bring him with you to Tullamore.'

My father was a little surprised, but said, 'Of course I haven't forgotten.' Hearing this gave me a greater incentive to play more music and without a word I withdrew into my bedroom and began playing with a fresher appetite. Meanwhile my mother made tea, and my father was pouring hot water into a basin. He was preparing to wash and shave and asked my sister Moira for a looking glass. When she found it he had her place the mirror in an upright position near the oil lamp. In a short time he was finished shaving and the tea was ready. My mother was about to turn on the radio when she said she thought she heard the sound of a car pulling up outside, and then we heard four knocks on the door. 'Good Lord,' my mother said when she opened the door, 'it's Jimmy Mac. Come in, Jimmy. You're just in time for a drop of tea.'

'No, no, not now,' said Jimmy. 'Maybe some other time. I just stopped to find out if Christy is still on for the match.'

'Indeed I am,' my father said, 'and is it all right if I bring the young lad along?'

'If he doesn't mind sittin' on the floor of the van,' Jimmy replied.

'No bother at all,' said my father.

'I'll pick you up at noon so, but I have to go now, I'm in a bit of a hurry,' and then he retreated away from the door.

My enthusiasm had me trembling inside my gut. I had to put my accordion aside and instead I opened my box of watercolours and began sketching a figure of a footballer but couldn't find the proper colour for painting the maroon jersey which was the colour of the Daingean team. Painting and sketching was a pastime that I still pursued. When I went to bed and blew out the candle I dozed off to sleep with the colours of football teams jumping around in my mind's eye. Next day, after we returned from Mass, we had a small snack just in time before Jimmy arrived. We had our overcoats on in readiness and within a minute we had climbed into the back of the van. The floor of the van was made of corrugated steel, and was very uncomfortable to sit on. It was a twenty-minute journey to Tullamore with no conversation for most of the way, that is until Jimmy shouted, 'There he is! Look at him!'

Tom Graham, who sat in the passenger seat beside Jimmy, shouted back to my father, 'It's Tom Quinn! We just passed him.' Tom was excited and said, 'He told us last week he'd be comin' with us in the van, but there he is, the auld rogue is bikin' it all the way by himself!'

My father was amused at what his friends were saying and added, 'Quinn is a strange man – he has peculiar ways about him.'

When we arrived in Tullamore Jimmy parked the van in the Market Square and we all headed to a bar near the Kilbeggan bridge. The inside of the bar was jammed with men young and old, either drinking or ordering pints of porter or 'small ones' of whiskey. Somebody bought me a glass of orange juice. It was gorgeous and very soon I was ready for another. We stayed in the pub for an hour until someone said, 'We should go, it's a bit of a walk to the park, and besides we can see the last half of the hurlin' game.'

When we got to the admission gate my father paid for both of us. Tom and Jimmy led the way to where there were long concrete seats near the sideline, about halfway along the field. It was a good choice that afforded us the opportunity to sit and rest while we watched developments unfold. The last twenty minutes of the hurling game was a hectic confrontation between two rival junior teams from the southwest of Offaly. I could see a fellow bleeding from his forehead and another had a bloody gash on his shin. The match continued without any serious incident until the referee blew the final whistle.

The day was bright and sunny with a nice calm breeze, and many of the spectators were in their shirtsleeves. In a short while we heard the sudden sound of the rolling of drums. Once, twice, and then the pipes. They were playing a warm-up march, 'A Nation Once Again'. The music had my full attention, as I thought it might be an opportunity to learn something I could play on my own instrument. Then the band marched across the field. Jimmy Mac was the first I heard shouting. 'Christy, will you look!'

Then Tom Graham joined in. 'Jesus Christ, will you look at him!'

Jimmy shouted again. 'Look, look, it's Quinn! He's marchin' behind the band.' St Colmcille's Pipe Band were playing up a storm and behind them, following in step, waddled Tom Quinn, with peaky cap and trench coat dangling from his arm. It was quite a sight for all of us and it gave us a good reason to cheer our hero as he followed the band in step with its pipe music. Indeed everyone agreed that Tom, our ever-helpful neighbour, was not to be denied his day in the sun. We could also tell from how he walked that he had had some refreshments before the game. In any case, his appearance behind the band was an exciting interlude that would forever stay in my memory.

After a short pause the Daingean and Rhode teams made their way onto the field and began limbering up while kicking the ball back and forth. They continued for a brief period before being told to line themselves up behind the band; it was time for the teams to parade around the field. Then they all started to march and this gave me an emotional feeling that I didn't understand. However, it was a spectacular sight with the sun shining, the colours of the teams and the lovely marching music. In the meantime Tom Quinn had disappeared into the crowd on the sideline, but it wasn't the last we'd see of him. After marching around the park the band stopped. There was a brief silence before they began playing again – it was our national anthem. Everyone in the park stood to attention and my father took off his cap and held it until the pipers finished the song. It was another emotional experience for me and I suppose for a lot of people in the crowd. In the meantime the referee was waiting in the centre of the field and when the band was finished he beckoned the captains of both teams and had them shake hands. Then he tossed the coin. This would decide who would play left to right. Rhode won the toss and decided to play against the wind. Then the ref blew the whistle and the game was on.

My father told me a little about how the game was faring out. The Rhode team were struggling and getting few chances to score and were falling behind on the scoreboard. My father pointed out that some of their players wore stockings that didn't match the colours of their jerseys, which were blue and white. The game continued in a one-sided fashion and at half-time Daingean led by ten points. My father was telling Jimmy and Tom about Rhode teams he had seen in the past. He remembered them for their cagey style of play and foxy use of their players, and they were known for pulling lost games out of the fire. My father liked the Rhode team for their personality and the possibility of surprise. He was probably the only person in O'Connor Park who believed in such an outcome.

Tom Graham bought me an ice cream and we all waited in the sun for the second half to begin. The Daingean team were first on the field, and received a huge applause. The Rhode team were late in coming out and when they did were greeted with boos and soft sounds of clapping from their small crowd of supporters. Then the game began with no scoring for ten minutes. It was back and forth when 'The Rabbit' Murphy scored a goal for Rhode, followed by a point from a free after Murphy was fouled in possession. After another couple of fouls resulting in two points, and with fifteen minutes left, Rhode were just four points behind. Daingean replied with a point, but then one of the Rhode forwards struck again when a high ball landed in the square and in a scramble for possession he booted the ball into the Daingean net!

Now it was just two points between the teams, and Rhode were pressing and passing to each other while the Daingean players were looking confused. My father's look to Jimmy and Tom said, 'What did I tell yeh!'

I asked my father for the score, but he was too excited and didn't hear me. Then Daingean were awarded another free, which they followed with a point, and it was three points of a difference. With five minutes left a Rhode midfielder dropped another high ball into the square. Nine or ten players converged quickly and the ball was lost on the ground somewhere when a Rhode forward booted it and it ended up in the corner of the Daingean net. The game was tied, and everyone thought it would be an even result. With minutes remaining, however, the Rhode men launched another attack and one of their forwards was pulled down on the 21-yard line. The resulting free was sent high and over the crossbar. Rhode had overtaken the hot favourites Daingean during the last five minutes of the game. From the kickout a Daingean man caught a loose ball and was on a solo run towards the Rhode end when he was unceremoniously shoved to the ground. The referee signalled a 40-yard free. Jack Dawley was selected to take the free for Daingean. It would be the last kick of the game. The referee's watch had no more time left. It was a chance for Daingean to level the game and force a replay. Jack Dawley placed the ball on the grass and walked backwards. Then he stood and looked at the ball. It was a test of character, but the bold Jack lost his composure and kicked the ball wide of the post. Rhode had won the senior county football championship. It was one of the most celebrated come-from-behind wins in Offaly's Gaelic football history and I had seen it happen.

My father was speechless, and so were Tom and Jimmy. We all left O'Connor Park and walked back to the town. Reaching Harbour Street, my father said, 'Let's have a drink in Wrafter's.' Wrafter's was bigger than the first pub and very soon it was full with lots of Daingean and Rhode supporters. When everyone had a drink in their hands some of the men began exchanging their opinions of the game. Several were angry with Jack Dawley, labelling him a coward and a windbag, but my father defended him. 'It's easy to talk; but we must remember that he was under terrible pressure.'

We were standing together in a small circle as Jimmy, Tom, my father and I had our drinks. Once in a while I would look up at the men as they chatted. I felt very intimidated and small in height and in my own mind I had a feeling of being disregarded by what was, after all, an adult world. My father bought another round of pints and asked me if I'd like another orange juice. I shyly said yes. At that point Jimmy reminded us that these would have to be our last, as we had to get home to milk the cows. We all understood. After matches on Sunday evenings some people would neglect their cows, leaving them late for milking.

We finished our drinks and headed out to Jimmy's van and soon we were out on the Daingean road. We had gone three miles out from Tullamore when Jimmy shouted, 'There he is, look!' My father and I couldn't see the road very well from where we sat, but then Tom Graham said, 'It's Quinn and he's walkin with his bike, he looks like he's unsteady.'

Jimmy pulled over the van in front of Tom as he stumbled along the edge of the road. 'We'd better give him a lift,' he said.

My father agreed. 'There's plenty of room back here.'

Tom opened the back doors of the van and Quinn crawled in onto the floor. He was tired, and began repeating, 'No better mates, no better mates.' Every time he said it he lifted his voice a little higher. He sat with his back to the side of the van with his legs stretched straight across the floor. Tom and Jimmy tied his bicycle onto the roof of the van, and when Jimmy started again for home, Quinn's voice became lower and lower. He said again, 'No better mates, no better mates, no bett . . . no better mmm . . .' And so he began to snore. He looked so peaceful that my father whispered to us, 'Quinn is asleep – we'd better not wake him.'

We were home at 6.30 p.m. It had been an exciting afternoon and after supper I withdrew to my bedroom with my friend the little Hohner accordion. The sound of the pipes from O'Connor Park was still in my ears and I could still hear some of 'A Nation Once Again'.

21

The Boys' School

It was a Monday in September 1953 when we were moved across the yard to the boys' school. I had been at the girls' school for two years and from what we were told we wouldn't get away with any codology in the boys' school because the teachers there were men who wouldn't spare the rod and spoil the child. Some of the older boys from there had told us awful stories about Mr Murphy and Mr McEnerny. Both of these teachers had reputations for physical abuse or so-called corporal punishment. Our transfer came after lunch break and we all walked in single file through the doorway of the boys' school. We were twenty-five strong and an average of eight years old. Inside we were greeted by Mr Murphy, a tall, red-faced man in his thirties. He quickly seated us behind higher desks and went around asking us our names and where we lived. There was another class of older boys in the classroom and Mr Murphy teased some of them about how smart us new fellows were.

As the weeks unfolded we came to know Mr Murphy, and I suppose he was sizing us up for whatever purpose. His pet subjects were Christian doctrine and the Irish language, and it didn't take him long to single out certain boys for verbal and demeaning abuse. He moved in on us gradually, that is, when he learned what our weakest subjects were, while ignoring our strongest ones. He would teach particular items one day and question us the next. I had a rough time trying to remember spellings in Irish and English and felt extremely vulnerable to his scoldings and hand-slappings with his long cane. Seamus Carr and I would talk together about what we thought of Murphy, which was essentially not very much. The biggest problem with this teacher was that he didn't like some children, not for their lack of ability but for how they looked. So he didn't like me because I was puny, and he mocked others for over-crying. He didn't like one lad because of his high-pitched voice, and others because they were poor. He beat Seamus Carr on the ear for being unhygienic and the same went for Gandhi. He also had his days of being reasonable and calm, and after a year Seamus Carr put a name on him that Seamus was very proud of, except I didn't know what it meant. 'Seamus, what did you say his name is?' I asked.

'Dr Jekyll,' he replied.

'Who is Dr Jekyll?'

'He's half-man, half-devil, and he changes back and forth.'

I was impressed and said, 'I'm going to write it down.'

'No, no!' cried Seamus. 'Suppose he sees it! Please,' he said, 'don't write it.'

'Maybe you're right,' I agreed. So I didn't write it anywhere because I didn't know how to spell 'Jekyll'.

Lunch break at the boys' school was usually half an hour. The bigger boys played football with a full-size leather ball. One time it hopped over in my direction as I stood nearby. I couldn't resist catching it on the hop and it almost knocked me down before I kicked it away. It was heavy and wet from the yard being soaked after it had rained the night before. Seamus Carr and Vincent Cuskelly (Gandhi) didn't like football, and neither did Willy Smith, who was of the belief that he was in fact Hopalong Cassidy. All four of us played cowboys, bank robbers, rustlers and Indian chiefs. We were convinced that we would be cowboys when we grew up and Willy Smith was already making a list of how many cows he'd have in his herd. I also wanted to ride the range like Roy Rogers and have my own horse and I wanted to camp out under the stars and I longed for a bedroll and rifle. Those were some of the ideas we shared and we would also run around thinking our upper torsos were cowboys, while below our waists was all horse. Our imaginations were aflame with stories, and when we graduated from reading funny comics like *The Dandy* to the 64-page westerns of *Buck Jones* and *Kit Carson* we were further convinced of our purpose in life.

Well, it wasn't going to be easy when after lunch break Murphy was waiting by the fire in the classroom. 'Come up here, Carr,' he shouted at Seamus.

Seamus walked slowly from his desk and stood before Mr Murphy.

The teacher shouted again, 'What were you and O'Brien reading at lunch time?'

Seamus went pale, and Murphy shouted again, 'What were you two little rats reading?'

Seamus didn't know what to say. Murphy was about to slap him on the ear when he blurted out, 'A prayer book!'

Murphy stood back and asked, 'You expect me to believe you?'

'Yes, sir.'

'Carr,' said Murphy, 'you are a purebred *amadán*! Hold out your hand!' Seamus held his right hand outwards, and Murphy had his cane ready. 'Now,' he said, 'this'll teach you.' And he came down hard on the tips of Seamus's fingers three times.

Seamus returned to his seat holding his hand under his left arm and I saw tears in his eyes. Murphy warned us all about reading comics, saying that they were the devil's workshop. The rest of the afternoon continued without interruption while Murphy stood with his back to the fire. He had given us pages to read of our catechism while he busied himself with a nail file.

Our story is one of children who were humiliated by a ruthless schoolmaster who should never have had a job as a national school teacher. He took advantage of children, whose complaints to their parents were taken for granted because many parents had experienced the same mistreatment during their own schooldays.

During lunch break Murphy had a habit of standing near the playground and watching us as we played football or other games. One day as we raced for the ball I was pushed and fell. Someone else pushed another boy and when I got to my feet I pushed and pulled a boy's jumper. It seemed like everyone was trying to knock someone to the ground. Seamus Carr ended up with a bloody nose and was trying to control the bleeding when Murphy rang the bell. It was time to return to class. When we were seated we were asked who started the fighting. No one said anything. Then Murphy came to me and said, 'It was you, wasn't it?' Then he looked at Seamus and said, 'It was O'Brien, wasn't it?' Murphy shouted, 'O'Brien, come here!' I went over to the area in front of the fireplace. Then Murphy said to the class, 'I'm going to have each and every one of you come up here one by one and kick O'Brien on the behind.'

Everyone was shaken and mystified by what Murphy wanted them to do. He shouted at me again, 'Who started the fight?'

Again I said I didn't know. Then he grabbed me by my shoulder. 'Bend over here by the desk. Come on, bend over.'

I bent down almost as though I was trying to touch the floor with my fingers. Murphy shouted, 'Carr, you're first.' And then he had everyone take turns as one after the other they kicked me on my rear end. When it was done I limped back to my seat and rested my head on the desk. Murphy was shouting at everyone, 'Let this be a lesson to you all!'

The school building was divided into two classrooms, with a wooden partition that separated our classes from the older boys' classroom. Mr McEnerny was the teacher in charge of the older boys and was also headmaster of the boys' school. He was in his sixties and was approaching retirement. He had a terrible reputation for cruelty and was notorious for using his fist, especially his knuckles, on the heads of his pupils. It was very rare for a parent to pay McEnerny a visit at the school. On one occasion, however, he beat a boy with an inexcusable amount of force, causing the boy's father to confront him. We all hoped that he would clobber him, but the confrontation ended with a shouting match and that was as far as it went.

Every two weeks the two teachers would swap classrooms and McEnerny would take over our class. The reason for the exchange was very practicable. McEnerny was tone deaf and so it was Murphy's job to teach singing to the pupils in the other classroom. On one of these occasions when McEnerny was in a leisurely mood he began asking us some general questions about the life of Jesus Christ. In response to each question we would stand up and raise our hands and shake our arms vigorously. Each one of us wanted to impress the old headmaster with the right answer. I remember McEnerny was wearing a brown pin-striped suit with a waistcoat and on it a watch chain reached from a buttonhole to where his timepiece was tucked inside a small side pocket. He had a big round belly that pressed against the downward line of buttons on his waistcoat, and below his bald head wire-rimmed spectacles rested on the bridge of his nose. My memory tells me that on one occasion he asked us who was the leader of the Fianna Fáil party. He pointed his finger towards Willy Pilkington and Willy shouted, 'De Valera.'

'Good lad,' was McEnerny's reply. Then he said, 'Here's one more. Tell me, who is the head of the Church?' We all knew the answer, and everyone raised their hands in a frantic wave of urgent expectation. But I wasn't expecting what came. With a sudden push of his hand I saw his forefinger pointing towards me and all the other boys sat down and waited for my answer. The room became quiet as McEnerny asked again, 'Who is the head of the Church?'

Pleased as punch, I stood up and shouted, 'Tom Flanagan!'

An eruption of laughter broke the silence of the room. I was dumbfounded. McEnerny was throbbing with laughter. Everyone was laughing except me as I looked around for support but received none. I sat down when McEnerny picked another boy who might know the answer. It was little Paddy Carlisle, who shouted, 'The Pope, sir.'

I wasn't impressed. I still stood by Tom Flanagan. McEnerny was so tickled with my answer that I could hear the bigger boys laughing when he told them the story on returning to his class next door. It seemed like the wooden partition groaned under the strain of the resounding laughter.

I had no idea that my youthful innocence would prove so appealing to local people; I heard that McEnerny told the story to the parish priest and his curates, plus all the school teachers and anyone else who would listen. I didn't know it, but I was a celebrity, because I truly believed that Tom Flanagan was the head of Daingean church, not the Pope. I never knew if Tom ever heard the story or what he would have thought if he had. I never spoke to him, but saw him many times in Daingean church as he polished the brass holdings on the altar rails or lit the candles on the altar before Mass. He also collected the money after people received holy communion. He would walk slowly down each aisle holding a wooden box at the end of a long handle.

He was perhaps in his sixties and his grey hair was mixed with black and he was usually unshaven. He also had his hair cut very close to his scalp, giving him the look of an escaped convict from a Charles Dickens novel. He dressed very shabbily, and wore a heavy black overcoat that was torn around the shoulders where the sleeves were joined. White thread had been used to stitch the torn areas, and more white thread had been used to sew the buttons of the overcoat. His trousers were never long enough to cover the tops of his heavy black boots, which were tied with brown shoelaces. He was tall and slightly bent and walked slowly with short steps. I never saw him talk to anyone and the word was that Tom, his brother and sister were fond of drinking bottles of porter together as they sat by the fire at home. In their own way they were colourful characters and so much part of the social fabric of our lives that people were unable to stand back and appreciate them for what they were. Tom Flanagan was the caretaker of Daingean's Roman Catholic church. I was almost ten years old when I stood fast and true and elevated him higher than the Holy Father in Rome.

22

The Matinée

At home I would talk of Seamus Carr and other boys who had been to the pictures. I wanted to see Hopalong Cassidy and the elusive Indians who ambushed stagecoaches. My parents were intrigued by much of what I was saying, at least for a while. I suppose it became a little tiresome when I invited some of my pals to play cowboy games around our haggard. My father was the first to speak, telling me to pay more attention to my homework and stop reading those comics. He was also beginning to add extra chores for me to do during my evenings after school. Then one day my mother said, 'Hopalong Cassidy is comin' to town. He's goin' to be in the pictures next Saturday, him and Gabby Hayes.' I had never heard of Gabby Hayes.

My mother's mind was made up. 'You and I will walk to Daingean next Sunday afternoon,' she said. 'It's time you saw the pictures, and it might calm you down.' On Sunday we arrived at the courthouse where the matinée performance was to be shown. We were a few minutes early, which made it easy to find comfortable seats. The stage or bandstand had a huge white canvas screen that almost covered the width of the enclosure. Near the front of the stage were long wooden seats that were filled with children of my own age. This area was normally used as a dance floor, but now it was full of impatient children who were shouting or shoving each other, while others were running back and forth. The noise was deafening, until the old caretaker entered from one of the side doors. He had an umbrella, and would stomp it on the floor. The silence that came was a short prelude, and then the lights went out.

As it began I saw movement on the white screen: soldiers marching, British soldiers. It was a newsreel and I had never seen anything like it. I was in a trance, and everything was moving so quickly. When

I saw the writing that introduced the next picture I could tell that Hopalong Cassidy was coming.

The picture began with William Boyd riding his white horse down a hillside. He was starring as Hopalong Cassidy and was on his way to break up a rustler's raid on a trail boss's herd. There was lots of gunfire and I saw rustlers holding their shoulders or falling from their horses. It was fantastic and Cassidy was a great shot with his six-shooters. I didn't want it to end, and when the rustlers held up their hands in surrender the picture moved back again to the hilltop. Then I saw them. It was the Indians on horseback, watching and waiting. My mother whispered, 'Look, it's Gabby Hayes and he's their prisoner.' I was looking at the feathers on Red Cloud's war bonnet and wondering what kind of bird he plucked them from. Hopalong looked tall and daring with his black hat and string tie. Near the end he rescued his friend and we all cheered him on. The picture stayed in my mind for weeks.

At school Seamus Carr, Gandhi, Willy Smith and I shouted our impressions of the picture to each other without hearing what any of the others were saying. We argued about who was going to be Hopalong or Gabby. Gandhi gave way and became Gabby Hayes. I would be the Indian chief because I had my mother's lipstick. Willy had his 'gun' with him and this made him an automatic choice for Hoppy. We were having the time of our lives when the bell rang again. It was back to the classroom.

Two more boys were introduced to the class. Murphy couldn't remember their first names, saying they were young Spollens and that they were the first set of twins he had taught. The two boys settled into our everyday routine but were soon in dread of Murphy's nagging criticism of their poor ability for doing sums or remembering spellings. What made matters worse was their tender sensitivities that brought on fits of uncontrolled crying. This enraged Murphy, who should have remained calm but didn't know how to cope or console or take control of the situation. The best he could think of was to yell the names of animals best suited to describe the two boys. Hearing this they roared and sobbed even louder while the rest of us looked on. Murphy continued his name-calling. 'Come up here, you two little weasels! Come here!' The two boys slowly walked to the space between the fire and the front row of desks. 'Now,' said Murphy, 'you pair of little girls. You think you can dodge your work by crying. All right, cry all you like, let's see how you like crying on the mantelpiece.' He caught the fair-haired boy and lifted him up and put him sitting on one end of the mantelpiece. Then he lifted the brown-haired brother and placed him on the other end. The mantel was at least five feet from the floor and below in its fireplace was a roaring fire. This I believe frightened the boys even further as they sat looking down on the classroom, while Murphy looked like he was enjoying himself or perhaps the vengeance he thought was his.

'As long as you two are crying,' he shouted again, 'I will leave you there. Stop crying and I'll take you down. If you want to stay on the mantelpiece, then keep on crying. I don't care, because I'm sick to my neck with the two of ye little wasps.'

Paddy Murphy was a blocky individual about five foot ten, with a red face and a full head of black hair turning grey. He was in his mid-thirties but looked older. I never knew for sure which county he came from, but at a guess I would say somewhere in the midlands.

During one of his deep moments of rage he confessed to us in class how much he disliked the town of Daingean and its people. He recounted the evening he arrived by bus, and when stepping off he put his foot into a deep pothole. To him, this was an omen of what he would have to put up with in what he called a 'godforsaken little hole of a town'.

One Monday morning he came to school with a black eye. He claimed he had been playing a football match when it happened. We wanted to believe something else, however, and maybe we were right.

Jimmy Reilly was a year older than the boys in my class. He was a well-built, quiet sort of fellow who loved football and the outdoors. He was doing part-time work for a farmer, which earned him some money for cigarettes and the pictures. In school he had little interest in learning, and Murphy did little to help or encourage him. I had a sense that Murphy avoided confrontation with Jimmy, in case of reprisals by his older brothers. I remember one instance when Jimmy had left his lunch on his desk. It was a rather large apple, which he intended to eat before he played football at lunch time. Murphy was questioning Jimmy about 'mitching' from school. 'You've mitched school a few times in the last couple of weeks. You told me you were sick, but I talked to a witness who saw you cycling near your home.'

Murphy had Jimmy against the ropes and Jimmy could see no way out. Murphy shouted, 'It's five slaps on each hand and I'm going to make each one count. Hold out your hands.' He held the stick up and was about to strike when he stopped abruptly and said, 'Whose apple is that? Is it yours?'

'Yes, sir,' replied Jimmy.

'Is it your lunch?'

'Yes, sir,' said Jimmy.

We all knew that Murphy loved apples and weren't surprised by what he intended to do. He spoke again in a lower tone of voice. 'All right, Reilly, I'll tell you what you can do. You give me the apple and in return I won't slap you. What do you say?'

Jimmy smiled grimly and was slow with his answer, and this irritated Murphy. 'Which is it going to be?' Then he yelled, 'All right, hold out your hand.' Jimmy was still hesitant and was on the brink of holding his hand out, but having thought about it he quickly withdrew and said in a soft voice, 'Sir, you can have the apple.'

Murphy took the apple from Jimmy's desk and placed it in the sunlight on the sill of an open window. We were all disappointed. We had hoped Jimmy would take the slaps and deprive 'Spud' Murphy of the apple.

There were many incidents of unusual punishments and I remember one that Murphy used as a way to divide us from our friends. It started when I failed a spelling test and received a warning from him. It was a minute or two before lunch break when he quickly dismissed us because nature was calling him to the lavatory. After eating our lunch we were soon in the middle of playing football with stuffed rags tied tightly with twine. It was a crude substitute for a ball but the best we had. Two stones were our goalposts and I played goalkeeper. The ball came close to the goalmouth and several boys began kicking it on the ground. It came at me and I fell as I grabbed it. Seamus Carr was also on the ground and was desperately trying to get back on his feet. Somehow the ball ended up in the middle of the yard when suddenly we heard the sound of Murphy's bell. As we headed towards the school door I noticed Seamus's nose was bleeding badly, and back in the classroom Murphy wasted no time. 'You know, of course, who did this,' he said as he gave Seamus a cotton handkerchief. Seamus held the rag to his nose but said nothing. Murphy was looking at me and said, 'It was O'Brien, I saw him. It's O'Brien, and I'm going to give you a chance to get your own back. Come out here, both of you.' He made us stand in front of each other. Then he said, 'Seamus, punch him on the nose. Go on, punch him.' Seamus and I were pals and Murphy knew it. When he started to shout, Seamus began to cry. 'Punch him, or I'll give you three slaps on each hand.' Seamus was confused and afraid. Murphy grabbed his hand and squeezed it into a fist. 'Do it, you coward, or you'll get it from me!'

I saw Seamus look at me and then it came. He didn't hit me too hard, but I was bleeding and Murphy was satisfied. My nose bled for the rest of the afternoon, and was still bleeding when I went home.

When my mother saw my bloodied nose she asked me what happened. I told her about Murphy forcing Seamus to hit me, and she became very upset. 'Wait 'til your father gets home,' she said. 'This time I'll ask him to go to town and talk to that lowdown blackguard. That bastard should be arrested.'

When my father heard the story he needed no one to tell him what to do. 'As soon as I eat this,' he said, 'I'm goin' to bike it to Daingean and have a word with him.' He stopped talking and began eating.

'Don't just have a word with him, Christy,' my mother said. 'Stand up to him and don't be a softie.'

That night when my father returned from Daingean I heard him talking to my mother about meeting Murphy in Andy Brock's bar. When my father mentioned me to Murphy – and the bloody nose – Murphy began by saying, 'Oh, Christy, don't say anything to me, I'm dying with a sore throat and headache and I'm aching all over.' It was enough to soften my father, who began to sympathise with Murphy. A few pints were bought by both and the sly Mr Murphy escaped what should have been a serious confrontation.

As I listened more, I could tell my mother was disappointed. 'We should have gone to the Guards about it,' she said.

The next day Murphy ignored me, except at one point after he slapped another boy he said, 'You don't go home and tell tales to your daddy, will you? No you won't, will you?' The young lad shook his head. Murphy said, 'I didn't think so.' And looking at me, he added, 'You're not like some I know.' The vindictive Murphy was already taking jabs at me, but at least he had eased off on the punching and slapping.

Nevertheless, he would find a way to get back at me; it was only a matter of when. Then one day he had twelve of us stand in a line by the wall. We were to study English reading and so we all held our books in front of our faces. We had done this before, so it was something we accepted. Murphy didn't bother us for half an hour. Then he came over to where we stood and began walking slowly from the beginning of the line. 'How many of you are showing a little bit of a beard?' he said. And so he began inspecting our chins, one by one. I was at the end of the line, and Murphy was coming closer as he probed at each jaw with his foot rule. Now and again he'd make his 'aha' sound, followed by 'A little bit,' or 'Nothing yet.' And then he came to me and held my chin with his hand. He pretended to look, then twisted my jaw and shoved me away at the same time. 'Aw, baby face!' he yelled. Everyone knew what Murphy was up to. He would have his day with me, no matter what. He had humiliated the young Spollans, Seamus Carr, Gandhi, and many others. Our parents thought we exaggerated when we told them of Murphy's spiteful attitude. In the end, it was useless to complain or try to explain because of a prevailing attitude of class respectability. Professional people were still held in esteem by ordinary Irish people. It was a peasant consciousness that favoured a 'let well enough alone' attitude and one that allowed Murphy and many like him to terrorise defenceless children in the classrooms of 1950s Ireland.

The first Monday after the summer holidays was a day of adjustments, with Murphy writing a curriculum of important lessons and a list of new books that had been introduced by the Department of Education. We were all an average of ten to eleven years old and many of us were glad to be done with farm work that kept us so busy during much of the summer. As the weeks continued I noticed that Murphy was especially vigilant towards the younger boys, which often bordered on cruelty. I asked Seamus Carr about it, but Seamus didn't seem to think that age made any difference.

I was convinced of Murphy's selectiveness. He would single out particular pupils because of their weaknesses or because of some personal dislike. He targeted a young lad one morning when he had us take turns at doing arithmetic problems on a blackboard. The blackboard was four feet wide and three feet in height and rested on a three-legged stand. Each boy was given a piece of chalk and told to add or subtract various numbers that Murphy had written. The young lad was eleven-year-old little Eddie Hanlon, who was having difficulty with a long division problem. Murphy wasted no time in goading the boy. Eddie had a habit of crying in a high-pitched voice and this of course irritated Murphy, whose response was no surprise to any of us. So once again he shouted and went on to compare Eddie to a young billy goat. In a short while Eddie became flustered by Murphy's constant barrage. He lost his concentration and this provoked Murphy to further extremes. After wrenching the chalk from Eddie's hand the highly strung lad started to cry, a very high-pitched cry, and Murphy started to shout louder, 'Stop it! Stop it!' Eddie was screaming louder than ever and Murphy was shouting 'What's wrong with you? What's wrong with you?' The young lad became hysterical and his crying screams were getting out of control. Suddenly Murphy grabbed the blackboard and slammed it down on Eddie's head. Eddie fell to the floor with the blackboard on top of him. Murphy was distraught and probably frightened. He had gone too far. He told us to take a break and go outside to the yard. As we were going out the door Eddie was still lying on the floor screaming.

We were shocked at the disturbance and while outside were curious about what was happening in the classroom. After a short while we could hear Eddie sobbing and soon there was little sound except Murphy's murmuring voice. In twenty minutes order was restored and we were allowed back inside. Eddie had calmed down and Murphy looked like a man who had been reprieved. We never found out what Murphy said to Eddie while we were outside, but whatever he said the effect must have been very persuasive in calming the boy in such a short time.

Everyone in our class was sure that Eddie's father would hear of the incident, and we all looked forward to Mr Hanlon confronting Murphy and giving him a good hiding. But nothing happened. The matter never came to anyone's attention and Eddie came every day to school as though nothing had ever happened.

23

Topping the Beet

The following months were a busy time with school and working in the fields at home. It seemed like my father was in full throttle during the evenings after he came home from work. He had sown three acres of sugar beet and now it was fully grown and ready for pulling. This job involved pulling two beets together, one in each hand, and beating them against each other so as to knock the clay away from the roots. Then they were laid on the ground side by side and when all the drills were pulled, the beets looked like rows of teeth turned inwards facing each other. When completed, the whole field was flattened, with the beet lying in long lines that also reminded me of fine-toothed hair combs.

Whenever I was available I would tie on leggings made of potato sacks, and wearing an old raincoat and cap I'd pull and slap the beets together and lay them down neatly on the ground. My hands were so bitterly cold from handling the beet stalks that I'd clap them against the sides of my upper body, criss-crossing my arms each time in rapid movement. We completed this work in a week. I had to miss two days of school so that I could help my father and had to make up an excuse for Murphy. This gave him a good reason for nagging and slapping me and reminding me how far behind I was in the class.

My father decided to let the beet dry or let the rain wash it before cutting the toppings. This was done with a sharp spade-like tool that was used in a downward chop. I was told that I should begin the work at the end of the following week.

At ten o'clock on a Saturday morning I began slicing the toppings, holding each stalk in place with my right foot. This prevented the beet from moving as the blade cut its way through. The work was very routine once I got used to it and very soon I was able to stand back and have a good view of my progress. It was as though I had beheaded a thousand of the king's soldiers. The field I was working in was next to the main road. During the late afternoon, as I was chopping and slicing, I heard a voice. 'God bless the work.'

I stopped and looked in the direction of the ditch that separated me from the road and saw a middle-aged man who was wearing a brown hat. He was standing on the outside embankment beside the road. I didn't recognise him at first. 'You don't have much more to do,' he said.

'Not too much,' I replied. 'I'll be able to finish it tomorrow.'

'Tomorrow is Sunday. You don't work on a Sunday, do you?'

I had forgotten and felt embarrassed. 'I forgot that today is Saturday.'

'Well,' he said, 'I must be on my way.'

I watched him mount his bicycle and cycle away. Then I noticed something as he continued down the road. Every thirty or forty yards he would lift himself slightly off the saddle and move his bottom sideways. When he was out of sight his name came to me and I remembered he lived next to the girls' school in town. Later on I would ask my father or mother what was it that made Mick Spollan so itchy on his behind.

After I had washed and settled in for the evening my family were all anticipating the music of the Ballinamere Céilí Band, who were scheduled to play on the radio at nine o'clock. They were making their debut on *Céilí House* and the local word was that they played some wonderful tunes. Two hours later the programme started, with Seán Ó Murchú exclaiming enthusiastically into his microphone, 'Céad míle fáilte go teacha céilí!' Then two taps from the drummer and the Ballinamere were on the air!

It was magic, wonderful and lively. Three great reels, one of them called 'Music in the Glen'. My father reached for a basin and began beating lightly on its bottom with the back of his hand. The broadcast lasted just half an hour, and when it finished we all felt a sense of loss. 'Isn't Dan Cleary a great man?' my mother said.

'Who's Dan Cleary?' my sister Moira enquired.

My mother looked at her. 'Were you asleep, or were you listenin' at all? Don't you know Dan Cleary is the leader of the Ballinamere?'

I was amazed. How did my mother know so much about the Ballinamere Céilí Band?

'The *Offaly Independent*,' she said. 'I read an article about them last week in the paper.' She added that Peter Kilroe from near Kilclonfert played the wooden flute with them. After my sisters went to bed she looked around the kitchen hoping to find the newspaper but it had disappeared.

A few nights later Dinny Doyle knocked at our door. When my father opened it he looked out and said, 'Dinny, what have you got there?'

Dinny came in and said, 'I've made a ring board, it's for the children and here's the rings. I've made them out of rubber from old wellingtons.'

'Holy God,' said my mother. 'Dinny Doyle, you are the most thoughtful of gentlemen.'

My father looked again at the new ring board. 'You did a powerful job,' he said. 'It looks great – you're a gifted man, and the hooks are all spaced to perfection.'

My mother offered Dinny some tea and the kettle was put on the fire. The ring board was shaped like a diamond and a piece of cord was hooked to its top for hanging it up. There were red and yellow circles on its front and the hooks were spaced on the edge of the circles. Dinny hung it up on the wall beside the dresser and we all had a go. Every time we hooked a ring or missed the board we yelled at each other or shouted words of praise. At first we didn't mind the commotion but later we became critical of our throwing ability. Dinny had to remind us not to expect too much from ourselves and that we would be a lot better after a bit of practice. We kept throwing for about forty minutes until Moira and Ann said they were tired. We didn't play again until the following evening. Meanwhile Dinny and my parents were talking about the beet and the chat reminded me of Mick Spollan and his itchy backside. 'Did my father tell you I saw Mick Spollan last Saturday evenin'?' I said to Dinny.

'How could I tell him when you didn't even tell me?' said my father.

I said I thought I had told him.

Dinny was amused by what my father said, but looked at me enquiringly. 'What did Mick have to say for himself?'

'He was ridin' by and stopped to have a look at what I was doin'. He must have heard me toppin' the beet.'

'He's a news mongrel, that's what he is,' my mother interjected. 'All he wants is news, news, and more news.'

My father laughed. 'I suppose he has very little else to think about.'

Dinny looked at me again. 'Paddy, you were goin' to say somethin'?'

So I told everyone about Mick and the way he lifted himself off the saddle of his bike. My sisters were laughing and my father mentioned something about the power of cabbage and peas, to which my mother replied, 'Christy, you're disgustin'!'

Dinny, though, was trying to be serious. 'You won't believe me when I tell ye the cause of it.'

'What?' asked my mother.

'Well,' said Dinny, 'when Mick was younger he was a member of the old IRA. The story is that he and other local lads were involved in an ambush against a lorry-load of Black and Tans. After shots were exchanged, Mick's unit retreated into one of the bogs with some of the Tans followin' them. Just when they got to the edge of the furze a shot was fired and it hit Mick in the behind. Somehow they were able to escape to a hideout. A doctor was located and operated on Mick, but wasn't able to dislodge the bullet. And so he left it where it was, jammed into an area near his spine. The doctor stitched the wound, and Mick recovered, except that the bullet is still lodged in his posterior, and that's why he has to lift himself a little when he's ridin' his bike.'

My father was lighting a cigarette. 'You never know who you're talkin' to.'

'That's right,' said Dinny, 'and when you see him nowadays it's hard to imagine he was an IRA man.'

My mother had been very quiet, and didn't say anything until Dinny was finished. 'Did you hear the Ballinamere Band on the radio Saturday night?'

'No, missus, I didn't. I had to go to Daingean to the chemist and now that I think of it, didn't I meet Bob Lynch on the street and we chatted for a minute. He told me about a new music organisation that started a few years ago in Mullingar. They had a meetin' there and now they're organisin' branches in different towns around the country. He told me that Croghan now has a new branch and that there's a meetin' in Daingean shortly. It looks like another branch is on their agenda next January.'

'Do they have a name?' my mother asked.

'Yes,' said Dinny, 'it's . . . it's somethin' like 'Cooleorí Éireann.' I can't remember the first word. But I do know that Croghan's branch members meet once a month in the schoolhouse at the auld crossroads.'

'Maybe Bob Lynch knows more about it,' my father said. 'I'll try to see him Saturday night.'

'Bob told me they have great music whenever they meet,' said Dinny, 'and a few good accordion players were there the last time.'

This aroused my curiosity, and over the next few days I kept reminding my father not to forget to talk to Bob and ask him about giving us a lift over to Croghan to hear the music.

My father called to Bob's house the following Saturday evening. Bob was very enthusiastic about going to the Croghan gathering. He said the next meeting would be Wednesday night week and that he'd call to our house and pick up my father and myself. We had no idea what to expect, except I looked forward to it and counted the evenings in between.

24

Croghan CCÉ

When that Wednesday night came it was cold, and heavy rain drowned out the sound of Bob's van as it pulled up outside our gate. Bob was early, explaining that he hadn't had time to go home after work and had come here instead. If he had gone home he would have been late for the session. We asked him if he was hungry and he said he wouldn't mind a sandwich. My father was impressed. 'Musicians are the same everywhere,' he said.

Bob was always a great man for a chat and usually had some fresh news because his job as a painter and decorator took him all over northeast Offaly. He had lots of information about the new organisation, which, he told us, was spreading throughout the country. He said it was called Comhaltas Ceoltóirí Éireann.

Bob soon finished his sandwich with the help of a mug of tea and then we were ready. I told my mother we wouldn't be late and my father said, 'Don't worry, we'll have Paddy home before eleven.' Bob thanked my mother for the sandwich and then we were on our way.

When we got there we could hear the music outside as we walked towards the doorway of the school. Inside the room was very bright, lit by two electric bulbs that hung from the ceiling. A couple of tables were pushed aside and four accordion players were sitting on a long wooden bench. I saw one whistle player, who managed to be heard despite the overpowering sound of the accordions. It was my first experience of hearing a live music session outside my home and it filled me with expectation and wonder. Bob was sitting beside me and told me who the musicians were. He said the whistle player was Joe Smullen and the man playing the three-row accordion was Tommy Smullen. Another accordionist was Joe Delaney, who at that time had his own céilí band. A teenage accordion player was asked to play a solo, and when I heard him I wanted so badly to know the tune and to have an accordion the same as him. I didn't know it at the time, but all these players had reel-to-reel recorders and also had access to recordings of Ciarán Kelly, Martin Mulhaire and several other box players. All of them had already been to some provincial and All-Ireland Fleadh Cheoils, which was another great advantage. I had a lot of catching up to do and wouldn't be able to enter the music mainstream for at least another ten years. Having heard the young fellow's solo performance – a real stunner – I had more questions. Bob told me that the teenager was Tommy Maguire and the reel he played was 'The Mason's Apron'. Then there was another solo, this time by Tommy Smullen, who also played a reel. This was another mighty bit of playing and the tune sounded very involved and complicated. Someone mentioned its name – 'The Moving Cloud'. There was wonderful enthusiasm among the listeners and the musicians were all eager to play for the small audience of thirty men and women. My father sat with his head down and was tapping his foot. I thought he might jump up and dance because he often danced at home when I played. Then Bob turned to him, saying, 'Christy, what do you think? Are you enjoying it?'

'It's a great night and wonderful music,' my father replied. My own thoughts were that if my father had a pint in his hand it would be more wonderful for him . . . music or no music.

On the way home Bob was very upbeat and chatted excitedly about the music and the players. 'You know,' he said, 'that young Maguire is goin' to win an All-Ireland in a few years. Jesus Christ, he's as solid as a rock.'

I was in total agreement, but even as I listened I had resigned myself to the fact that my biggest problem was not having a proper accordion, and the prospect of getting one lay beyond not one horizon but one after the other.

When Bob pulled up outside our gate he was in an inspired mood and continued talking without turning off the ignition. I was trying to open the back door of the van so I could get out, and was relieved when my father said to Bob, 'Why don't you stop the engine and come in for a few minutes?'

'Wha'? Wha'? All right, Christy, I might as well.'

It was very inspiring to be in Bob's company and once we were inside we all sat around the fire. He continued to talk about the music and was cursing himself for not having his accordion with him. He told me he had recently bought a new nine-coupler Paolo Soprani. I marvelled at how easy it was for him to find and buy one. When I went to bed I didn't sleep until well after midnight. Sometime in the night I dreamt of acres of beet being gathered up and piled into heaps and then loaded into huge accordions that served as crushers with their bellows pumping in and out. I woke up when one accordion refused to squeeze its bellows.

25

The Grand Canal

The Grand Canal ran half a mile from the back of our house and on quiet nights we could hear the chugging sound of the boats. My father was able to guess if a boat was sailing empty or if it was carrying a load of porter. He also remembered the sound of some of the engines that powered particular boats and their numbers, like 39M or 40B. He was sensitive to the sound of the boats because of his experience as a boatsman for some years before he was married in 1944. He talked to us many times about his old friends – men who had given him songs with the words written on cigarette boxes, men who were from other counties, and men who personified their humble beginnings by sharing what little they had. There were other men whose egos and selfishness left a lasting impression on the young Christy O'Brien, whose give-and-take nature would help influence my own values.

My father had lots of ghost stories and tales of mysterious drownings, and the names of loughs he said were haunted or just plain unlucky places. He had stories of two boats tied together during gale-force winds or storms and how they ploughed their way through thirty feet of high waves while crossing Lough Derg on the River Shannon. Once he and his mates were marooned on an island for a week and found shelter in the home of a hospitable family. A gramophone was brought into the kitchen and several gallons of porter tapped from one of the Guinness barrels on the boat. He said they danced for several nights listening to the same 78 rpm record over and over and over. The record was worn out by the end of the storm.

During the time when I was topping beet, Daingean's small harbour was a busy stopping point for beet boats. Most of these boats or barges were used for delivering porter from the Guinness brewery in James's Street, Dublin. The Grand Canal waterway was linked from Dublin to the River Shannon and from there the boats sailed with their cargo to Limerick city. It's been said that the slow boat travel was ideal for conditioning the porter. The barges also transported sugar beet to Carlow's sugar factory and also to Tuam sugar factory in County Galway. When visiting my Aunt Mary's, I would pass over the bridge at the top of Daingean, where I would see huge piles of beet yet to be loaded onto the boats. This was usually done in late August and September.

My father was in the cowhouse washing our cow's udder with warm water and disinfectant when a car pulled up outside our gate. Its driver was a man from the town who said a fellow from one of the boats had been in an accident and that other boatsmen were dragging the canal under the bridge. The missing man was an old friend of my father's with whom he had once boated. His name was Ned Cummins from Edenderry. Hearing the man's name and the likelihood that he had been drowned, he told my mother he had finished washing the cow and that he was biking to Daingean. He threw on his overcoat and within minutes was on his bicycle pedalling hard for the town.

It was a couple of hours later when he came home. When he came into the kitchen he looked very distraught and as he sat down he explained to my mother how they had found Ned Cummins' body near the bottom of the canal right under the very boat he was to steer out of Daingean earlier that evening. My father was very emotional and as he spoke he broke down crying. 'Poor Ned,' he cried. 'Poor Ned, oh poor Ned.'

'How did it happen?' my mother asked.

He recovered a little and said, 'They thought he might have stood on a bootlace as he walked along the side of the boat. He had a couple of pints in Cronley's bar, and then left for the boat. I was in the old warehouse when they brought him in – poor Ned – and they left him there for the night. We looked at his nailed boots but didn't see any-thin' wrong with the laces.' He was crying again. 'Poor Ned Cummins, poor Ned. He left a wife and four children.'

My mother made tea and my father brought it with him to the bed-room. He said he was tired and I could hear him crying when he closed the door.

I wasn't allowed to play my accordion for two weeks as a mark of respect for Ned, so I'd sneak away with my mouth organ and try out some new bits of reels or jigs on the roadway. In later years my father explained that boatsmen were very loyal to each other. All along the canal towns their reputation as honest and reliable men was noted and appreciated, especially during the Second World War when they would bring tea and sugar from the bigger towns to country areas that were hit hard by food rationing. When rumours began in the late 1950s that commercial travel on the canals would soon be a thing of the past, my father and his boatsmen friends were stricken with disbelief and scepticism. In the end it was just a matter of time before the old boat culture of the Royal and Grand Canals would be no more.

Some of our most delightful times were when Dinny Doyle came across the fields for a house ramble, which might be during the day or late evening. Tea was very often the launching pad for chats about music, or some neighbourly interest. He always included me or my sisters with chitchat, questions about how we were doing in school. On one of his visits he spoke about the invisibility of the fairies, and how he heard them playing fiddles over at his side of the bog where the quickenberry and beech trees grew. He said he was setting snares for rabbits at six o'clock in the morning and the sun was about to rise when he heard a faint sound of music. At first he thought it was his imagination, but as he walked towards where he thought the music came from, it got louder. When he got to the quickenberries the sound had moved further away to where the beech trees grew among the furze. When he went to where the sound was in the trees, it had moved back again to the quickenberries. He went back and forth a few times but the music moved again and again. At that point he gave up on the possibility of seeing the fiddlers and concluded that they were in fact the 'wee folk' or the fairies. He said the music was delightful and full of great soul and they had tunes he never heard before.

When he finished the story we were all silent for a few seconds. We were sitting looking at Dinny, waiting for him to tell us more, when he said, 'Paddy, how's it goin' in school?' I told him that Murphy had sent me down to the back garden to cut hazel rods for beating us, and had slapped me three times because I had selected rods that weren't stout enough. He sent another boy to the garden with a warning about what he'd do if the boy returned with a bunch of reeds instead of the sturdy rod he needed to put manners on us.

Dinny was flabbergasted. 'What kind of a devil would do such a thing to young children?' My father told Dinny about having gone to the town and having a word with Murphy.

Then I told them about a recent incident during spelling class when he picked on the young Spollen twins, who started crying. Murphy shouted at them, 'Come up here. Come here, you pair of little sissies.' When he had them standing in front of the roaring fire he yelled that he was tempted to throw them into it. Hearing him say this frightened the two boys out of their wits and their crying became louder, with tears flowing from their eyes. Murphy reached for the big fire tongs and put it around one fellow's neck, yelling that he'd give him a good reason for crying and then started to squeeze the tongs. We were all frightened when we saw what he was doing. It goes without saying that his scare tactics made matters worse, but fortunately he removed the tongs, instead yelling at the boys to go and stand facing a corner in the room. He had them stay in that position until the class was finished.

Dinny looked at me with disbelief. 'Paddy, are you sure this is the truth?'

'If you are makin' this up,' my mother intervened, 'it'll be a shame on you and a stain on yer soul.'

I was adamant and felt disappointed. 'You can ask any of the lads I play with,' I said. 'Any of them will tell yeh. I'm not lyin'. That's what he did, you should ask the young Spollens.'

'It's all right, Paddy,' said Dinny, 'we believe yeh. Don't worry, we believe yeh.' He said some people could be very cruel and that something should be done about this wicked animal. Maybe he was right, because at that time I was too young and inexperienced in the world to be able to fully appreciate the difference between good and evil. However, some time later I noticed a change in Murphy's treatment of Seamus Carr, a sort of easing off on the slapping and very few questions regarding homework or days out of school. It all began to make sense when one day I saw Seamus give an apple to Murphy just before lunch break. At least twice a week Seamus would have a huge apple in his school bag which he'd leave on the teacher's desk. Seamus never said anything to me about it; indeed nothing was said by anyone. It was a case of letting well enough alone.

On a lighter side, I chuckled privately to myself as I saw myself in school taking a sugar beet from my satchel and offering it as a gift to Murphy. The consequences, of course, were too terrible for me to contemplate, but I loved to think about it!

26

Milking the Cow

I was glad the work with the beet was finished. My parents talked about all the work that went into growing it and getting it ready for the boats. They concluded that the whole process of preparing it was too much and so my father never grew another sugar beet. We did, however, make some money from the transaction with the beet company and with it my mother bought us clothes and a mattress for herself and my father. She also bought me a better mouth organ, which was longer, and I could play all of 'The High Level Hornpipe' on it. It was my reward for enduring the long hours of grubbing, thinning, weeding, pulling and topping and the loading of cartloads of beet. I hoped I'd never have to do it again.

With the beet work out of the way I had more time for homework from school, swapping and reading comics and playing the mouth organ or the Hohner accordion. I was also developing an understanding of where some musicians hailed from, as Ciarán MacMathúna announced their names, the tunes they played, and the town or village where they lived. History and geography were subjects I loved at school, and I began to give the map of Ireland a closer look as I searched for Tulla and Kilfenora in Clare, or Castleisland in County Kerry. It was a time of mystery, and a kind of romance prevailed as I listened to the accordion music of Francie Brereton of Nenagh, County Tipperary or flute player P.J. Maloney from the same county. A major irritation was trying to learn particular tunes. Anything I already knew I had picked up by ear, which was how musicians learned their music, especially if they lived in areas where house dances were common. This meant they heard many of the same reels, etc. played over and over on different occasions at various house dance gatherings. Because I had very limited access to the music, however, my only source was the radio.

Far more often than not I would have to help my father with milking the cow during the dark winter evenings. He would wait until
A Job of Journeywork was over and then I'd accompany him to the
cowhouse. He would have me hold the hurricane oil lamp while he
washed the cow's udder before he began milking. My mother often
teased him about how the cow would give her more milk because, as
she said, she had 'the touch' or the kindness in her for animals. She
thought the cow understood this and responded by giving her more
milk. One evening as I stood holding the lamp I saw that my father
was struggling to get milk from the cow. 'What in the name of Jaysus
is wrong with her?' he said. 'Or is it me doin somethin' wrong?' I
thought about this and couldn't come up with an answer. 'Paddy,'
he said, 'do you remember the day on the bog when you played the
mouth organ, and Phil Rourke's cattle nearly trampled the turf?' I
said I did. 'Now I want you to go inside and bring out the mouth
organ and don't let your mother see you with it. Put the lamp down
here on the straw.'

I ran into the house and found the mouth organ in the corner near
the fireplace and I secretly put it into my old overcoat pocket. My
mother was washing Moira's hair and my three other sisters were
in the bedroom arguing about something. Nobody noticed me going
or coming. I ran back to the cowhouse where my father was waiting.
When I confirmed that I had the mouth organ he said, 'Start playin'!
Remember I told you that cows love music? It calms them.'

'What'll I play?'

'Anythin',' he said, laughing a little. 'Just play anythin', anythin' at
all.'

I took the mouth organ from its blue box and began playing a
march called 'Kelly, The Boy from Killane' and followed it with an
old Fenian melody called 'Down By the Glenside'. My father began
milking and I kept playing. I was watching the bucket beginning to
fill. It was slow at first as my father kept on squeezing the spins of
the cow. I was also watching the cow and saw that her ears were now
pointing outwards.

'By God, Paddy, the music is doin' the trick. Look,' he said. 'That's
a good girl,' he said to the cow as the milk came shooting out of her
spins. 'You're a real auld cod, aren't you, Polly? Now we know what
she likes, and it isn't hay, turnips, or mangels, it's music! Wait'll your
mammy sees this – she won't know what to say, and Paddy, don't

you tell her about playin' the mouth organ. We'll tell her some other time. When we're finished here we'll go back to the house and say nothin' and see if she'll notice the full bucket.'

Back inside, my father lifted the bucket of milk onto the table that stood against the back wall of our kitchen. It was where we kept the skim milk and the cans that we had bought from travelling tinsmiths. When my mother came out of the bedroom she saw me and my father. 'Did ye milk the cow?' she asked. I said we did. My father was washing his hands and said nothing.

My mother saw the bucket on the table and went over to strain the milk. Then she started to laugh. 'Which of ye did it?' she said.

'Did what?' said my father.

'There's twice as much here,' she said, 'much more than what you got from her last night! Paddy, where did ye get the extra milk?'

'It is extra milk indeed,' I said, 'but it came from the cow. Honestly,' adding that the cow was in a very giving kind of humour.

'Yes,' said my father, 'I had no bother gettin' the milk from her at all. Paddy is right, the cow was in good humour and liked the way I touched her.'

He turned his head away as he said it and gave me a wink. I think my mother saw him because she said, 'You two are a connivin' pair of rogues.'

27

The Hoax

It was a weekend in October when we were able to organise our forces for an Indian raid on Fort Laramie. I had already done my share of scouting and located an ideal area for ambushes, rustler hideouts, or anything to do with the landscape of Western films. New members were joining our posses and outlaw gangs, good lads and bad lads. One of our most devoted recruits was Jimmy Quinn, who was the youngest of Tom Quinn's family. Others were Andy McCormack and his brother Seán. Also the Pilkington brothers, Pat, Willy, and John, who were convinced they were the James gang. Despite warnings from my mother about a bull patrolling the moors, we all decided to scout the place and meet afterwards in a spot beside a ditch that ran alongside the main road. Arriving at the meeting place, our gang eagerly reported that the bull was nowhere to be seen. The Pilkingtons were sure it was a ploy to keep us off the moors. And so we galloped off to find a suitable area for the attack on Fort Laramie. We found a small sandpit and the McCormacks were told to defend it, with Jimmy Quinn as its commander. The rest of us were the attacking Indians, with Seamus Carr wearing several feathers from his mother's hens. Gandhi wore his sister's lipstick for war paint. Most of us had bows and arrows, while the sandpit defenders wore gunbelts and hats, and two lads had plastic rifles.

It was going to be a no-nonsense showdown. It began with the Pilkingtons yelling Indian war cries, 'Yi-yi-yi! Ya-he-ha! Yah-hee-hah!' We could see Willy Smith's head peeking out of the sandpit, then he ducked, just in time as a war lance missed him and Jimmy Quinn shot down its thrower. We were circling, ducking, dodging, hiding and running backwards and regrouping, and then the soldiers came out of the fort and charged us and some of us were captured. Seamus Carr and Jimmy Quinn held a pow-wow and decided that

Willy Smith be burned at the stake. Suddenly we heard the sound of *moo, moo, moo*. It was the bull, but we couldn't see him. Vincent 'Gandhi' Cuskelly came running over. 'I saw him,' he gasped, 'I s-s-s-saw him tha-tha-tha b-b-b-bull!'

'Let's get across the drain to the field,' I shouted.

We all ran and climbed over the drain and fence and jumped across into my father's field. We ran to its far end where we wouldn't be seen from our house.

Jimmy Quinn spoke with urgency. 'Where can we get a stake, Pat?'

'Wait a minute,' I said, 'and I'll get one.'

Someone else said he was getting a spade from my father's shed. Half an hour later we had a stake embedded in the ground and Seamus Carr had returned with an armful of sticks and twigs. Willy Smith was happy to be chosen to die at the stake. John Pilkington tied his hands behind his back and shoved him up against the post. Willy was grinning while John wrapped twine around him and Seamus Carr put sticks and brambles around his feet. Then it was time for the Indian war dance. With more whooping and yells we danced around Willy, who was still grinning and seemed to be enjoying himself.

We screamed and yelled more Indian war whoops as we danced around, pounding the ground with our feet and bending backwards and bowing downwards. 'Yi, yi, yi, yi! Ah-ee, ah-ee!' And then there was silence and we stood waiting.

Jimmy Quinn was sweating and wanted more. 'Anyone got matches?' he shouted.

We looked at each other and Willy stopped grinning. We didn't have any matches and I said we didn't have any at home. Quinn was insistent and said he was going home to get some. As soon as he got to the road Willy shouted at me to cut him loose. Seamus Carr undid the twine and Willy, who was looking relieved, said that Quinn should die at the stake instead of him. Then someone came up with an idea to frighten Jimmy when he returned. I was asked if there were any dry ashes in our ash-pit at home. I thought there was. One of the McCormacks told me to go and get some, and Vincent 'Gandhi' Cuskelly said he'd come with me. Someone else told us to get two buckets of ashes. My mother was in the kitchen when we got to the house. I said that myself and Gandhi wanted to take out the ashes, and that we wanted a bucket or two for a job.

'You two are up to somethin', aren't you?' she said.

We told her we were sowing a tree in the bog!

She said no more and gave me an old bucket and handed a big paper bag to Gandhi. We filled them both and rushed out to the field where the other boys were waiting. All the sticks and brambles were gone from around the stake, and all we needed to do was pour the dry ashes in their place. Seamus Carr was nervous and reminded us to hurry, that Jimmy would be back in a minute. In the meantime Willy Smith had left and was on his way home.

Everything was ready when Jimmy came back to the field. When he was within 30 feet of us I saw he had the matches, but as he came closer he knew something was wrong. Seeing the naked stake he enquired, 'Where's Willy?'

We pointed to the ashes and I said, 'We burned him.'

Jimmy was stunned. He went pale in the face and said, 'You didn't. You couldn't have.'

'Look at the ashes,' we said, 'that's all that's left of him. We had to do it. He was a traitor!'

Some of the other lads looked at their feet and two of them had their hats in their hands.

Jimmy was convinced. 'This is murder,' he said, 'that's what it is! You fellows are dangerous, and . . . and . . . this is terrible! Poor little Willy,' he yelled. 'What are we goin' to do?'

Seán McCormack looked hard at Jimmy. 'You're the one that wanted to burn Willy at the stake!'

'I didn't! I didn't!' Jimmy replied.

'Then why did you go home for the matches?'

Jimmy had forgotten about the matches and had dropped the matchbox on the ground. 'We were only playin'! That's all it was!'

But Seán was not letting him off. 'Then Jimmy, why did you go home for the matches?'

Jimmy looked worried and started to cry. 'I don't know. I don't know.'

'Listen, everyone,' I said. 'We shouldn't tell anyone about this, just say nothin'. We burned a traitor and that's all there is to it.'

Poor Jimmy was bewildered. 'What'll I do?'

'Go home and say nothin',' I said. 'We're all goin' home anyway, but we have to hide the stake and bury the ashes.'

Seamus Carr said he'd make a cross for the grave.

Jimmy couldn't stand any more and started running to where his bike lay against the garden wall of our house.

The following Monday we saw Jimmy in school, but he wouldn't have anything to do with any of us. Willy Smith was absent for whatever reason, which would ensure that Jimmy's misery would continue. In fact Willy didn't appear in school for the whole week. Unbeknownst to us, his father had told Murphy that his son had an abscess in his jaw and had to have a tooth removed.

The following Sunday we were all at Mass, including Jimmy, who sat near the front of the church with his sister. When the priest and six altar boys walked in from the sacristy and stood in front of the altar Jimmy saw that one of them was Willy Smith!

Jimmy's reaction was immediate. He stood up in the pew and screamed, 'Baaaahhhh! Eeeeech!' Pushing his way along the pew, he reached the aisle and ran frantically until he got to the church door and disappeared, with his sister running after him.

We could still hear him screaming as he disappeared into the distance. When we returned to school our schoolmates were full of talk about the incident in the church. *What's wrong with him? Is he all right?* His sister brought a letter from her mother stating that Jimmy was in bed with the mumps and would be out for at least a week.

It was two weeks before Jimmy returned. He ignored us for the best part of a month and we didn't play cowboys and Indians again until the following summer.

Out with the Wren

Christmas was a few weeks away, and my father was looking forward to going out with the wren. My mother had made arrangements for hiring Gilbert McCormack to take us to Thomas Pender. My sisters were looking forward to the season's holidays. We were also complaining about how narrow and sooty our chimney had become. Kathleen and Patricia had written to Santa, telling him that they had asked their daddy to sweep the chimney. Ann was worried that Santa would dirty his lovely red suit or get stuck. I didn't believe in Santa but went along with my sisters, or maybe I didn't want to be left out or not get a present.

It was late November and the weather was frosty at night and cold and damp during the day. I had my usual evening chores of collecting sticks and small twigs for the morning fire. I also had to pull hay for the horse, cow and calf. Sweeping the yard in front of the house was another small job that I had to keep up with. At night, when the moon was up, its yellow light shining on the swept yard outside our door, somehow its warm glint inspired my instinct for playing the accordion. I could never understand this attraction, even when I learned about the power of the moon and the way it controls the tides.

My sisters continued to badger my father about sweeping the chimney. Finally their persistence paid off and he came home from work carrying a sweeping brush with five lengths of cane that were extensions to be assembled all the way to the brush head. The brush itself was circular and had prongs that would loosen the soot. The next day he covered everything in the kitchen with potato sacks and newspapers. My mother and sisters disappeared into one of the bedrooms. I was given the job of loading a wheelbarrow in the kitchen and wheeling the ashes and soot outside to the dung-heap. It would be a long chore with many trips of loading, reloading and dumping. The entire job was completed in half an afternoon. My father was visibly pleased with his achievement, and looking up the chimney he said, 'It looks well enough now! Pat, come 'ere and have a look.'

I was surprised at its width and how each of its four sides looked so clean, and I said something about it being a long time since it was last done.

'Oh,' said my father, 'I'd say twenty years.'

We removed all the covers and unscrewed the five canes of the brush. Then we washed and dried our faces and hands. My sisters and my mother came from the bedroom, and everyone had a look up the chimney before we relit the fire. The girls were as happy as a flea in a rug.

'Santy will be delighted!' Ann yelled.

'It looks lovely,' Moira agreed.

My mother was also very pleased. 'Christy,' she said, 'that was a job that really needed to be done.'

'There's plenty of room for the oul' fella now,' said my father, look-ing at each of us.

Throughout the twelve days of Christmas our family were absorbed with the spirit of the season. My father and I had searched Phil Rourke's moor and bog areas for a tree, but all we could find was a holly bush. My father had a bush saw and cut the little bush close to the ground so that its central limb was long enough to put into a small bucket. Arriving home, we sat it in a bucket and packed several stones around it until it felt steady and could stand up by itself. My father liked to encourage us and told us to hang Christmas cards on the holly and we made a yellow paper angel for the top of the tree. When it was finished we hung ivy over the doorway, and on the window panes and along the shelves of our dresser. Our kitchen had become a kind of greenhouse and had a cosy feel to it, especially when we lit a couple of tall red Christmas candles and stood them upright in jam jars wrapped in coloured paper.

It was an inspiring time for music, and I didn't waste any of it. As I practised and played I felt the flames of the tunes run through my veins. Before leaving for a drink in town my father would dance on the kitchen floor, or sometimes dance without music and whistle softly at the same time. I was never able to recognise what he whistled; it was an accompaniment he developed just for himself, I suppose.

A couple of nights before going out with the wren Paddy Brien came for a ramble. He had cycled from his home in Clonadd, and thought nothing of the three-mile journey. He brought with him a tambourine, and some vizards that he wanted my father to try on. Paddy, then in his late thirties, was a remarkable man. He had very alert eyes that were always full of humour or, as my mother would say, full of devilment! He was a great joker and full of conversation and my sisters would giggle and titter uncontrollably while listening to his observations or jokes. Once when they were on a giggling spree my mother became embarrassed and ran all four of them into the bedroom. Paddy was talking all the while and didn't notice anything odd.

'Well, the Lord Jaysus,' said my father. 'Where in the name of Christ did you get this?'

'At an auld flea market in Tullamore,' said Paddy.

My father put on the vizard – it was a baboon's face – and looked in the mirror. Then he turned around to face us. 'Is there anyone here that would like to fall in love with me?'

My mother cringed. 'Surely to God you're not going to wear that! If anybody sees you on the road, they'll run for their lives!'

My father looked at it. 'Be the cross of Christ,' he said, 'what an ugly-lookin' candidate. He looks like everyone belongin' to him is dead. Paddy, play a tune and we'll try this one out.'

I began playing and my father took to the floor and did a clown's dance that he made up. He was poking his behind outward and shaking his head from side to side and making *Ya! Ya! Ya!* sounds. It was difficult for me to concentrate because my mother was laughing so much she almost fell off her chair. My sisters were peeping around the bedroom door and Moira squeaked a loud laugh and the other girls screamed and ran back inside to their room. My father put on another vizard, opened the door, went outside and closed it. Then a *tot-tot-tot* knock and Paddy shouted, 'Come on in!'

My father came inside with the vizard on his face and my mother's headscarf on his head.

'Who are you?' cried Paddy.

'I'm an old woman, and I'm learning to dance!' he said in a low voice. Then he looked at me. 'Young man,' he said, 'play me a fling.'

I quickly obliged and my father reached for Paddy to be his partner. Paddy put his own vizard on and the two of them hopped around the kitchen.

I squeezed out the tune 'Some Say the Devil is Dead and Buried in Killarney'.

The two men danced, facing each other, then twirling around and facing each other again. Paddy was shouting, *yowh, yowh, yowh,* and my father was making a howling sound like *hoo hoo hoooah*. Everyone was laughing uncontrollably and my mother had to dry her eyes with a dishcloth. My sisters were shrieking and giggling, and our youngest sister Patricia began crying when she saw Paddy's vizard. I was beginning to tire and so slowed the tune to half its pace. My father noticed and said, 'Paddy, rest yourself for a while.'

Paddy Brien sat down and wiped his forehead with a neatly ironed handkerchief. 'Janey Mac,' he said, 'that's hard work, Christy.'

My mother made tea and Paddy started to tell one of his nonsense jokes, which he called his 'bag of lies'. I remember it began with Paddy going to Daingean to buy a round square and how his aunt was missing and a search party went looking for her. Later he was listening to the wireless and heard a man say he had seen his aunt cycling over Ireland, so that must have been her. We all drank the tea and my father explained that Gilbert McCormack would drive them on Saint Stephen's Day and that he'd pick up Tom Brewer at the terrace after meeting Paddy and Tom at Gilbert's house in Daingean. Then they would drive to our house where my father and Mick Hayes would be waiting.

Christmas Eve was an evening of preparation and excitement, especially for my sisters, who were expecting Santa. My father had been busy sweeping our front yard. My mother was making plum pudding that she rolled into a round lump and encased in a white cloth. Then she tied it when all of its sides and corners were pulled together. It reminded me of Dick Whittington's travelling bag that hung from the end of a stick on his shoulder.

The early night was bright and clear, with glittering stars from horizon to horizon. Standing inside under the cleaned chimney I looked up and could see the stars mixing in with twirling blue smoke from our fireplace. Moira was standing close by. 'Let me have a look,' she said.

I stood back and she stepped under the hurl. Looking up, she said, 'The chimney is shinin', and I can see the moon movin'.'

I looked again and said to her, 'It's the smoke in the breeze; when you look through it, the moon seems to be racin'.'

Moira had the last word. 'Santy is goin' to love how clean the chimney is,' she said.

My mother and sisters left a glass of milk and two slices of currant cake on the table before we retired at bedtime. It was a small snack for Santa – something to help him on his journey.

Next morning it was gone and replaced by some toys. A doll, a tea set, a small stuffed teddy bear, a cap gun and a Mountie's hat, another small doll, and some tiny cars and a plastic tractor. Everyone was pleased that Santa had recognised our house! He had been here. My sisters went outside to look at the roof beside the chimney. Ann said she saw marks on the thatch that, she said, 'had to be him'. She was thus a confirmed believer. We ate a Christmas dinner of two chickens, potatoes, carrots, and lots of gravy and afterwards tea and plum pudding. My father washed his down with a bottle of porter. Lemonade was carefully divided between my mother, sisters and me. Outside the weather was overcast but the interior of our kitchen gave us a feeling of security and cosiness as we sat near the fire. I was toying with the keyboard of my accordion when my mother asked me to play 'Jingle Bells' or 'Rudolph the Red-Nosed Reindeer'. She knew some of the words and sang along with me when I played. Late in the evening we had chicken sandwiches and stuffing, with tea and some more plum pudding.

The next day was Saint Stephen's Day, and in the morning my father began trying out some old clothes and a pair of pyjamas given to him by Tommy Brien. He had his vizard and a walking stick for pretending to be lame when out with the wren.

Gilbert McCormack arrived at noon and Mick Hayes was due in half an hour. Saint Stephen's Day had arrived almost as quickly as Christmas Day was gone. My father had his 'duds' ready and put on his vizard when he heard the sound of Gilbert's car pulling up outside.

Mick Hayes didn't like to be late, and late he was by twenty minutes. Everything was fine until he came to the top of Killoneen Hill, where the rear tyre of his bicycle went completely flat. There was nothing else he could do but wheel his bicycle the next mile to O'Briens' gate. As he was coming down the hill he could see Gilbert's car in the distance. The two Brien brothers were walking around, stretching their legs. Tom Brewer was playing his mouth organ in the back seat of the car. After about fifteen minutes Mick was within shouting distance of everyone. As he came closer, my father could hear him cursing and groaning, and then he stopped for a rest. Tommy Brien saw him and ran down the road to help him carry his accordion.

'Lord Jaysus, give me patience,' groaned Mick. 'Wouldn't you fuckin' know it, the very day I wanted to be early, the fuckin' bike let me down. I got a puncture on the top of the hill. It's little wonder that people say this godforsaken road is haunted.'

'It's all right,' said Tommy. 'Don't worry about anythin'.'

Mick left his bike inside the gate and joined everyone in Gilbert's car. Then they were away up the road, out with the wren!

Their first stop was Edenderry, a journey of twelve miles. When they arrived Gilbert parked the car and everyone climbed out with their vizards on, and Tom and Mick led the way with accordion and mouth organ. My father played a tambourine, while the Brien brothers took up the rear with Laurel and Hardy-style dancing and clownish gestures.

Tom Brewer opened the door of a pub and in they went as they played and danced. My father did a small sort of a skit and acted the part of an old lady who wanted a dance. He pulled a fellow off his stool and the two did a jig. The Brien brothers were hooting and clapping. Some more of the bar's clientele joined in and were trying to keep up with the jig. Someone went around the bar making a collection with an old hat, and three pints and two orange juices appeared on the counter. Another man began a rebel song while the wren boys were having their drinks. Tommy Brien called for another jig and Mick obliged with 'Haste to the Wedding', while Tom sat on his hunkers and did a frog dance. He was joined by a married couple from the bar who lost their balance and fell on the floor!

All of a sudden Tom Brewer was ready with his foot drum, mouth organ and tambourine and began with a hornpipe.

'Who is the little fella?' somebody asked.

'Jaysus, he's a humdinger,' said the barman.

'Where are they from?' another enquired.

'Not from around here,' said the man drinking beside him. 'These are a great batch of wren boys, no doubt about it.'

'It's a pity they're leavin'.'

After Edenderry, Gilbert drove them to Rathangan, where they did a couple more bars. All went well and they were welcomed everywhere they went. Other towns and villages included Rhode, Walsh Island, Portarlington, Tullamore and Killeigh, and they finished their tour in Andy Brock's bar in Daingean. Mick went on a cursing spree when he realised that the huge weight of coinage in the side pockets of his topcoat was tiring him out. After they arrived in Daingean he made an excuse to carry Tom's drum from the car. After opening the trunk he saw a slot in the drum's casing and loaded all the coinage into it. When he hauled it inside the pub everyone was having a drink and no one noticed Mick with the drum.

When it was time for more dancing Mick rested his pint and began playing. My father took to the floor with Paddy Brien and they were dancing to a polka when suddenly there was a loud crash as Tom's drum hit the floor. The little man had tried to harness himself to his drum, but it slipped from his grasp and fell onto his toes. He roared a loud 'Fuck!' and backed away from the drum, and with a ferocious kick he buried his boot in the stretch of skin that covered its circular frame. 'You low-down fuckin' git!' he groaned. 'And just when we are finishin' up!'

Everyone in Brock's pub was either laughing or stood dumbfounded at what had happened, and nobody had ever seen Tom so angry or embarrassed. He tore away his vizard and walked out the door with my father running after him. Outside on the towpath my father tried to console Tom with words of praise. 'We wouldn't be able to do it without you,' he told him.

When they returned to the pub Tom was greeted with a round of applause and Andy Brock stood him a glass of whiskey. More music and dancing preceded a round of songs from local men and my father sang 'Rockin' the Cradle'. Everyone was well on it when Andy Brock was seen drying his misty eyes with an immaculately clean handkerchief. 'Last call!' he cried. 'Last call!'

Someone from outside the counter was called to help him fill a stream of pints and whiskeys.

It was an hour after closing time when the bar was cleared and everyone adjourned for a last hurrah on the sidewalk. Mick and Tom played more jigs and hornpipes and men were dancing with other men. Young ladies on their way to a dance across the street were commandeered for a crash course with the younger fellows from the pub. A corkscrew was doing its duty with bottles of porter coming from the pockets of men intent on 'makin' it a night'.

The power of the bottles would soon wane and cede to the frosty air of midnight. Mick, as ever, felt it most and Tom complained about cold hands from blowing the mouth organ. The two Briens decided to take a walk over to Gilbert's house on the other side of the street. Gilbert had already gone home to wait for them until they were finished 'doin' the town'.

After the two men had warmed themselves they went outside with Gilbert and got into his car. Then they drove over to Brock's bar and collected Tom, Mick and my father. The money was easy to remove from Tom Brewer's drum since he himself had made such a sizeable hole in its front side. Gilbert was paid with a sackful of coinage that amounted to many half-crowns, red ten-shilling notes and two-shilling bits. My father was left in charge of counting and dividing the rest, which he did the following day. He told us at home how they did in the many pubs they stopped at.

'Gilbert McCormack has the patience of a saint,' my mother said. 'How he put up with all of you, I'll never know.'

When my father finished counting there was a total of fifteen pounds, seventeen shillings and threepence.

Each man was given three pounds, three shillings and ninepence, which was paid out the following weekend. Bit by bit we were told of our father's adventures on Saint Stephen's Day. He said they ran into a few other batches of wren boys; one group had no music, which he thought was unbelievable. Near Rathangan, Gilbert's car almost ran out of petrol, but all in all they were very pleased that the car had not gone to ground with a puncture. My father concluded his story of the day with a remark that gladdened me. 'The next time,' he said, 'we'll have Paddy with us with the accordion.'

29

The New Teacher

In another week we were back at school, and with it came the same old insecurity and dread that caused so much nervous tension in me. I haven't written much about the fear I had of Murphy when he was the master at our boys' school, and I can't speak on behalf of my schoolmates. And yet I can easily assume that most of the youngsters were sharing the same sense of dread that I felt. We didn't know what to expect or what kind of mood this adult bully might be in or what lessons he'd pick from his bag of tricks. All we knew was that he enjoyed keeping us on the edge of our seats, and enjoyed ridiculing or deriding us for small mistakes and misspellings.

During the month of January some of us were told that we were to be moved to the older boys' room, which was beyond the partition. The news of this sickened my stomach with thoughts of the knuckled fist of McEnerny, who sat on his throne behind his desk not a stone's throw away. It was another month before we were marched in a single file from our classroom to where McEnerny stood, cane in hand, waiting. I still see him with his back to the fireplace, his small spectacles resting near the top of his nose, and his heavy cane pointing us to three rows of empty seats.

'Sit down there,' he calmly said. 'And what is your name?' he said to Seamus Carr. He continued to ask us all our names, and when he was finished he handed us copies of a new Christian doctrine catechism. We were told to read it for the rest of the afternoon. After another month nearly everyone had experienced a taste of the old headmaster, who in fact wasn't as brutal as we were led to believe. He was an experienced teacher who was overly fond of honesty, even if honesty was inspired by stupidity. I don't remember him ever hitting me, probably because he was a friend of my father's. One cold winter my father had carted a load of turf to McEnerny's school. It had assured continued heat for a couple of weeks, and this was something the headmaster never forgot.

McEnerny announced his retirement just before Easter, telling us that he'd miss us and that he had had some of the best times of his life in this old school. I looked across at Seamus Carr and saw he was smirking behind his English book. After class he told me he thought McEnerny was going soft in the head from his migraine, or maybe it was something else.

After Easter our new headmaster was introduced to us by Murphy. 'This is Mr Coffey,' he said.

We were all standing as a mark of respect but said nothing and I remember Mr Coffey looking over his dark-rimmed glasses and waiting for us to make some sort of response. We had nothing to say. Mr Coffey continued to eye us, and, pulling out his handkerchief, said, 'All right, boys, you may all sit down.' He removed his glasses and rubbed his handkerchief all over his face and then settled his glasses back on his ears and nose. He was a small little man with a round belly and a shiny bald head. 'Now,' he said, 'let's get to know each other.' He looked at Ollie MacEvoy and asked, 'Son, what's your name?'

'Ollie.'

'Ollie what?'

'MacEvoy.'

'Well, Ollie, where is County Roscommon?'

'In Ireland,' responded Ollie.

Mr Coffey laughed and said, 'Ollie MacEvoy, are you trying to be a little latchico? You are trying to be a little latchico, aren't you?'

'Yes, sir. No, no, sir.' Ollie was red in the face. He never heard the word before, none of us had.

Mr Coffey turned to Bunnie Hanlon. 'You,' he said, 'where is County Roscommon?'

'The west of Ireland,' said Bunnie.

'Ah,' cried Mr Coffey, 'we're getting closer.'

He looked at me. 'You, with the fair hair, where do you think it is?'

'Across the Shannon,' I said.

He seemed pleased with what I said, and looked at us all. 'County Roscommon is indeed on the western side of the River Shannon, no doubt about it. And another thing I want you boys to remember is that County Roscommon is where I was born. It's where I grew up, in a little town called Elphin. Now get your maps out and we'll find it. A sweet to the first boy that finds it.'

Our small maps were out in a flash.

Austin Hanlon found it before any of us and Mr Coffey gave him a sweet. This was Mr Coffey's way of encouraging a pupil. He said, 'Good boy, good boy,' and Austin began to blush. He was afraid some of his classmates might tease him about the sweet on his way home after school. Mr Coffey told us to study the map of Ireland while he sat at his desk. Then he began writing with his head facing downwards. He didn't look in our direction for a long time. Finally Seamus Carr whispered, 'What is he doin'?'

'I don't know,' was my hushed reply. 'Maybe he's writin' a letter to his mother.'

30

Singing Lessons

It never occurred to us that we weren't entirely rid of the bully Paddy Murphy. However, it later transpired that Mr Coffey, like McEnerny before him, had no ear for singing songs and this meant that he'd have to switch classrooms with Murphy so that Murphy could stand in as our singing teacher.

Nothing unusual occurred during the weeks approaching summer, that is until one day when we were being drilled by Murphy, who was trying to teach us a Latin hymn! Over and over he had us read the words of a hymn he expected us to sing at Sunday Mass. None of us had ever heard the hymn before, which meant we would have to learn its melody and lyrics with less than four days to Sunday. Murphy seemed to think we were familiar with the hymn and so he began to sing it. I suppose he expected us to join him as he sang but we just stood in silence, not knowing or attempting any of the melody. In less than a minute Murphy's feathers changed colour and his face was looking like he was going to explode. His neck and face were red and blue, which was a sure sign of his anger and frustration. 'It's worse you're getting,' he shouted. 'What am I going to do with you? You're all a shame and a disgrace.' He hit the tuning fork hard against the edge of Mr Coffey's desk. *Zaaing-ooo* – it trembled a troubled A, and then he began with another hymn, '*Genitori, Genitoque*'. We knew this one, or half knew it. We all sang together but Mr Murphy wasn't finished. He started at the far end of our line and began poking his ear close to each boy's mouth. I didn't know the hymn very well, a few words here and there, as Murphy moved slowly along trying to hear each one of us. Vincent 'Gandhi' Cuskelly was standing beside me making hissing sounds that came out between his teeth like a sewing machine in labour, *zeests-zeests-zeests*. I thought of singing louder to hide Gandhi's misfortune. I didn't want Murphy to hear how Gandhi was doing, but quickly gave up on the idea. Poor Gandhi had no ear for music and when Murphy was two boys away he became more nervous. This changed the tone of his voice and so it became deeper and louder. In truth he reminded me of a gander in distress! *Zawzests, zawzests, zaawzeeet!* One after the other. It was the sound of nonsense but the best that my friend could do. And then Murphy was upon him! I saw the master's face as he listened. He twisted his head and his mouth curled like he had put his nose close to the inside of a rotten egg. With the narrow end of his tuning fork he tried to pry open Gandhi's teeth.

'Open up,' he yelled. 'I've heard better from squeezing the handle of a bicycle pump. Come on, open up.' It was no use. Gandhi was petrified with fear, and Murphy, in disgust, moved away and came to the next boy, who was me. I was making my own sounds that were a mixture of more gibberish, but I was keeping it low and soft so as Murphy wouldn't be able to make out what he was hearing: *Chau, chau, chau.* It didn't make any sense to me either. Murphy pushed closer to hear more of it but then backed away after a couple of seconds. His face was clouded with a heavy frown or perhaps disbelief. In any case I sensed he was glad to be done with Gandhi and me. The loud singing of the other boys had shielded us somewhat, but in the back of my mind I couldn't help but remember Gandhi's bad breath and how my sisters complained about mine.

Mr Coffey had heard Murphy shouting at us from where he sat next door and enquired from us about what happened during singing class. We told him about the new hymn that Murphy had expected us to sing and that we had never heard it before. Mr Coffey looked at us in search of a weakness in our story but quickly concluded that we were telling him the truth. 'I will speak to him about this misunderstanding,' he said, 'and try to prevent it happening again.' We were very gratified on hearing this. It was the first time we ever heard a schoolmaster saying he'd speak on our behalf and we felt very relieved by his fair and sensible attitude.

31

Céilí House

It was another weekend and I was looking forward to hearing *Céilí House* on Saturday night. We had heard the radio man mention something about a band from Galway that had won the All-Ireland at one of the major Fleadh Cheoils. It was a time in my young life when I was beginning to anticipate some note patterns in the tunes and also developing a better understanding of how jigs, reels, etc. were shaped. Indeed it was a very slow process of learning new tunes from the radio and then hoping they would be played again on later programmes. Any time I learned a tune it motivated me for more and more playing and practice. Romantic notions about travelling to Galway or Clare and meeting box players from the radio consumed me and disrupted my concentration. As an example, one evening after school I walked into our kitchen carrying a load of hay in my arms and was about to lay it on the fire when my mother shouted, 'Paddy, what are you doin'?' I turned immediately and went out the door to the calf house. When I came back my mother said, 'You're thinkin' too much about that bloody music. You should rest yourself from it.'

On Saturday night's *Céilí House* Seán Ó Murchú was his usual exuberant self. His high-spirited voice sparkled with excitement as he introduced the Aughrim Slopes Céilí Band from County Galway. With them was a guest artist from the band, whose name was Paddy Carthy. Paddy was a wonderful flute player and had lots of good tunes. The band opened the programme with 'The Galway Rambler' and 'The Bunch of Keys', two very fine reels, and then a selection of double jigs that began with 'The Bride's Favourite', coupled with 'Whelan's Fancy'. I was deeply touched by this kind of music, its style and the rolling pace of the jig playing. As I listened I craved a tape recorder, knowing the benefit it would provide – if only I had one that very night. My mother and sisters were also enjoying the

My parents Christy and Molly O'Brien in the haggard at the end of our old thatched house in 1944, just after they were married.

My father coming home from work at quitting time in about 1953, after a day out on the bog cutting turf for a neighbour. He's smoking a Woodbine cigarette, and that's a sleán, a turf spade, he's carrying on his shoulder.

My father out cutting turf in a neighbour's bog in around 1953. That's his workmate Tommy Wright standing in the background.

Flute player P.J. Moloney and accordion player Francie Brearton at a Fleadh Cheoil in around 1958. Brearton was my first accordion hero.

My father and his workmate Leo McGill on their bicycles, heading home from working a day in the bog.

Paddy Brien and my father in their vizards, preparing to go out with the wren boys. This was taken in our new house at Castlebarnagh in around 1962.

My mother and me at about two years of age, taken in around 1947 in the haggard behind our house in Castlebarnagh.

I was eleven years of age when this photo was taken in 1956, at the Daingean National (Boys') School. Not many people had cameras at that time, so a travelling photographer would visit the school each year to take pictures of the pupils for their families.

I am standing in between Tom and Johnny Rourke, neighbours from the next farm over at Killoneen Hill. The boys' mother, Bridgie Rourke, snapped this picture after we'd finished sowing potatoes one June evening in 1957.

I was probably thirteen when this photo was taken in 1959, again by a travelling photographer.

Standing in the street with my accordion at the 1964 Fleadh Cheoil in Clones, County Monaghan, where I competed in the All-Ireland Senior Duet with fiddler Maura Connolly. After a recall, we were awarded second place.

Another itinerant photographer took this picture of me in around 1960 when I was fifteen years of age, again at Daingean National School.

music as far as I knew. However, I never realised until years later how deep and far away I was in my thoughts when listening to the music on *Céilí House*. I suppose I could have been light years away from everyone else in our kitchen. When I heard more of this céilí band my thoughts began racing back and forth, imagining that I was walking among the stone walls and green fields of County Galway. I was enjoying a musical journey of imagery where people danced at crossroads and where pubs were alive to the sound of Paddy Carthy's flute. I was in another world, where music was the dominant force of who I was. Years later I talked about these old radio days to other musicians of my generation and they also spoke of the magic, excitement and frustration of hearing those new tunes. More than anything we wondered if the magic would ever be repeated. There is a tune called 'The Smiles and Tears of Erin', which to me is a cultural metaphor for a time of yearning among young musicians in many parts of Ireland during the latter half of the 1950s.

32

Making the Hay

Our Aunt Maggie was a frequent visitor to our house before she was married. I was very fond of her because she was always in a happy mood, and always brought sweets, lemonade or oranges when she visited. I remember one warm summer when she and her boyfriend were helping us out at 'piking' hay (which is an old country term for raking and piling hay into cocks). Everyone was in a great mood for teasing and cod-acting with each other. My Aunt Mary said something funny to Aunt Maggie, implying that she had her work cut out for her if she married her young man, whom Mary referred to jokingly as 'the Longford fella'. Everyone laughed and the hay was forgotten when my two aunts began pushing each other. My mother joined in and the women were screeching and shouting when she pushed her sister against a haystack. Maggie's fiancé Johnny McCreamer was covered with hay and didn't know who was throwing it on him. Two young ladies with short pants – cousins of my mother – were having a whale of a time trying to bury Johnny in the hay. One of the girls tripped over Johnny's legs and fell. My father pushed my Aunt Mary, who was wearing a very wide sun hat. Someone else was poking her head out of a pile of hay and began pulling hard on my father's leg. He fell.

While all of this was taking place I was standing a little bit away and at first I thought they were fighting but soon realised it was all a good-humoured shindig. It ended with everyone on the ground or lying in small piles of hay. My mother had brought a basket of scones and a couple of bottles of strong tea, which she had tucked away under the shade of a tree. After a few shouts of 'The tea is ready!' everyone gathered together to eat and drink. Johnny McCreamer, who later married my Aunt Maggie, praised the timing of the snack, telling my mother, to her amusement, that the shortest way to a man's heart was through his belly. I didn't know what to make of what he said. Then all of a sudden someone noticed Black Bob, our new horse, walking across the field and dragging the 'snake rake' behind him. My father jumped to his feet, ran across the field and caught the horse. 'You're thirsty, aren't you?' he said to the animal. Then he unharnessed him and brought him under the shade of a tree and tied the reins to one of its branches. Without saying a word he went across the hayfield and disappeared behind the house and when he returned he was carrying a bucket of water. The horse proved to be extremely thirsty and drank all of it in the space of a minute. My father joined us again for more tea and another scone. 'Sometimes we forget about how an animal might be feelin',' he said. 'I think Black Bob knew we were drinkin' somethin' and decided to get himself a bit of attention.' We all nodded in agreement.

Meanwhile Mick Mangan had just come in from the road to tell his wife, Aunt Mary, that he was on his way home. Having joined us in conversation he enquired, 'Did any of you hear about the Electricity Supply Board goin' around askin' people if they want to have the electric light put into their homes?' Neither my parents nor anyone else had heard anything about it, but soon they were all talking about what the Electricity Supply Board (ESB) were up to, and my father suggested that it might be dangerous to have electricity in any of the old thatched houses. Mick went on to explain that it might be difficult for everyone to agree to getting it in because so many would rather hang on to their oil lamps. He said it would probably take time for people to get used to the idea. Mick was looking very grave and said that another issue would be cooperation between a group of neighbours. The Electricity Supply Board needed three to four houses within a mile radius of each other in order to make it cost-efficient to bring the electricity to the area. If one or two homes objected you might not have electricity for another five years or so. Mick looked very solemn as he talked, and everyone listened. It was the first time I heard people talking together about the prospect of electric light in our homes and even then I knew within myself that I was all for it. And why not? Wouldn't it put an end to the problem with the radio? No more waiting for batteries to be charged and hopefully more music into the bargain!

The weather held up that week and the hay was saved and made into three dozen cocks to be brought into the haggard later. The work

with the hay and then the straw was a very uplifting time for everyone. It cheered us up, and with the bright sunny weather there was
also the lovely scent coming from the new-mown hay. It was the
smell of summer and with it was the call of the cuckoo, which could
be heard not far away in a neighbour's field or perhaps in a tree by
the banks of the canal.

33

The Piper and the Pigs

When my parents were busy saving hay or turf it was always at the expense of something else that deserved attention. What was usually needed was a reminder of some sort, not that a reminder was the only way my parents could see what was staring them in the face. One ignored problem was having three young pigs, one six months older than the others. We kept them in a shed that leaned against the gable end of the cowhouse. The outside corners of the shed were supported by two round poles with stout planks bolted to each pole supporting three walls. On top was a corrugated iron roof. Below, all along where the edge of the floor and the walls met, the pigs were succeeding in burrowing their way under the bottom ends of the walls. They were also eating into the bottom ends of the wooden poles, undermining the stability of the entire shed. This could have been prevented if my father had the time to 'ring' the pigs before they got older, especially the eldest one, who was looking like a formidable character and would prove very hard to control during the painful exercise of squeezing a ring into his nose. The question of what should be done was put aside for some time. Then one day a bagpiper came to our gate at the road and stood there while he played a tune. He wore a long beard and his pipes were decorated with green tartan colours and with tassels hanging from three different drones. He played for a long while before stopping. My mother sent me to the gate to give him sixpence – he thanked me and marched away up the road playing a Scots march.

It was then my mother noticed the pandemonium coming from the pig house. The pipe music had had a frightening effect on the three pigs, who were squealing and running around inside the shed in an uncontrolled state. The pig house was shaking and almost ready to collapse. At one point I saw one of the poles being lifted by the snout of the bigger pig and the bottom plank being pushed outwards by one of the younger pigs, who was trying to escape. My mother ran to get a bucket of pigshire – a mixture of boiled turnips and mangels, bran and skim milk pulped together – in the hope that it might have a calming effect on them. As the sound of the pipes diminished in the distance she gave the pigs the food and very soon they settled down again. This was on a Saturday afternoon and when my father came home after half a day's work the story of the piper and the pigs was relayed to him by my mother, who usually told him of the day's events while he sat eating his dinner. The story didn't surprise him. 'We'll have to ring the big pig first and maybe Tom Nugent might have a pig ringer,' he said. 'Do we have any rings?'

'Haven't I had them here for months?' my mother replied. 'I bought a packet of them in Cronley's weeks and weeks ago.'

'Let me see them,' said my father. She had them hidden in a drawer and when we saw them my sisters and I took pity on the pigs. 'These'll quieten them,' said my father. The rings were in a couple of sizes and were of an oval shape, and turned inward with enough space for the nostrils to pass through. One or two of them on the big pig's nose would prevent him from rooting at the bottom of the shed, or any other adventure he might use his snout for.

'Who are you goin' to get for the job?' my mother asked, and I knew my father was joking when he said, 'You can hold 'em, can't you?'

Caught by surprise, my mother shouted, 'What!? Are you losin' every bit of sense you have?'

'I'm only pullin' yer leg, woman,' my father laughed. 'I'll ramble up to Tom Nugent's after I finish atin' this.'

'Bring Paddy with you,' my mother said. I was delighted. It made me feel important.

After a mug of tea my father said, 'Paudgeen, are you ready?' I was, and so we walked the half-mile to Tom Nugent's house, where we were greeted by his sister Nancy. Tom was out walking for exercise. He wasn't long out of hospital due to a complication with his knee. Nancy was a wonderful lady who I remember giving me little bars of chocolate and telling me how mannerly I was. She always called me after a cousin of my mother's who died in America from drinking moonshine during the Depression in the 1930s, so she often said to me, 'Hello Pat Dunne.' She would say I was the spittin' image of my mother's cousin, who came home from America to visit everyone before he went back again and died, somewhere in Ohio. Nancy made some tea and had lovely buns for us to eat, some of which had pink and white icing on top. I was in heaven with her kind attention and generous nature.

When Tom came back from his stroll he was using a walking stick and was limping a little. He sat down on a chair near the table and Nancy poured him tea. 'Tom, you wouldn't happen to have a ringer for ringin' pigs?' my father asked.

'Indeed, I do,' said Tom. 'Whose pigs are you goin' to ring?'

'My own,' said my father, 'and I was hopin' you might ring them if I held them for yeh.'

'If you're able to hold them I should be able to do it,' said Tom. When my father told Tom about the bigger pig Tom took off his cap and scratched his head. 'By God,' he said, 'I hope he's not too big. It's hard work tryin' to ring an oversized pig.' My father was anxious and asked Tom when he'd be able to come down to the house. 'Maybe tomorrow,' said Tom.

'Tomorrow is Sunday,' said Nancy as she looked at the two men. 'Surely to God you're not goin' to ring a pig on a Sunday.'

'We will,' said my father, 'because one of them has grown bigger than expected and we've got to do it as soon as possible.'

The next day Tom came down to our house. It was late in the afternoon and Mícheál Ó hEithir was broadcasting a Leinster senior hurling final between Wexford and Kilkenny. My father was sitting close to the radio and the match was tied when suddenly Mícheál yelled, 'It's a goal! It's a goal!' My father began jumping on the floor. In a moment the game was over and Wexford had beaten Kilkenny. My father had not seen Tom come into the kitchen and said, 'Tom, are you long here?'

Tom never missed a chance for a joke. 'About half an hour,' he replied.

My mother was filling the kettle and said, 'It's time for a drop of tea.'

My father went outside but came back in a matter of minutes. 'Hush, keep your voices down,' he told them. 'I was over at the pig house and the big pig is asleep with his nose stickin' out under the door. Maybe we can ring him while he's asleep. Tom,' he continued, 'do you have the ringer handy?' Tom took it out of his pocket. 'Here,' said my father, and handed Tom one of the rings. Tom slipped the ring into the curled slot on the ringer and held it ready for squeez-ing. The tool had the look of a pincers but was loaded with two extra claws. It never made sense to me what these extra claws were meant to do. My father had a hopeful look on his face and said, 'If we steal out nice and quiet we might be able to do it.' I followed the two of them to the pig house door. The pig was still asleep and was making little whimpering sounds. His pink nose was indeed way out under the door, leaving plenty of room for Tom to put the open ring around one of his nostrils. It was a chance both men badly needed.

Tom got down on one knee and put the ring on the appointed spot near where I saw the pig's breath pulsating from out of its snout. He didn't have time to wait and my father who stood behind him whis-pered, 'Now!' Tom pressed the pinchers and squeezed quickly with his two hands. It was a clean squeeze and the ring entered the sleep-ing pig's nose with full force. The pig woke in shocked torment and jumped backwards, almost taking the ringer with him. He was plung-ing and squealing inside the shed, with the other pigs joining in. The pig house vibrated and the two men stood against its door in case the big pig came running at it. The commotion inside was deafening and lasted for maybe five minutes before the pigs started to tire and the noise from within became more subdued with short little grunts that were superseded by a soft snore that Tom said was from the big pig. 'That'll keep him quiet for a while,' my father said. But we still had to ring the other two. Tom was in agreement that it would be better to leave it alone for another week, and with that in mind I followed them back inside the house. My mother was full of remorse for the pig and told Tom and my father that they were heartless devils, 'no better than Oliver Cromwell'. The two men laughed when they heard that.

The following week Tom came again in his horse and trap while, as he said, he was 'out for a spin'. He had the ringer with him and said he should have left it with us the last time he was here.

'No harm done, Tom,' said my father, and then they were on their way again to the pig house. When they opened the door the big pig retreated back into the far corner.

'Is it possible he remembers us?' said Tom.

'It's hard to know,' said my father. 'Let's see if the other two remem-ber us.'

'We have to put the rings on their noses first,' said Tom. They had the two pigs ringed in less than ten minutes, the result being a chorus of squeals that made my sisters run back into the house. They had not been at home for the ringing of the big pig but had heard the story from our mother. The same story was told over and over by men who worked on farms and bogs around our locality and it became part of local pub gossip when drinking men tired of talking about the weather.

34

The Birth of a Calf

Tom Nugent came for another visit. It was the week before the summer holidays and our cow was in calf.

'Tom,' said my father, 'we were just talkin' about yeh.'

'Be the Holy, I hope it was somethin' good.'

'We're beginnin' to worry about the cow,' my father said. 'She's looking very heavy.'

As usual my mother was making tea. Tom was looking forward to a mug and said, 'After we have a drop we'll go out to the shed and I'll have a look at her.' When the tea was drunk Tom and my father went to have a look. I followed them, and inside the cowhouse we watched Tom as he talked to the cow while feeling her underneath. 'She's due in a couple of days,' he said, 'but it could be any time.'

'Is it possible she's goin' to have twins?' my father asked.

'I don't think so,' said Tom, 'but anythin's possible. She's a fine animal, isn't she? God bless her. I'll come down tomorrow night. Somethin' is tellin' me she wants to do this alone, some cows are like that, so 'twould be better to keep an eye on her from now on. They like to be alone when they calve and often wait for the time when nobody's around. It's like a game with them and this one might be like that.'

Tom was known and respected locally as a man who was good at overseeing a cow calve. He was very intuitive and somehow could read into a cow's behaviour when their time came. He was also very gentle and kind and could coax his way into a cow's confidence. He was another remarkable man, and a great neighbour.

The next night at around nine o'clock Tom, true to his word, arrived and this time he was seated on a motorbike that he had bought from Paddy Byrne in Daingean. The bike was a noisy contraption but nevertheless we were relieved when its owner removed his wind glasses to reveal his face.

'Jesus Christ,' said my father, 'Tom, it's you!'

'Who else could it be?' said Tom.

'When did you get the bike?' my father asked.

'Just today,' Tom said. Then he asked about the cow.

'She seems to be the same,' said my father. 'I'd say she must be sick for calvin'.'

'Let's have a look before we go into the house.'

When they were finished they came into the kitchen and continued talking about the cow, and Tom was saying that she might calve sometime that night and that it was just a matter of when.

So we all settled down for a long night of watching and waiting. Tea and sandwiches were made, and more tea, followed by more tea. Now and again Tom would go out to the shed to see the cow and the old hurricane lamp was lit and had to be refilled with oil. When he returned he said, 'She's just standin' there waitin'.'

After another ten minutes my father went out to see her. It was a little after midnight when he came back and told us that she was still the same. My mother had begun to doze off in her chair and when her head fell forward she woke up and declared, 'I can't keep awake.'

'Why don't you go to bed, and you too, Paudgeen,' said my father. I protested and told everyone I wanted to stay and that anyway I wasn't sleepy.

'Molly,' said my father to my mother, 'you go ahead. We'll be all right, and there's nothin' you can do now anyway.'

Tom was sympathetic. 'Missus,' he said, 'you should go to bed and get a wink of sleep. We may need you to put us to bed in the mornin'.' Tom also had a way with people and the result was that my mother excused herself and went to her bedroom.

I was surprised at myself when at one o'clock I noticed I wasn't sleepy, and I said then that I'd go out to see the cow. I had never been up so late and felt excited by the whole experience. I tiptoed outside with the lamp until I came to the door of the cowhouse and looked inside. The cow was still standing quietly alone, no sound, no movement except for one ear that moved backward when she sensed I was behind her. I went back to the house. After another ten minutes Tom and my father decided to have another look. This time, as Tom stood at the rear end of the cow, he said he had a feeling somethin' was wrong. Suddenly he rolled up his shirt sleeve and I saw him shove his hand inside the cow's posterior. When he withdrew his hand he looked at my father. 'I'm afraid,' he said, 'that the calf is turned inside her.' My father looked worried, as this was his only cow.

'I'll have to turn the calf,' said Tom, and then he looked at me. 'Paudgeen, would you go and get a rope as quick as you can.' I ran outside to the far shed where I knew I'd find one. When I returned, Tom was busy trying to locate the calf's hind legs. 'Ah,' he said, 'I think she's goin' to be all right. Paudgeen, give me the rope and I'll tie it. The poor thing. She wasn't able to calve by herself with the calf turned inside her. Cows have died because they didn't have someone to help them. Now we have to pull the calf out.' I had never seen a calf come out of a cow and I was stunned by what was happening. 'Pull,' said Tom, and my father and I pulled until I saw the calf's two little hooves appearing through the cow's behind. We pulled harder on the rope and then I saw a pair of long, thin legs coming slowly outwards. We had to pull still harder until the long glistening body followed, sliding into its new world. Tom cradled it in both arms to prevent it from dropping onto the floor and then he gently lifted it down onto a bed of new straw. Our cow had calved!

We untied the cow and she turned immediately to her baby and began licking its small body. My father had removed the water bag and cleanings – the term we gave to the afterbirth – and what emerged was a beautiful white-faced, brown-coated bull calf. Tom retied the cow to its manger and my father came back from the house with a bucket. He milked a full bucket of beestings and poured some into a milk bottle. Then he put a baby sucker on its top so the calf could suck it. The little calf couldn't get enough. He was ravenous! The milk was gone from the bottle in less than two minutes and my father had to refill it from the bucket. Halfway through the second bottle the calf tried to stand on its legs. Slowly it lifted itself onto its knees and with sheer willpower it rose and stood beside its mother. It was a struggle at first but once on its legs an air of confidence took over. The cow looked back at her accomplishment and I thought I heard her give a sigh of approval.

'It's hard to beat the instinct and wonderful nature between a mother and its newborn,' said Tom.

'It's a gift from God,' said my father, who was now lighting a cigarette. Then he looked at me and said, 'Paddy, run on in and put the kettle on. We'll be in in a minute.' Tom and my father put the calf in its new calf house, which was prepared with plenty of straw. When they came into the kitchen the tea was brewed. I asked my father what the cow and calf were doing. He said the calf was asleep and the cow was chewing her cud.

35

The Two Bulls

My father had often talked to us about his younger days when he lived in Ballycommon. He was very proud of once having been a member of a batch of wren boys from there. He spoke highly of the Boland boys, Joe and Mick, who played accordions, and their sister Annie who did likewise. The Bolands were out with the wren with my father, who remembered some of their favourite reels, including 'The Salamanca' and 'The Silver Spear'.

Well, one evening after cycling home from Daingean my father mentioned that he had met Joe Boland in Tullamore. 'Yeah,' he said, 'I met him on the street. He got down off his bike and we chatted for a good while. We hadn't talked to each other in several years. I told him about Paddy and the music and Joe said he'd stop by next Saturday afternoon, on his way to Kildare.'

When I heard what my father said I was alive with excitement. My mother had never heard Joe play the accordion but said, 'Didn't he play with the Gallowglass Céilí Band at one time?'

'I believe he did,' said my father. 'I think he played with them the year they won the All-Ireland céilí band competition.' After hearing about Joe's intended visit I went to the back room with my accordion and began practising a jig called 'The Lark in the Morning'. It was a tune that my father said he first heard from Joe, and I wanted to be able to play it without missing a button.

The conversation soon changed when we saw Jimmy Spollen passing our window and then a gentle knock on the door.

'Come on in, Jimmy,' shouted my father, who was sitting by the fire. Jimmy came in and sat by the dresser. He was a tall man who wore a battered hat and his overalls smelled of diesel oil. I heard him speak from where I was practising and could tell who it was. I abandoned the accordion in favour of fresh news that I knew Jimmy would be telling my parents. He had called in to settle on a date for thrashing our corn and wheat. Jimmy was in charge of the mill, with his brother Jack taking care of the tractor. They were a popular pair who were hired during harvest time by most of the small farmers around our locality. The two of them worked well together, though many people thought they weren't on speaking terms. The reality of it was that Jack being so quiet frustrated Jimmy and so he gave up trying to talk to him. On the other hand, Jimmy could be quite talkative and had lots of things to tell us as he sat and engaged my parents in conversation.

'Did you hear about us gettin' in the electricity?' he asked. 'You didn't!' My mother was taken by surprise.

'God blast it,' said Jimmy, 'I did. And bad luck to it. It's one of the greatest nuisances a man could ever have!'

'Why is that?' my father asked.

'You'll think me to be a right fool when I tell yeh.'

'Not at all,' said my mother as she handed Jimmy a bottle of stout. Jimmy took the bottle and stood it on the floor beside him. He wanted to finish his story before having a drink. 'I went to bed last night,' he said, 'and when I'd settled meself and turned a few times and was ready to doze off I had to get out of bed again.'

'Why?' my mother interrupted, 'did you forget to say your prayers?'

'Now Molly, don't start laughin' at me, although I suppose I deserve it.' It was then he reached for the bottle of porter and held it to his mouth. After a good swallow he continued. 'I wouldn't mind but I've made the same mistake over and over.'

'What mistake?' said my father.

Raising his voice, Jimmy shouted, 'I forgot to turn off the god-damn light!' We all looked at him in surprise and Jimmy was a little embarrassed.

'Sure there's no harm done, Jimmy,' said my father.

'That's what you think,' said Jimmy, 'except I almost broke a couple of me toes when I tripped against one of the legs of the bed. How did it happen? Well it happened when I turned off the light and I found meself fousterin' around in the dark tryin' to find where the bed was, and I'd no flashlamp, so I had to turn the light back on and watch the bed as I turned it off.'

'Ah,' said my mother, 'you'll get used to it after a few weeks.'

Jimmy wasn't finished. 'Look at me face,' he said. 'You see the pieces of paper stuck to me chin and jaw?' We hadn't paid much attention before to the little blood-soaked paper patches on Jimmy's face. 'You know what's the cause of this?' he asked.

'You might as well tell us,' said my father.

'I blame the ESB,' said Jimmy, 'because ever since they put in the electricity I can't shave without cuttin' me face!' Even though Jimmy was very serious about his predicament, my father and mother were on the verge of laughing. 'Every time I try to shave I'm standin' in me own light and when I took the mirror off the wall and held it with one hand under the light I cut myself tryin' to do two things at the one time. I tried shavin' lyin' on the floor and I cut myself again, not to mention the mirror bein' in the way of the light. And another thing – we had an outside light put on the gable end of the house thinkin' it would be handy at night for anyone that might bring a cow to the bull.' (Jimmy's bull was often hired to service local farmers' cows when they were 'round'.)

'Anyhow,' Jimmy continued, 'when the light is on it shines right in over the door where the bull is in the shed.' Jimmy looked very grave and said he thought the light was making his bull over-anxious because a man came to the yard with his cow a couple of nights ago and the bull began pounding his head against the door of the shed. 'When I came outside to see what was wrong,' Jimmy said, 'I saw the cow and assumed that the bull could smell her scent – nothin' too unusual about it. But when I opened the door for the bull he ran out of the stable and across the yard and threw himself at the cow. It was just by sheer luck that he didn't knock her down. The owner of the cow wanted to know what was wrong with him. I said he never did it that way before and that I thought the cow would surely be in calf and that she looked no worse from the experience. Blast it, I was glad when the cow and the man were out the gate and on their way.'

'What about the bull?' my father asked.

'All I know,' said Jimmy, 'is I put him back in the shed and noticed that as I brought him towards the door he looked back a couple of times in the direction of the road where the cow had gone and made a forlorn roar a couple of times. You know, Christy, it worries me a bit because I never seen him runnin' at a cow like that before. All I can say is he was all right before we had the bloody light on.'

'Well,' said my mother, 'you know what you should do?'

'What?' said Jimmy.

'You should put a shade on the light so the bull doesn't catch its glare.'

'Be the Jeepers, Molly,' said Jimmy, 'a great plan and by God it might do the trick. It very well might.'

Another knock came to the door and my father was still laughing as he shouted, 'Come in,' and into the kitchen stepped Mick Crowley.

'God bless all here,' Mick said. 'I hope I'm not interruptin' anythin'.'

'Not at all,' said my father, 'we were just talkin' about Jimmy's bull.'

Mick sat down. 'I just buried a bull in the bog the other day; it was Big Mick's bull.'

'What happened to him?' Jimmy asked.

'I'll tell you what happened,' Mick started, 'the bastard tried to gore me. Only for Big Mick's little terrier I'd be dead.'

My father was curious. 'I thought the bull was tied to a stump of a tree.'

'The fucker broke loose,' said Mick, 'and when I was walkin' back to Big Mick's house the sneaky devil spotted me and came runnin' with his head close to the ground. He took me by surprise.'

'Good God, what did you do?' said my mother.

'I ran as hard as I could,' said Mick.

I made the mistake of laughing a little but my mother looked and me and said, 'Paddy, stop it! It's no laughin' matter.'

Mick, though, had a sense of humour. 'It's all right, missus,' he said, 'it's all right. The little dog delayed the bastard and I just had enough time to climb over a stone wall.

'Be Janey,' said Jimmy, 'you're a lucky man, Mick, somebody was prayin' for yeh.'

'So I suppose Big Mick had to put him down?' said my father.

'He wasted no time,' said Mick, 'he shot him dead that same evenin'.'

'That was hard luck on Big Mick,' said my mother.

'There was nothin' else he could do,' my father added, 'a wicked bull is a terrible thing to have around, especially where there's children.'

'And me, too,' said Mick, who was in a good mood from telling his story. But he wasn't finished. 'Big Mick gave me the job of buryin' the bull,' he said, 'and I dragged him with the tractor into the far end of the bog and dug a deep hole just beside him so as I'd have nothin' to do but push him in with the back of the tractor. I was down about 6 feet and ready to climb up when the bank collapsed from the weight of the bull. I heard a kind of creakin' sound just in time to look up and I could see the bull beginnin' to slide in, on top of me! I jumped out of the way and got out of the hole just in time. I was a lucky man but thanks be to heaven my reflexes are tip-top, otherwise who knows? Anyway, the point I'm tryin' to make is the bastard of a bull tried to murder me when he was alive and when he was dead he tried to murder me again!'

When we saw that Mick was laughing, suddenly everyone in the kitchen burst into laughter and I saw tears in my mother's eyes as she lifted her apron. Jimmy was also laughing a little, making sounds similar to a duck quacking, and he abruptly finished by slapping the side of his leg. 'I'm afraid I have to leave ye all to it,' he said, standing up. 'It's near milkin' time.'

My father also stood up. 'Jimmy,' he said, 'I'll see you to the gate.' This was a small business meeting disguised as a gesture of hospitality.

My mother put the kettle back on the fire. 'Nothin' like a drop of tea to lift one's heart, Mick,' she said. 'You could have been killed with such a dangerous animal like that on the loose.' When my mother heard a story about anything to do with life and death she would often say, 'We're livin' in strange times,' and when she said it this time Mick looked at her and said, 'I heard on the radio about the Americans goin' to put a man on the moon, maybe next year.'

'Oh, come on,' said my mother, 'you must be coddin'!'

'No, no,' said Mick, 'they're very serious about it.'

'God almighty,' said my mother, 'what are they doin' that for?'

'I think,' said Mick, 'they're tryin' to beat the Russians to it.'

My father returned to the kitchen and sat near the table. 'Did you hear that, Christy?' my mother asked him. 'They're goin' to send a man up to the moon!'

My father was lighting a cigarette and blew a mouthful of smoke into the air. 'Nothin' surprises me,' he said. 'From now on quare things are goin' to happen.'

'You never said wiser words, Christy,' said Mick. 'I heard about a strange thing that happened somewhere down in Wexford.'

'What was that, Mick?' said my mother. 'Well, as you all know, the ESB is installin' electricity around the country. Anyway, they were workin' somewhere in County Wexford and were diggin' holes in the ground for puttin' down a line of poles and it so happened that the spot where one of the poles was to be sunk was where a lone bush was growin'. Some people call them fairy bushes.'

'We have one below, near the bog,' said my father.

'Well,' said Mick, 'to make a long story short, the ESB men dug the hole and firmly sunk a pole in the usual upright position, makin' sure it was in line with the other poles. Apparently everyone was satisfied with their day's work and when they quit in the evenin' nobody noticed anythin' unusual – not until the followin' mornin', that is. So when they walked into the field to begin their work they saw that the pole was layin' at an angle of 60 degrees! Apparently some of the workers were local men who had warned the foreman about it bein' dangerous or unlucky to desecrate a fairy bush and that the little people would seek revenge.'

'That's somethin' I'd have nothin' to do with,' said my father.

'Yer right,' said Mick. 'This is the God's honest truth and can't be denied. The foreman said 'twas the wind that did it and he didn't pay much attention to any of it. So they went ahead and sunk the pole a little deeper in the same spot. All was well – until the next mornin', that is, and this time the pole was lyin at an angle of 45 degrees. Funny thing, there were no reports of wind the night before, so the question remained, what in God's name was happenin'? Anyhow, the stubborn foreman was still not convinced and ordered the men to sink the pole again and jam several big stones around its bottom. As far as everyone was concerned it was another job well done and the pole stayed upright and solid throughout the day. In the evenin' they retired again and as they left the field they looked back and saw that the pole was in the same upright position.' I could see that Mick was delighted with having such a strange story. He waited for my mother to pour the tea, and when he had a couple of mouthfuls of it he said, 'So the next day when the work crew walked into the field they were astonished to see that the pole was lyin' at the opposite angle from the day before! How in the world could this be? The foreman had to change his plans and reroute all the poles and it cost the ESB a week's worth of work.'

'By God, Mick,' said my father, 'if what you say is true—'

'True?' Mick interrupted. 'By Janey, didn't I read it in the *Irish Press* last week, and 'twas also mentioned on the wireless.'

My mother had been quiet for a while. 'My God,' she said, 'it makes a person wonder about what to believe in. I've heard people say that there's no such thing as the fairies, but what does a story like that tell yeh?'

'It tells me,' said my father, 'that I wouldn't mind a pint or two.'

'You don't need an excuse for a pint,' said my mother, 'does he, Mick?'

'I must admit,' said Mick, 'I wouldn't mind one meself.'

36

Joe Boland

On the afternoon of the Saturday Joe Boland arrived at our gate and left his bike lying against one of the pillars. When he walked into our kitchen he looked very tall and I would guess he was probably in his late forties. 'Well, the hard man, Joe,' said my father, 'yer a man of yer word.'

'No bother at all, Christy,' replied Joe. I was a little disappointed when I saw that Joe had no accordion with him. In my own mind I assumed that a well-known musician would always have his instrument with him wherever he went. Joe took off his cap and laid it on the back table and sat down near the door. My mother said she would make tea but Joe declined. He didn't drink tea during the day, he said, as it would keep him awake at night. My father and he began talking about old times and chatted a bit about what Joe was doing in Kildare. Then Joe looked at me and said, 'So this is the musician.' I nodded my head in agreement. 'Why don't you play a bit of a tune or two?'

'You hardly have to ask him at all,' said my mother. 'He's been practisin' all week.' I was a bit embarrassed when she said this and was glad I had my back to everyone when I heard it. My accordion was, as usual, hidden under an old coat in the corner near the fire. I pulled it out and found a chair.

I sat waiting as my father talked, but Joe saw me and said, 'Go ahead, atta boy!' I was nervous and couldn't think of what to play.

'Play "The Lark in the Morning",' my father said. 'It's one Joe used to play when we were out with the wren.' By this time I was a bit fed up with the tune and didn't feel like playing it. So I suppose I hummed and hawed, hoping I'd think of something else. In the end Joe coaxed me into playing the jig, so I fingered the tune as best I could but unfortunately I didn't get through it without missing a few buttons. When I'd finished, Joe clapped his hands. It was my very first applause from an outsider but it didn't make me feel better because I felt I hadn't played very well. Then my father asked Joe to play a tune.

'Oh God, no,' said Joe, 'I haven't played in years.'

'Ah, come on,' urged my father, but Joe was adamant, saying he was completely out of practice. I was shocked into disbelief and terribly disappointed and wanted to run outside and hide. I was twelve years old and desperately needed help with my fingering on the keyboard, or perhaps some other tips or advice. Joe didn't help me in any way and I sensed afterwards that it may not have occurred to him that I really needed a few tips or something that would whet my appetite for playing. Instead he asked me to play another tune, and I wearily played a waltz that I had recently learned from the Galloway Céilí Band. Joe never heard it before and asked where I got it. When I told him he said, 'It's a catchy little tune.' By this time my father was anxious for more conversation and so they began talking again about Joe living the life of a bachelor and working for a big farmer somewhere in Kildare. I wasn't interested and nobody seemed to care or understand that music was my conversation, and one that would take me many years to develop.

37

Mr Coffey and Mr O'Connell

In school Mr Coffey continued to impress many of us with his sense of fair play, although he often over-burdened us with homework. His constant use of the word 'latchico' was still a wonder to us all. We had asked our parents and various people what the word meant but nobody had any idea. However, most parents seemed to think that if Mr Coffey called us a latchico it meant that one of us or even all of us were rascals of some sort. Soon we were all calling each other latchicos when playing at lunch break and some of the schoolyard bullies had taken the word to mean something to bolster own importance when imposing their 'law' on the weaker boys.

'Come up here, you little latchico.' Mr Coffey was looking at Seamus Carr! 'Come up here,' he said again. Seamus walked slowly up to Mr Coffey's desk. 'Bring your English book with you, go back and get it.' Seamus retrieved the book and walked up again to where Mr Coffey was sitting behind his desk. 'Give it to me,' he said, and Seamus handed him his book. Mr Coffey was looking over his glasses at Seamus and then he lifted the book and held it out in front of him. 'When I saw what you were doing with your book I had to look twice because I could not imagine anyone doing what I thought you were doing. But now that I see the book in my hand I can say without any doubt that YOU'VE BEEN EATING IT! Have you not? Have you not, you little latchico?'

'Yes, sir,' said Seamus. Mr Coffey continued to stare at Carr over the rims of his glasses. 'Don't you know that cows and goats are the only creatures that eat books? Young fellow, I ask you, are you a cow or a goat? Are you?'

'No, sir,' said Carr.

'Then why are you eating your school book?'

'I don't know, sir, said Seamus.

'You don't know? You don't know? Go back to your desk and sit down, you little latchico.' Then he pointed his finger towards me. 'Come up here and bring your composition with you.' The composition was my homework, a short story from my imagination that I had written the night before. 'Now,' said Mr Coffey, 'let me see your writing,' and as soon as I gave him the two pages of my story he began reading it. 'Aha,' he said, 'very good!' He read some more and was about to hand it back to me when he said, 'The handwriting looks different from here onwards.' He pointed his finger at the page. I was afraid he would spot it and he did. 'Why is that?' he asked me. Even though I was trembling inside, I held my ground. 'It was getting late, sir, and my mother was trying to get us all to bed, and I had to speed up my writing.'

'Oh,' he said, 'oh,' and handed me back my two pages. I had escaped and nothing more was said. As a matter of fact I was stuck the night before with the story and asked my mother for help. When she read what I'd written about robbing an orchard, she said, 'Let me finish it. It's quicker this way,' and so she wrote the rest of the story. So it was my mother's handwriting that Mr Coffey saw. To this day I'm sorry it wasn't the tyrant Paddy Murphy that I pulled my bluff on instead of Mr Coffey, of whom I have great memories and great appreciation for his teaching methods. I remember him telling us in class that we were just as good as the pupils in the west of Ireland and that we could be even better if we worked a little harder and got rid of some of our lazy habits. He seemed to think that being lazy and neglectful was a trait in schoolchildren that was particular to the midlands. Maybe he was right when he called us all a crowd of little 'latchicos'.

Mr Coffey's term in Daingean boys' school lasted a little over two years. I was sorry when he told us that he was moving to a new teaching position near his home in County Roscommon. Our new headmaster was a twenty-eight-year-old man who was already known to us as Mr O'Connell. He had arrived as replacement for Murphy, who had applied for a teaching post near his home area and had somehow got the job. We were all delighted to see the last of him. In contrast, Mr O'Connell was a mild-mannered sort of fellow who represented a new breed of school teacher. He taught us Irish history in both English and Irish. He also concentrated on geography in both languages, which included some major western countries, their rivers and mountains and many big cities in the USA, England and

Scotland. He was an old-style Irish nationalist and great admirer of Pádraig Pearse, who signed the 1916 Proclamation and was one of the leaders of the Easter week rebellion that was initiated at the GPO in Dublin on Easter Monday of that year. It was during one of our singing lessons that he asked us, any one of us, to sing a song of our choice. No one volunteered, and Mr O'Connell was about to move on to something else when I stood up and said, 'Yes, sir.' And off I went with 'Down Erin's Lovely Lee'. I had learned it from an All-Ireland senior football brochure that my mother's cousin bought in Croke Park in 1957 when Louth senior footballers beat Cork by two points. I had won a bet of half a crown with her cousin Jack Dunne and when he gave me the coin he also gave me the little booklet. The song in its middle pages was the first thing I noticed and I was attracted to its words. I didn't know it was a Fenian song and when I finished singing it the class was silent.

Mr O'Connell was astonished. 'Good lad, Pat, good lad.' He then put his hand in his trouser pocket and pulled out some change. He took a sixpence from a bunch of pennies and gave it to me as a reward. I was mystified and felt a small bit embarrassed because a teacher had never given me money before. Mr O'Connell was proud of me and began telling the class about the meaning of the song, and that it was written by a Fenian sympathiser. He continued to talk about the bravery of O'Donovan Rossa and Captain Mackey and our singing class became a history lesson. From that day onward I always felt that I was a favourite of the young headmaster. He seemed very interested in my sketching and painting with water colours. However, I don't believe he ever knew about the other more committed side of me, which was the music, and I never knew if he had any liking for Irish traditional music.

38

The Circus

On another occasion our mother was in Daingean doing some shopping for groceries when she met Father Cronin on the street. He was one of the priests who was attached to the local reformatory, which was a school for juvenile delinquents. He was in jolly humour and stopped on the towpath to talk to her.

'Missus,' he said, 'did you hear about the circus? It's coming to town and it's supposed to be a big one.' My mother hadn't heard about it and asked when it was coming. 'In two weeks,' said the priest. 'I believe it's going to be put up on the green beside Larry Weir's pub. They're bringing with them lions and tigers and elephants.'

'My God,' said my mother.

'My God, indeed,' said Father Cronin. 'It should be a sensational exhibition, and it might be good for the town.'

'How did you hear about it?' my mother asked.

'We were sent a letter, to the senior brother at the school, asking permission for the circus to be set up across the street from the reformatory. So we all decided it would be good for everyone to see the animals, sort of educational.'

When my mother came home she couldn't wait to tell us. My sisters were excited and asked about the elephants and lions and would they be dangerous. I had never heard of a circus before and so in school I asked Seamus Carr about what to expect. Seamus seemed to know more about it than any of us. He said it was a sort of travelling zoo and that he heard about a huge snake that could squeeze a man to death, and a woman that walked on a wire that was way up in the air! I didn't know whether to believe Seamus or not, so I asked 'Gandhi' Cuskelly and Willy Smith if they knew anything about it. Both of them knew about the high-wire woman but argued about the size of the elephant. Another sensitive issue was which end of the elephant was which. Was it the end with the long thick tail or the end with the short little tail that the elephant used for eating? None of us had ever seen an elephant eating and so we didn't know which was what. Our parents laughed at us and said we'd have to wait until the circus came before we'd learn the answer.

A week before its arrival I noticed some posters in shop windows and on the walls of Daingean bridge. Written in bright red lettering was 'DUFFY'S CIRCUS – THREE NIGHTS ONLY WITH TWO MATINÉES'. In school Willy Smith, Seamus Carr, Gandhi and I continued our little debates about what to expect from the circus – it was now a few days before its arrival. My three friends were armed with more information and were competing with each other as to who knew more about the animals. At lunch break Gandhi began talking about some sort of a striped horse that his sister told him about. 'There's no such thing as a striped horse,' Willy Smith said.

'There is!' Gandhi replied, and tried to say its name, but he stuttered a little when he started the word. 'Zee, zee, zee, zee,' came sizzling through his tightly closed front row of small teeth. 'Zeb, zeb, zeb.'

Seamus Carr helped him. 'I know what it is,' he yelled.

'What?' said Willy.

Carr was feeling confident. 'It's a fuckin' zebra,' he shouted.

Jimmy Quinn had now joined us. 'What is that?' he asked.

'A striped horse,' said Carr. 'I saw one in a cannibal picture.'

'Ha, ha, ha,' Quinn laughed.

I had never heard of a zebra so I said nothing. Willy Smith silenced the others when he said he'd ask the teacher what a zebra was. 'I dare you,' said Jimmy. Willy was certain he would and told Quinn he'd ask Mr O'Connell 'right after lunch'. Gandhi had remained silent throughout the discussion but was red in the face with excitement.

As soon as we were back in the classroom Willy stood up and waved his hand. Mr O'Connell was correcting essays when he noticed Willy. 'Okay, okay,' he said in his County Clare accent, 'what is it, Willy?'

'Sir,' said Willy, 'what is a zabra?'

Mr O'Connell couldn't believe what he heard. 'A what?' he said. A small look of panic came across Willy's face. Mr O'Connell recovered and said, 'Willy, are you sure you have the right name of whatever it is?'

'It's a zabra sir, a striped horse,' Willy began again.

Mr O'Connell started to smile. 'Aha!' he said. 'You may now sit down, Willy. I think I know what you're asking.' Then he said, 'It's a zebra, isn't it?'

'Yes, sir,' said Willy.

'And you want to know what it is, right?' said Mr O'Connell.

'Yes, sir,' an impatient Seamus Carr chimed in.

'Oh,' said Mr O'Connell, 'so you want to know about the zebra. Maybe you all want to know about the animal with the stripes.'

'Yes, sir,' the whole class shouted as one. 'So,' said Mr O'Connell, 'the said zebra is from here,' as he pointed his ruler at a map of Africa that hung on the wall. 'It's not exactly a horse, although it is almost like one. And of course its whole body is covered with stripes.'

Someone behind me had another question. It was Paddy Mooney and he wanted to know why the zebra was striped. Mr O'Connell said it was to confuse the lions and tigers who hunted the zebra herd, and when all the zebras ran together the lions and tigers couldn't pick one out when hunting for food because they all looked as one. He said that the sight of all the zebras together gave the lions headaches and the tigers became dizzy, sometimes losing their balance and falling to the ground. We all laughed at how Mr O'Connell described these unusual animals and after school we had a quick get-together to talk about what he'd said.

Gandhi, however, wasn't satisfied. 'How could a zee, zea, zebra not be a horse and be almost like one at the same time?' he asked. This was a fair question. We all looked at each other hoping for an answer.

When the circus came we were thrilled to see its long cavalcade drive into the town. Curious spectators and pupils from our school gathered to see how the 'Big Top' was assembled on the green. The parade had passed by our house on its way to Daingean with a dozen or so caravans rolling along the road carrying animals and a wide range of equipment. My mother asked my father if he'd like to see it but he wasn't interested. So, on Saturday afternoon my mother, my sister Moira and I walked the mile into Daingean to see the matinée performance scheduled for three o'clock. When we arrived we were twenty minutes early but inside the big tent a sizeable crowd was already seated. We were lucky to find three seats near the front, because lots of people preferred seats among the rows that weren't too near the ring. The prospect of lions or other animals in the tent dampened the courage of parents with small children. But my mother wasn't unduly concerned and was looking forward to it all. Moira and I didn't know what to expect and sat beside her in a quiet mood of expectation. Our mother gave us each a sweet and while we waited, a brass band began playing music. As it continued, a green curtain was pulled back to reveal a small bandstand with musicians wearing blue uniforms. They were playing bugles, trumpets and saxophones and I noticed a small drummer who was hopping on his seat in rhythm with the music. Each musician had a small beard growing on the top of his chin and long, dark sideburns. When they increased the tempo of the music the lights went out, except for where a man with a tall hat came to the centre of a ring that was laid out in front of us. He was wearing a long red coat and had a whip in his right hand. A clown came running from behind, pushed the man in the red coat to the ground and then disappeared.

The music returned to a very slow pace and two huge elephants came into view, with a young lady leading them to the centre of the ring. My impression of the elephants was one of amazement, although I thought them extremely lazy because they moved so slowly. The girl had them climb onto small round wooden platforms that gave them little room to manoeuvre. Then with the music reaching a crescendo each elephant stood on one leg and all of us clapped loudly in appreciation of the acrobatic efforts of the massive beasts. Next two clowns ran into the ring carrying a long, narrow board and placed it halfway over a round barrel. A girl sat on one end and one of the elephants put his foot down on the other end. The girl was propelled upward, caught a trapeze that was hanging overhead and began swinging back and forth, higher and higher, until she landed on a very high platform above all our heads. She stood for a moment, then reached for a long pole and slowly walked forward onto a wire that was held tightly, stretching across to another platform. When she was halfway to the second platform the crowd in the tent fell totally silent and my mother, holding my hand, began to squeeze it. The girl finally made it to the other side and we could hear a loud sigh of relief from the crowd as everyone began to breathe again.

This daring girl was joined by two other girls who swung back and forth on trapezes before each one let go and caught another trapeze before swinging their way to an opposite platform. It was very tense stuff, with oohs and aahs from the spectators. It ended with a loud sigh of relief from the audience when the girls finished their performance.

Then came the zebras, two of them, and also four horses, all trotting in a circle around the ring with two clowns jumping from one animal to another as the brass band played German polka music. Then came the big snake. It must have been twenty feet long. It had a very thick mid-section, and a bearded man, stripped to his waist, played and toyed with it. (It was years afterwards that I figured out that it must have been a boa constrictor from the Amazon, in South America.) At one point the snake wrapped itself around the man. It was a dangerous stunt that they must have practised many times before. Thankfully there were no mishaps and the man gave the big snake a handful of something to eat when they finished their performance.

Next two cages were pushed into the ring, one cage with two yellow-and-black-striped tigers and the other with two brown lions with heavy black manes. All four animals roared in unison and appeared very wary. A lion-tamer ran into the centre of the ring and bowed. Then he opened the door of one cage and lured the tigers out. Cracking his whip, he directed them to sit on two prepared plat-forms, while a young girl placed a large hoop onto iron holders that were stuck in the ground. The hoop was a target for the tigers to jump through. But before that a clown came running into the ring with a lighted torch. He held the torch to the edge of the hoop and a flame lit it, creating a ring of fire. The tamer's whip cracked and cracked again as we all watched in awe. The first tiger leaped towards the burning circle. It was a clean jump that carried him right through the flaming ring. The man with the whip cracked it again and the second tiger leaped towards the flaming hoop. His leap was as masterful and accurate as the first. A huge applause came from everyone and I could hear my mother say 'Good God almighty' as we watched the tigers being escorted back to their cages.

The lions were next, and when they were released from their cages the animals became emboldened and it was a struggle to get them onto their platforms. The lion-tamer abandoned his whip and began to use a chair as the lions roared in protest and all the while the hoop remained aflame. Then the animals began backing away and the lion-tamer succeeded in pushing one lion onto a platform and the second followed, but just as it did the first lion leapt to a nearby chair. Meanwhile the audience became concerned and the tent was becoming very quiet. Then all of a sudden the first lion sat down on the grass while the second lion took a short run, dived through the air and landed on the ground!

Within the blink of an eye he had cleared the inside of the flaming hoop and I could hear a sigh of relief from the audience followed by more exciting applause. Things were then happening very fast and it was hard going for the lion-tamer but he had succeeded and everyone thought he was very brave. After he had caged the animals he advanced to the front of the ring and bowed several times, left, right and centre. Then he withdrew behind a curtain only to return again, and this time he wore a long black cape that he swept around the front of his body as a gesture of conclusion.

On the way home we talked about what we'd seen. My mother was awfully impressed by 'the man with the lions'. 'He knows no fear,' she said. 'Nerves of steel, that's what he has.'

Moira was more impressed with the snake. 'It gave me the shivers,' she said.

My mother asked me what I thought of the circus. 'It was great,' I replied, adding that walking the high wire made me tense and nervous and that I thought there should be a net or something underneath to catch anyone who might fall.

The following Monday in school was a tough day for me. Mr O'Connell had called in sick and I made the mistake of sketching an elephant and a zebra on my copy book. I showed it to Gandhi and he passed it along to Willy Smith and soon everyone wanted one. Then several boys gathered around me to watch as I sketched more elephants and zebras. After an hour of it I began to tire. When I said I'd do no more and that I was tired a couple of bully boys took offence and threatened me. Willy Pilkington came to my aid with strong words of reason, and because he wasn't a lad to tangle with, the bullies faded into the background. The effect of my drawing wasn't lost on Mr O'Connell, who somehow heard of the quiet behaviour of our class when he came back to school the next day. Apparently he was impressed with me when he saw a sketch of an elephant that I had done for someone.

39

Black Bob

I was getting a little taller and with that came a small promotion from my father, who saw me more and more as someone who knew how to work with a horse, and in this case it was Black Bob.

My father had sold our young two-year-old pony and bought an older quarter horse. We had had the horse almost three years when I was given the job of yoking him to a cart so that I could work at hauling home the turf and packing it into a shed. My father woke me one Friday morning with a half cup of tea and said, 'Paudgeen, drink this – it'll wake you up.' He had given me half cups of tea in bed before and I often wondered for years why a half cup. The stinginess annoyed me and I wanted to ask him why, but instead I reached for the cup and began sipping it. Then he said, 'Paudgeen, do you think you can begin to bring home the turf from the bog? You can catch Black Bob and yoke him to the cart. Do you think you can do it?'

'Yeah, I can give it a try,' I said.

'You can take it nice and easy, no need to kill yourself and don't work the horse too hard.' Then he left the room and prepared for his day's work at Jimmy Mac's farm. In a matter of moments I jumped out of bed and put my clothes on. When I came into the kitchen I looked out over the half door in time to see my father walking his bike towards the gate. He had his two-grain fork lying at an angle on the left side of the bike with its handle resting on the handlebars, and the fork went all the way down beside the centre of the back wheel to where one of its prongs was hooked between the chain case and the frame of the bike. It was a sight that was common during those days when people helped each other in hay fields or at thrashing corn. After he was gone I made myself more tea and cooked a couple of eggs in a cup that I balanced on hot coals. After I'd eaten and washed my face I went outside to the shed to find the winkers. It was time to catch Black Bob!

He was grazing in what we called the L field and I'd no problem when I walked to where he stood and put the winkers on his head. I yoked him to the cart and then we were on our way to the bog. I loaded the turf bare-handed and started to cart it home. Black Bob was an easy-going horse and it was no bother driving him back to the yard, where I undid his belly band and lifted the shafts of the cart upwards. The load of turf keeled over backwards and tumbled down onto the yard beside the door of the turf shed. After five loads I threw the turf from the yard into the shed. It was around seven in the evening when I finished, not before I brought Black Bob back to the L field and turned him loose. I looked after him as he ran off and saw him tumble and roll on the grass. He made some snorting sounds like he was blowing his nose. Maybe it was his deep appreciation of his freedom that made him so giddy. Just when I thought he was finished he broke the silence with a litany of farts that seemed to echo their way around the field. I laughed quietly to myself and walked the short distance back to the house. I spent the rest of the evening with the accordion revising tune ideas that had been nagging me during the day while I was working with the turf. It was as though I found expression for the music through the loading and unloading of the cart, combined with the sweet smell of the furze and heather. All of it lifted my spirits as Black Bob and I cantered back and forth. The outdoors and the work involved stimulated my quest for new music even though I had little to go on except what I heard on the radio. The jigs and reels from Ciarán MacMathúna's *A Job of Journeywork* programme were slowly coming alive in my consciousness amid images of heathery bogs, yellow-blossomed furzes and the ever-green sight of Killoneen Hill in the distance.

Little Johnny Rourke lived with his family on Killoneen Hill, which was just over half a mile from our house. His father was one of our greatest neighbours and a friend of our family. Phil Rourke had often ploughed our front field with his strong iron plough and two sturdy horses. There were eight children in the Rourke household and their mother was a good friend of my mother's. Mrs Rourke, or Bridgie, was the most stout-hearted woman that anyone ever knew, and never came to our house without something for us children. Apples, oranges, chocolate, a bottle of lemonade – and she once gave me a pen and coloured pencils because I did a painting of Blessed Marie Goretti, who was beatified by Pope Pius XII. When she saw the painting she became convinced that I had supernatural gifts and told my mother how she knelt and prayed in front of a painting I did of a saint. She said she prayed with a request to the saint after propping it up on the table at home. Afterwards she told my mother that her request was granted! I was listening to both of them talk about it and Mrs Rourke glanced at me approvingly many times. Her sense of appreciation drew me closer to her and her family and when my father asked me to go up to Rourkes' and help Phil with dropping potatoes I was ready and willing and ran up the road after school to Phil's bottom field where he was putting down his potatoes. Young Johnny was standing nearby watching us. He was just six years old and very tanned from the early summer weather. As we grew up we became firm friends and his appreciation of my accordion music consolidated my respect for him. On the evening after dropping the potatoes Johnny's mother took a photo of the two of us in their back yard. Mrs Rourke began comparing our two very different heights and became a little impatient. 'Johneen, Johneen,' she said to her eldest son, 'will you look at how tall Paddy Brien is, look at how tall Paddy is!' She went on, 'Johneen, Johneen. Wake up! Grow up! Grow up!' Of course she didn't expect an instant result but I do have a hunch that my painting of the saint was propped up again later that evening.

40

Joe Delaney

It was a late evening in September 1959, just after my thirteenth birthday. I was weeding mangels in our back garden when I heard something outside on the road. I stood up to listen and could hear the door of a car slam shut. I ran around to the front of the house in time to see Bob Lynch walking into our front yard.

'I see you've been drawin' home the turf,' he said. 'Oh, and by the way, I've somethin' I want to tell yeh.'

We went inside and sat down. My mother was busy combing Moira's hair after shampooing and drying it with a towel. 'Bob,' she said, 'tryin' to rear four girls would test the patience of Jove.'

Bob lit a cigarette and said, 'Missus, it'll be worth it when you get old. You'll have someone to hand you a drink of water.'

'That's a poor consolation, Bob,' she replied.

Bob blew a burst of smoke from his mouth and nose. 'I can't stay very long. I thought I'd drop in since I was passin' the house and tell Paddy about a fiddle player that's married to my sister.' I was listening very intently as Bob continued, 'I should have mentioned it long before now but in any case I'd like Paddy to meet him and hear him play a few tunes.'

'Who is he?' asked my mother.

'His name is Joe Delaney. He owns a garage in Edenderry and he's a true blue traditional player on the fiddle.' Bob was enthusiastic and went on to say that he had some business in Edenderry early the following week and that he'd stop on the way and pick me up. 'You can meet him for yourself, Paddy,' he said. 'We'll stop at Delaneys' house, it's near the square in the town and I'll introduce you to Joe and his wife. I can go and do my bit of business and leave the two of you at the music.'

I was delighted. It was something I really wanted. In fact I'd always be grateful to Bob for his kindness and great consideration to me as a young beginner musician. We settled on the following Tuesday night for Bob to call and take me to Edenderry.

Bob arrived as promised shortly after eight o'clock. I was ready with my overcoat on and had my accordion in its black wooden case. I heard him pull up at the gate and rushed out the door so he wouldn't have to get out of his van. I opened the passenger door and put my accordion behind the front seat and sat in. It was a twenty-five-minute drive and Bob smoked and chatted all the way. When we got to Edenderry he steered the van slowly all the way down its lengthy main street until we came to the Delaney home and parked directly outside. Bob lifted the heavy knocker and tapped gently three times. It was dark outside on the street except for a few lights here and there. We saw no light coming from inside the house and were beginning to think that Joe and his wife were gone to bed. But then a light came on and in a few seconds the door opened. It was Bob's sister. 'We were expectin' you,' she said, 'come on in.'

I was very relieved and followed Bob into the house. 'Keep goin' straight ahead,' Mrs Delaney said, 'he's waitin' for you. Turn left at the door.'

Bob stopped and said to his sister, 'I have to leave for an hour on business, but I'll be back around half nine.'

When he was gone Mrs Delaney introduced me to her husband. Joe had risen from his seat behind a table and was making his way towards me. He was leaning his right hand on the edge of the table as a sort of support. 'I'm Joe Delaney,' he said, 'or what's left of me.' I didn't know that he was referring to the loss of his left leg. It had to be removed many years earlier when it was mangled in a machine accident. When I met him he was using some kind of wooden leg. He was a big man, or he may have looked bigger to me because I wasn't fully grown. He was also very matter-of-fact and very friendly. He was probably in his early sixties, with white hair combed from left to right. His strong facial features gave him the look of a man who was very comfortable with himself. Somehow he reminded me, in later years, of the movie star Lon Chaney. I saw that he had his fiddle lying flat on the table and its bow placed in line atop its four strings. A book of music lay open on the table in front of him. It was one of Francis O'Neill's collections of Irish dance melodies.

'Bob was tellin' me you play the single-row accordion,' Joe said.

'Yeah, I try to,' I replied.

'Take it out of the box and try a tune,' he said, 'or maybe we can play somethin' together.'

When I had the accordion on my knee I began with a hornpipe that I had finished learning. It was 'The Echo Hornpipe'.

'That's a nice one,' Joe said when I had finished. 'What did you say its name was?' When I told him he said that maybe it was in the book. Reaching for his reading glasses he thumbed through the pages of O'Neill's until he found the hornpipe section. Looking down through his glasses he moved the pages carefully back and forth, licking his thumb to catch an elusive page. 'By the holy,' he said, 'look at it, it's here.'

He took the fiddle and bow from the table, checked the tuning and stroked the strings up and down. Then he was playing the hornpipe and I saw a slight touch of a smile on the side of his mouth. He was enjoying the tune. His playing of the hornpipe was a little different from the way I had it. Then he put the fiddle back on the table and asked me to play another tune, so I had a go at a double jig called 'Saddle the Pony'. I was a little nervous, but the tune wasn't too difficult and the second time around Joe joined in and we played it over about four times. 'Well,' said Joe, 'we don't have any difference of opinion on that one.' He was referring to us both having the same setting of the tune. We played a few more and Joe talked for a while and remarked about various players that he heard on the wireless. He was especially interested in Seán Ryan's fiddle music and was very impressed with Seán's ability at composing jigs, reels and hornpipes. He told me he thought Seán was one of the best traditional fiddlers in Ireland. I wasn't sure what he meant by 'traditional' and it would take me a number of years to find out. Then the door opened and Mrs Delaney came into the room carrying a tray of tea, currant cakes, sugar and milk.

'Ah,' Joe said, 'my beloved, you are a gift to the music of Ireland.' Mrs Delaney blushed a little and left the tray on the table. She was a pleasant sort of woman with black hair and may have been in her late forties. She withdrew without saying anything and gently closed the door. 'Women love a little bit of a compliment,' Joe said. 'It goes a long way in a marriage. Now, you do the pourin'.' We drank the tea and ate the delicious cakes. Joe spoke again about music and some other players. Suddenly he said, 'Did you ever hear of the harper Turlough O'Carolan?'

'Who?' I said.

'Turlough O'Carolan. He was born not too far from here, just inside the Westmeath border.' I had never heard of O'Carolan and Joe continued, 'His music is in O'Neill's book, and wait 'til I see. Yes, yes, here it is. He was born in 1670 and died in 1738.' I was amazed at hearing this piece of news. 'Wait 'til I play you a few of his tunes.' He began with 'Planxty Irwin' and followed it with 'Planxty Drury'. He also played 'O'Carolan's Concerto'. When he finished he said that O'Carolan composed the concerto as a wager and won the bet because he was able to compose the tune in the same style as an Italian harper who was touring Ireland at the time. Joe told me that O'Carolan composed in the old Gaelic style of melody and also in a baroque style that was all the rage in Ireland during those days. I was fascinated by all of this, and the experience with Joe consolidated my instincts regarding the strong feeling I had when hearing some of the tunes he played. After a short while he put his glasses back on and began playing more jigs and reels from the book. One jig that stood out was 'The Old Grey Goose' and Joe told me it had been recorded in the USA by the Sligo fiddler Michael Coleman. I hadn't heard of him either, but Joe set me right and then switched to talking about the piper Barney Delaney, who recorded on some cylinders for Captain O'Neill and Sergeant Early.

'Was he a good player?' I asked.

'He was,' said Joe, 'and very stubborn. O'Neill wrote about how difficult it was when he tried to get him to play.' Joe began to laugh. 'You know,' he said, 'Barney Delaney was a cousin of mine.' I hadn't heard anything about Sergeant Early or Barney and I must have looked very engaged because Joe kept talking. 'Yeah,' he went on, 'a second cousin; and you know he was born and reared between Geashill and Tullamore. He emigrated to America in 1881, probably for the same reason that so many people left this country.'

Then we heard a knock on the front door. Bob Lynch was back and he came in and sat down beside the table. 'How did you two get on?' he asked.

'Oh,' said Joe, 'we played a few and we were just talkin' about Barney Delaney the piper before you interrupted us.'

Bob laughed. 'A piper, you said?'

'Yes,' said Joe, 'not the bagpipes but the Irish uilleann pipes, and a great instrument, especially for the playin' of slow airs. And another thing – people years ago were known to say that the Banshee will stop cryin' when she learns to play one.'

'Holy smoke,' said Bob, 'I've never heard of that one.' I was hoping that Joe wouldn't go on too long talking about the Banshee. I had heard enough about her from people whose stories gave me the creeps. So I was relieved when Mrs Delaney came into the room to retrieve the tray. She said she had made more tea and asked Bob if he'd like some. 'You always had an eye for a man in want,' he said to his sister. Joe laughed when he heard Bob. A good sense of humour was important to Joe, and his brother-in-law had a way with words. There was plenty of chat while we drank more tea and Mrs Delaney brought some extra currant cake and some brack. This reminded me that Hallowe'en would soon be upon us.

When we'd finished, Bob lit a cigarette and stood up from his chair. 'Paddy,' he said, 'I think we should be on our way.' Then looking at Joe he said, 'Oh, by the way, Joe, I knew I wanted you to play somethin' for me but I couldn't think of it 'til now.'

'What one is it?' Joe asked.

'It's one of the greatest reels ever,' Bob said. 'It's called "The Salamanca".'

I had heard my father talk about it but had never heard it played.

'Well,' said Joe, 'I haven't played it in ages but I'll give it a go anyhow.'

'Good man,' said Bob. Joe checked the tuning again and then eased into the reel. He didn't play it too fast, which helped me to hear the tune better, but as I listened I wasn't sure I liked it. Bob, on the other hand, knew the tune and didn't take his eyes off the fiddle while Joe was playing. It was clear that he was under the spell of the tune and when Joe finished he said, 'Thanks, Joe. It's one I could listen to for ever.'

Joe grinned at Bob. 'For ever is a long time,' he said.

As I was putting my accordion into its box Bob said to me, 'We have to go now, but you'll meet Joe again, isn't that right, Joe?'

'For sure,' said Joe. 'My wife and I will be goin' into Daingean in a couple of weeks. Bob will let you know and we can have another tune in his house.'

After we said our goodbyes we were out the door and into Bob's van. I was home in less than half an hour.

41

Jimmy's Return

It was two years since Jimmy Quinn had emigrated to England with his mother and sisters. All the eldest boys were already gone and lived within the shores of John Bull, which was how their father referred to England. Jimmy's father refused to go there and remained at home.

Then one evening when I had finished working with Black Bob I took the notion of getting onto his back and riding him back to the L field, where I would turn him loose. I found a tar barrel and put it beside the horse and used it as a way to climb onto his back. It went very well and my sisters cheered me on as Bob and I sauntered out of the front yard. As I was riding along the path that would take me towards the L field I'd no idea that Jimmy was cycling on the road and could see me riding the horse. He had returned from England and was on his way to visit us. Seeing me riding a horse was something Jimmy didn't expect, and I wasn't aware that it made him feel a little jealous. When I returned home Jimmy was in the kitchen playing rings with my sisters. He was wearing a gun belt and holster and had a very determined look on his face. 'Hey Pat,' he said, 'I see you got yourself a horse.'

'He's not mine,' I said, 'it's my father's.'

'Oh,' said Jimmy.

'Aren't you goin' to welcome Jimmy home?' my mother asked me.

'Welcome home!'

'Pat,' said Jimmy, 'you look different than when I saw you last time.'

I didn't know what he meant. 'I suppose I am,' I said.

Jimmy had forgotten he hadn't seen me for two years and none of us were thinking very clearly with the distraction of the ring game and my sisters shouting and teasing each other. The game was narrowing towards the final ring and everyone got caught up in the excitement.

My youngest sister, Patricia, was Jimmy's partner so when she threw the ring that won the game he yelled and hugged her and promised her the biggest apple to be found around Killoneen. She was all smiles and a little bashful about the attention. Jimmy said he was going home to get the apple and left us in a frenzy of excitement and laughter. My sisters were now convinced of Jimmy's gallantry and my mother said he must have had good schooling while he was away in England.

After half an hour he returned with the apple. It was, as he said, huge. Jimmy handed it to Patricia and she held it and felt it and tried to bite it but couldn't get her teeth into it. 'Let me get a knife,' my mother said.

'No, no,' said Jimmy, 'this is Patricia's apple and she is the only one allowed to eat it.'

'How can you expect her to eat it if she can't get her teeth into it?' my mother replied.

'Let me help you, Patricia,' and with his penknife he cut a small lump from the apple. He handed her a piece and she began chewing. Her mouth twisted a little and her forehead began to frown. It was a baking apple and she said it was sour. Jimmy said, 'Let me put a little bit of sugar on it,' and when he did, Patricia's face returned to normal. We played a few more games of rings until nine o'clock and then Jimmy said he had to go. He'd promised his mother he'd be home before half nine.

During this time my father was in bed resting. He had been complaining of severe pains in his stomach and intended to see a doctor. When Jimmy was gone home he came out of the room and sat by the fire holding his stomach.

'Is it bad?' asked my mother.

'I was goin' to shout from the room,' he said, 'the noise of everyone was makin' me feel very down.'

'I think you should see the doctor tomorrow,' my mother said. 'You've been puttin' it off for too long. You know, you may have ulcers.'

He said nothing but the next day he came home from work at two o'clock and with Gilbert McCormack's hired car he went to the doctor in Tullamore. When he got there the doctor sent him to the hospital for an X-ray, the result of which was that he indeed had a huge ulcer. The doctor put him on a diet – no fries, cut down on tea and Guinness. It was a disappointment for my father. We weren't very aware of what an ulcer really meant or what kind of food or drink would aggravate it. It would take some time for my father to get used to the doctor's orders. It also affected the time I had to practise the accordion because my father didn't react well to noise at this time, whether it be music or verbal exchanges between my mother, sisters and me.

He went through months of pain, and many times he spent alone in the cow shed hanging by his hands from the crossbeam over the door. He told us afterwards that the pain was so bad that he would swing and pull himself up and down in search of relief. But no relief came, despite ridding himself of the frying pan and constantly drinking minted milk solutions called bismuth. Meanwhile, he had become friendly with Father Mullen, who had caught my father's attention during Sunday Mass, when he could be seen pressing his hands against his lower chest, and sometimes during the service he would sway from side to side before the altar. My father sensed that something was wrong with the priest and decided to visit him one evening when he was in town on an errand. When he got to the curate's house the priest was walking up and down in the back yard. When he saw my father he said, 'I know who you are, and you're the right man in the right place.' My father didn't know what he meant until the priest said, 'Would you mind milkin' me cow? I would do it meself but I'm not feelin' too well.' There was a bucket nearby. 'You can milk her into that,' Father Mullen added.

'I'll have her milked in two shakes of a lamb's tail,' my father said, grabbing the bucket.

The priest showed my father where the cow was housed and spoke to him while he milked her. He told my father about an ailment he had in his stomach and in a hushed tone of voice said it was cancer. My father was shocked when hearing about such a serious disease, the mere name of which made many people nervous. Then my father told the priest about his stomach ulcer and how he saw no sign of it disappearing and how worried he was about it. Father Mullen was very consoling and said it would fade away and not to worry. These were reassuring words for my father and when he finished milking, the priest said, 'Good man, you've done me a great favour. I hope I can return it.' After that my father went about his business.

Some weeks later he was passing by the curate's house again when he saw Father Mullen waving at him to stop. When he got off his bike the priest said, 'Christy, would you mind milkin' her again? This awful pain is at me and I've no energy for doin' anythin'.'

'Don't worry, Father, it's no trouble at all,' replied my father. The priest had the bucket in his hand and my father took it and went to the cowshed. On another occasion my father cleaned the cowshed and put in fresh straw for bedding the cow. Father Mullen was unable to express his appreciation of my father's help as much as he would like to but somehow gave my father a strong sense of belief in the priest. My father spoke to us at home about Father Mullen having something special. He said the power of heaven was in him.

It was several months later when we heard the priest had been taken to the hospital in Tullamore and shortly after that he died. My father was devastated and talked about him being a huge loss to the parish. He went to the funeral and afterwards to the graveyard and helped cover the coffin during the burial. When he came home he was very quiet and after supper the extreme pain in his stomach began again. My mother urged him to go to bed, saying that maybe the rest would help.

In the weeks that followed the stomach pain stayed with my father. Many times he wasn't able to eat and he tried to ease the pain by bending back and forth and pulling from the crossbeam of the cowshed. I also remember him sucking a variety of lozenges and peppermints, but nothing seemed to deaden the pain. He was becoming desperate and one evening after supper he told my mother he was going to visit Father Mullen's grave. 'When are you going there?' my mother asked.

'Next Saturday evenin', after confession.'

Jimmy Quinn returned to school on the first Monday of October, and everyone had a question for him. Mr O'Connell welcomed him back and said he should listen to how the classes were conducted for the first week so as he could adjust to what was going on. Jimmy began to accompany me home after school. He would cycle slowly beside me as I walked along and we chatted about various western heroes, including the Lone Ranger and Buck Jones. Jimmy had become more devoted to the game of 'Good Lads' versus 'Bad Lads'. During his stay in England he feasted on many of the new sixty-four-page comics that were available. He had become immersed in Western stories and went to the cinema whenever a Western was shown. He was in his own world, in which he referred to himself as 'Kid Cutler'. Eventually I became a little afraid of his change in personality and tried to move our conversation to other interests such as football, hurling or music. Jimmy had no interest in any of it, while I on the other hand was getting more involved with my accordion and had graduated from painting pictures of saints to sketching and painting landscapes. My interest in Gaelic football and hurling was another passion, and I looked forward to the match broadcasts on Sunday afternoons. The clear voice of Mícheál Ó hEithir gave me a variety of heroes other than those of the Wild West. Names of great footballers from Offaly and other counties were more exciting and heightened my imagination so much that I still recall their names and where and who they played for, even though it's now a long time ago. Mícheál's radio broadcasts were so clear and exciting that I developed a visual understanding of the game, with its backs defending and forwards on the attack. I had also begun to copy and paint the All-Ireland winners from black and white photos of the teams featured in the Monday sports edition of the *Irish Independent*. I wanted to see the teams in colour. It would be a great sight, the blue and gold of Tipperary or the black and amber of Kilkenny and later the green, white and gold of Offaly.

Jimmy was a regular visitor to our house to play throwing rings with my sisters and me. Each game featured four of us, two a side. Jimmy usually partnered with my youngest sister, Patricia, and even though they were underdogs they would still manage to surprise us. One evening we played several games that developed into a show-down of sorts with Patricia hooking big numbers and Jimmy cheering his head off. With Jimmy's promises of bigger apples and a bag of sweets she rose to the occasion with everyone cheering and shouting with laughter. These were special times for us all.

It was a couple of weeks later when Jimmy said he had noticed something 'different' about me but somehow he couldn't figure out what it was. 'I can't put my finger on it,' he'd say.

During another evening of rings we were almost at the end of a game when Jimmy shouted, 'Pat! Pat!'

'What?' I replied.

'I've got it,' he said. 'I know what's different about you.'

'Well,' said my mother, 'what in holy Moses is it?'

Jimmy was cackling a laugh that reminded me of a woodpecker. 'It's your trousers. You're wearin' long corduroy trousers!' We all looked at him in silence, waiting for him to say something else. A small twitter came from behind me – it was Moira. Then another sound of someone holding her breath before bursting into laughter, followed by everyone roaring their heads off. Everyone was laughing except Jimmy. Was it possible he didn't know what we were laughing at?

'Jimmy,' my mother said, 'Paddy has been wearing his long trousers for almost a year.'

'But . . . but,' Jimmy stammered, 'he wasn't wearin' them before I went to England.'

'That,' said my mother, 'was over two years ago.'

'I know, I know,' said Jimmy, 'but now he looks so different since he began wearin' them.' Everyone turned towards me, looking at me up and down, hoping to see something that Jimmy had seen that the rest of us had missed. To my relief Jimmy began throwing his six rings at the board. And so the game resumed. Jimmy was a peculiar lad but always entertaining and extremely self-assured. A year later he went back to England and I never saw him again.

My father's stomach pain became a major concern for all of us, especially our mother. I remember it was a Saturday evening when he returned home and told us that he had been to confession and got a few worries off his mind. He said Father Doran was very easy on him. After he was finished in the chapel he cycled all the way to the graveyard to where Father Mullen was buried. When he found the grave he said an Our Father and three Hail Marys, which was the small penance given to him by Father Doran during his confession. As he knelt there he asked the dead priest to cure him of the ulcer. He prayed some more and then he loosened his belt and pulled his shirt open. When his stomach was sufficiently naked he took some clay from the top of the grave and rubbed it on the painful area. After he was finished he cycled directly home, arriving at our gate at half past eight. It was an early hour for him to arrive home on a Saturday evening, especially if he had been to Daingean. He was unusually quiet as he sat by the fire while my mother prepared tea. Shortly afterwards he moved into the corner by the fire and before he finished his tea he fell asleep.

Meanwhile it was time to listen to *Céilí House* on the radio, and Seán Ó Murchú was in terrific form as he introduced the Leitrim Céilí Band from County Galway. I was again carried away by so many great tunes and several selections that included some of Seán Ryan's jigs and hornpipes, tunes that Seán had just composed. My mother was busy ironing freshly washed shirts, blouses and undergarments.

My sisters were trying on different clothes that they were swapping and were in their own world of giggling and teasing each other. I was trying to hear Seán Ó Murchú's introductions and shouted at them to keep quiet; but it was no use, one giggle ignited another and not until my mother intervened did they lower their voices. Seán Ó Murchú introduced another selection, 'The Yellow Tinker' and 'The Hare's Paw'.

'A great auld tune,' said my father, who had woken up.

'Where did you hear it?' my mother was curious.

'In Daingean. I heard young Tommy Smullen play it in Watt Nolan's.'

'When was that?'

'Jesus Christ, woman, wasn't I tellin' you about the music in Watt's pub? It must have been a month ago.' I was beginning to feel irritated with their talking as I tried to hear the bands playing the final selection of reels. As I listened I managed to retain a few bars of two tunes played on the programme and while they were fresh in my memory I grabbed my single-row and went to the bedroom to try them out. My imagination was once again refreshed and in the darkness of my room my mind was teeming with the names of several band members, 'The Bucks of Oranmore', the stone walls of Galway and the wonderful flute music of Paddy Carthy. Then I squeezed the accordion with vicious intent and began.

42

The Man Who Didn't Like Music

My father had secured a new job at Bord na Móna's new briquette factory in Mountlucas, which was two miles from our house. The local newspapers usually referred to it as Croghan briquette factory following a debate between local councillors, Bord na Móna experts and some clergymen who had wrestled with the problem of where the factory was to be built.

As he settled into the job – loading lorries – he became friendly with many of the drivers who drove to the factory to pick up briquettes or regular lorry loads of turf. One evening, after he came home from work, he said to me, 'I met an accordion player at the factory today.'

'Who was it?'

'A man by the name of Dominic MacCarthy, Did you ever hear of him?'

'Yeah, I did. He's from Clara,' I said. I told my father that I had heard Dominic playing on Ciarán MacMathúna's *A Job of Journeywork*.

My father said he had told Dominic about me and that Dominic said he'd drop in to hear me play next week, when he would be passing our house with a load of turf. In the meantime we had a surprise visit from Mick Crowley, of whom I wrote earlier.

As soon as I saw him I was reminded of the time he showed me how to fill his pipe and the awful sickness after I smoked it. Of course that was six years earlier, on the afternoon they abandoned the turf cutting after it began to rain. My memory of Mick was that he loved the company of children and his presence afforded me the liberty of playing hide and seek with my sisters as he watched us with a grin on his face. On the same day, during a tea break, I began begging him to let me smoke his pipe. He laughed and said he would when he and my father were finished. Shortly afterwards it started to rain and after waiting half an hour we gave up and headed home. When we returned to our house we all sat around the kitchen drinking tea. When Mick took out his pipe to have a smoke I begged him again.

Mick looked at my parents for approval and my father said, 'Mick, go ahead or you won't have a minute's peace.'

'First you have to clean it and fill it with fresh tobacco,' Mick said to me with a grin. As he spoke he emptied his pipe and began scraping it with his penknife while I stood by in close attendance. Mick didn't have much new tobacco left in his purse so he told me to run outside to the turf shed and find a small bit of white turf. When I returned he had me pack the turf tightly into the pipe. 'Good boy,' he said, 'now I want you to light it while you hold it in yer mouth.' I scratched a match on the side of the matchbox and when it lit I tried lighting the pipe but the match burned out. I lit another and put it to the turf and it began to turn red. I was pulling hard on the stem, sucking in the air. 'Keep at it,' said Mick, 'good lad.' I lit another match, and then another. With two more matches wasted I began to despair and was about to give up when the pipe ignited! 'Good lad, good lad,' said Mick, 'keep pullin' on it.' I did, and then went outside so as I would be alone to enjoy my success.

Walking towards the back haggard I came to the hay reek and as I stood there I felt a strange sensation of dizziness. Everything around me started to spin and I collapsed on my knees and the pipe fell out of my mouth. I fell against the hay when I tried to reach for the pipe. The entire haggard of hay and straw reeks were turning upside down and my stomach became sick, a dry sickness that had me retching. Although I was lying on the grass I tried holding on to the hay reek because I was afraid of falling further to the ground. Suddenly I began to throw up. I was breathing deeply and pushing hard at trying to empty my stomach until it seemed like there was nothing left. In a short while my father came looking for me and when he saw how I was he said, 'You'll never smoke a pipe again!'

Like a lot of people in Ireland Mick 'took the boat' and sailed to England where he found employment in Manchester. When he came home to visit he stopped by our house to catch up with all the local news. 'My God, how you've grown up, lad,' he said to me. 'And the long trousers look good on you. Now tell me, did you ever get goin' on the pipe?'

I shook my head. 'No,' I said. I didn't want to talk about it. My father was frying kippers for one o'clock dinner and my mother was knitting a cardigan. Mick declined to eat anything, opting instead for a mug of strong tea. He had given up smoking and had put on some weight. My father said he was looking well and my mother added that England must be agreeing with him. I could see by the expression on his face that Mick was pleased. The three of them chatted about old times, the Irish economy, and the prospect of the coming Christmas. Mick asked my father if he had any intention of going out with the wren and this led to me being asked to play Mick a tune on the accordion. I was in no mood for playing because I was tired of my small repertoire. However, after my father pressed me a little I grabbed the box and did a bit of fingering on its keyboard. The sound of a few notes reminded me of a jig called 'The Geese in the Bog' that I hadn't thought of in months. I began playing the tune and it went better than expected. When I'd finished my father said, 'That's a great one, a haymaker. What do you think, Mick?'

Mick didn't say anything and his silence didn't go unnoticed by any of us. 'Do you like music?' my father asked him.

Without a moment's hesitation Mick replied, 'I hate it.' My father was visibly shocked. He looked at Mick like he had two heads. 'Do you like any kind of music at all?'

'None of it,' said Mick.

I put away my instrument quickly and went outside to the haggard and from there I walked to the bog to clear my head. I had never met anyone who disliked music, not just my music but other kinds of music as well. It was unbelievable! I thought about it and wondered if something strange had happened to Mick while he was living in England. When I returned to the house Mick had gone back to Daingean. 'Good Christ,' my father was saying, 'I never thought such a man existed.'

'Just imagine,' said my mother, 'not likin' music. It's beyond me to even think about it!' As for myself, I couldn't imagine it either.

When my sisters came home from school we told them the news of Mick and the music. All of us began voicing our opinions on the matter and it was funny with everyone talking at the same time. We probably sounded like a bunch of turkeys in distress as we tried to understand the cause of Mick's problem.

'He needs a good woman,' said my father, 'a big woman, a woman that would beat the shit out of him once a month!'

My mother was sympathetic and said, 'God help him.'

My sisters and I were laughing at my father's remedy, which was his way of making a joke of the matter. My eldest sister Moira suggested that Mick could be cured if he went to Lourdes, while Kathleen added, 'A week in Lough Derg might do the trick, it might help him feel the sound of a tune.'

My father decided that a big heavy woman wasn't, after all, the answer. 'Listen, the best thing for Mick,' he said, 'is to bring him up to the Grand Canal and tie a rope around him and then throw him into it and then pull him out, and then throw him back in again.' My father was very funny with his use of words. He had a great sense of timing and would raise or lower his voice depending on the need for emphasis. He was able to give credibility to nonsense and lifted the spirits of people who knew him. We settled on his 'cure' for Mick's problem and laughed at the image of Mick struggling at the end of a rope while trying to stay afloat in the Grand Canal! This story – Mick Crowley and the Music – stayed with our family for many years. It is one that my sisters and I never forgot.

43

The Miracle

December was a month of frost and cold east winds that blustered across the Midlands. It was near the end of 1959 and with Christmas two weeks away, songs of the season were played frequently on the radio. On one of those cold afternoons a lorry pulled up outside our gate. I was walking back to our front door carrying an armful of turf for the fire. When the door of the lorry opened a tall man stepped down. It was Dominic MacCarthy. He was wearing a chequered tweed cap and a large grey overcoat and as I went inside he followed me into the kitchen. 'Hello Mr MacCarthy,' my mother greeted him.

My father was on his knees under the back table trying to set a mousetrap with fresh cheese. 'Dominic,' he said, 'sit down and make yourself at home. I'll be with you in a minute.'

'Take your time, Christy,' he said, and then to my mother, 'Missus, I hope you don't mind me sayin', but I'm dyin' for a drop of tea.' The kettle was already boiled and so she prepared the teapot. Dominic looked at me and said, 'So, I hear you play the box.' I nodded. Dominic had big, round blue eyes that reminded me of marbles and he sported a narrow grey moustache, much like Clark Gable. His eyes followed anything that moved, without much movement of his head, and it seemed he was able to take in all that was around him.

When given the tea he lit a cigarette, after offering one to both my father and mother. 'The missus doesn't smoke,' my father said as he took one. Dominic lit his cigarette with a lighter, which was something we hadn't seen before, and nor had our dog, Rex, who broke into a fit of growling when it lit up. Dominic was amused by the dog and would open and shut the lighter, teasing him, and each time he did it Rex would growl with more conviction.

My father began talking about what he perceived as one particular mouse that had somehow succeeded in removing the cheese from the trap, leaving it empty and unsprung. 'He's a foxy little snake,' he said. Dominic said that there was probably more than one mouse involved, perhaps a half dozen. My mother started to laugh, and looking at me she said, 'Paddy, why don't you play a bit of a tune for Dominic?'

'Yes, yes, Paddy, go on, give us a tune,' said Dominic. The accordion was under the front table and as I reached down I had to put my head under the tablecloth so as I could find it. When I began to play I saw Dominic watching me with keen interest and after the first tune he asked me to play a few more. After I played a couple of my new reels he lilted a bit of a jig and asked me did I know it, but I had never heard it before. Then my father asked Dominic to give it a go but he declined, saying that he couldn't manage the box because it didn't have a second row of buttons.

I noticed that my father was anxious for a bit of serious conversation, which he began by telling Dominic that Mick Crowley was home on a holiday from England. Dominic didn't know Mick at all but when he heard the story of how Mick hated music his eyes stopped moving. 'What do you think of a man that doesn't like music?' my father asked Dominic.

'He's a fuckin' animal,' said Dominic, 'and that's all I will say about him.'

My mother defended Mick, saying he was a God-fearing man and that everything else about him was normal.

'He's still an animal,' said Dominic. My father was enjoying Dominic's assessment of Mick's 'ailment' and was on the brink of saying something about cattle being attracted to music when Dominic pointed at the accordion. 'Would you mind handin' me the box for a minute?' As he held it on his lap he asked, 'Have you ever played this one?' and began playing a Scottish jig. I listened to the melody of the tune and marvelled at Dominic's ability. He had a light and tender touch and later, when I became more experienced, I was able to say that his fingering rhythm was of a staccato style. After playing the first part of the jig he stopped and said, 'I was playin' this a week ago and now I can't for the life of me think of the second part of it. I was hopin', Paddy, that you might know it.' I said I was sorry and that I had never heard it before. I also felt a bit sad for Dominic, who was looking up at the ceiling as though expecting divine intervention. When I asked him where he got the tune, he said, 'Jimmy Shand, the man himself.' Jimmy Shand was a famous Scottish accordion maestro whom Dominic greatly admired. He said he had visited Scotland some years earlier and had made it his business to seek out Jimmy's address in Glasgow. When he eventually found the man's house he knocked at the door and it was opened by Mrs Shand, who invited him inside. This was one of the highlights of Dominic's musical career.

As I heard him tell the story I felt he was reliving the experience as he described Jimmy in glowing terms, saying in the end that he was a pure gentleman. He gave up on trying to remember the second part of the jig and so passed the accordion back to me. I was tempted to try another tune when my mother poured more tea. The conversation took a turn when Dominic asked my father how his health was doing. 'I can't complain,' said my father. I noticed that Dominic was interested in learning more. 'You were havin' trouble with your stomach, Christy, weren't you? I remember one day at the factory you were in terrible pain. At the time you said it was an ulcer.'

My father looked at Dominic and then at my mother. He was clearly surprised. 'Well,' he said, 'I haven't had any trouble with it lately. Come to think of it I haven't had any pain in a while, or maybe it just didn't cross my mind.'

My mother was visibly moved by what my father said. 'Jesus, Mary, and Joseph!' she said, blessing herself. 'It must be the clay from Father Mullen's grave that cured you. My God, it's a miracle! That's what it is, a miracle!'

Dominic was looking back and forth at my parents. 'What are ye talkin' about? What miracle?'

'Dominic,' my father said, 'you may not believe it but about three months ago I was in horrible pain from the ulcer. Father Mullen had died a few weeks earlier. I knew him fairly well and sometimes I'd milk the cow for him, or clean the cow shed. He told me he also had an ulcer – which eventually led to stomach cancer – and could hardly stand up in the church when sayin' Mass. I went to see his grave shortly after his burial, the same evenin' that the ulcer was painin' me. I knelt down and asked the priest to take me out of this unbearable sufferin'. After I prayed I took a fistful of clay off the top of the grave, pulled up my shirt and rubbed my stomach with the clay. The strange thing about it is, since then I've forgotten all about the ulcer, that is until just now! So now that you've asked me about it I can't remember when the pain stopped.' My father's face was alive with wonderment. 'Jesus Christ,' he said, 'it might be a miracle.'

My mother told Dominic that my father always sensed that Father Mullen had some power of a spiritual nature. 'By God,' said Dominic, 'I wouldn't mind knowin' where he's buried. I've got a boil on the calf of me leg and it's irritatin' the hell out of me.'

'Well, it's easy enough,' said my father. 'He's buried in the new cemetery just past the reformatory.'

Dominic was clearly impressed and said he wasn't a great one for going to Mass or praying too much, adding that he didn't think he was as well in with the Lord God as was my father.

'Don't you worry about it,' my father said. 'It's not the Lord God you'd be dealin' with. Father Mullen is the man that cured me. God had nothin' to do with it.'

After drinking the second mug of tea and smoking another cigarette Dominic stood up from the chair and looked at me. ''Twas good to hear you play, but you have to keep at it.'

'Will he be any good?' my mother asked.

'Oh he will, but he has to keep practisin', because practice makes perfect.' He looked at me again and said, 'In a couple of years you'll feel the difference in your fingers.' I felt encouraged by Dominic's words, but remained silent.

My father walked with Dominic to the roadside where the lorry was parked and there they talked for a short while before Dominic climbed back onto the driver's seat. We heard the engine revving and then a growling moan as the big vehicle began its journey towards Daingean, where he would meet the Tullamore road which would finally take him to his home in Clara.

When my father came back in he was very excited about the prospect of his ulcer being cured. 'My God, isn't that a fright,' he declared. 'And what's more, I'd forgotten all about it.'

My mother looked very solemn. 'That's the way with miracles. People never know when it happens, or maybe us mortals aren't supposed to notice the moment it occurs.' She may have been right.

Nevertheless we were still curious about our father's health and every so often would ask him how he was feeling. 'Never better,' was his response. The ultimate test was when he went back to the frying pan. After a few weeks of eating rashers and eggs for breakfast we were amazed at how comfortable he was with his stomach. We talked more about the miracle and concluded that something wonderful had happened when he knelt beside Father Mullen's grave. My father's faith in the priest as a holy man in life was transcended into a profound spiritual belief when he took clay from his grave and pressed it tightly to his stomach.

44

The Man Who Loved Himself

I believe it was several months before we saw Mick Hayes again. It was a dark November night when he cycled to our gate and leaned his bicycle against one of its pillars. As he opened the gate our dog, Rex, let him have it with a barrage of barking and prodding his head through its iron bars. Rex was then fully grown and had developed a strong interest in barking at anything that moved. Seeing Mick's headlight at the gate infuriated his imagination and he went berserk with his teeth bared and saliva dripping from his jaws. Mick was about to turn away when my father came from the house and grabbed Rex by the scruff of the neck. My father's intervention did little to calm the dog, so he carried him away and put him in the dairy house and closed the door. I could hear Mick cursing as he leaned his bike against the wall of the house.

'You sly little fuck,' he roared, 'bad luck to every bone in yer body you lousy little fuckin' tyrant.'

Rex had quit barking by the time Mick and my father came into the kitchen. My mother had made a griddle cake and was levelling a bed of coals on the hearth. 'Hello missus,' said Mick, 'I see you're makin' a griddle cake. I hope I'm in time for a bit of it.'

My mother stood up from the fire. 'God almighty,' she said, 'we were just talkin' about you an hour ago.' Mick was pleased with her welcome but began complaining of rheumatism and aches in his legs. He said he had not ventured outside for several months and hadn't been to Daingean in almost a year. As soon as he was seated by the fire he said to my father, 'What breed of a dog is it you have nowadays?'

'He's a Kerry blue terrier.'

'Well,' said Mick, 'he's a noisy little bastard. For a minute I thought he might jump through the gate tryin' to get at me.'

'It's only because he didn't know yeh,' my mother said. 'The next time you come he'll be more friendly. His name is Rex. It helps to know a dog's name.'

'I've put a few good names on him already,' Mick chuckled.

I was always expecting to hear a tune from Mick and on this occasion I had the loan of a C#/D Paolo Soprani accordion that was similar to his. When he saw it he asked me who owned it.

'Barney Bateson, of the back road. He loaned it to me for a month.'

'That's very decent of him. Not everyone would be so trusting,' said Mick.

'Except for you, Mick,' said my mother.

I began playing a few tunes, after which Mick showered me with praise and said, 'You don't expect me to play after that?'

'After what?'

'After the way you've just played. Paddy, you've come a long way and you're playin' lovely tunes, tunes I've never heard before. Where did you get them?'

'Off the wireless.'

'Off the wireless,' Mick said thoughtfully. 'What a great world we live in. By God, isn't it a wonder what that little talkin' box is doin' to the youth of this country.' As he chuckled he repeated, 'Off the wireless, off the wireless,' shaking his head as he said it. Everyone else had remained silent while Mick and I had our little music chat. My father never attempted to converse very much about me and the music, or what was played on the radio, and if any of it was mentioned it would unsettle him and he'd change the conversation to suit his own understanding of the world. Finally, after I finished another tune he turned to Mick and asked, 'Are you goin' out with the wren this year?'

Mick looked at him with genuine surprise. 'God no,' he said, 'I'm afraid, Christy, I'm gettin' too old for it.'

These were among the last things I ever heard Mick say, because when he went home that night little did I know but that I'd never see him again.

45

The Price of a Tune

When Christmas came my three youngest sisters were keeping its spirit alive with high hopes of Santa again visiting and bringing them toys. The mystery of how he travelled so easily around the world intrigued them and they would ask me how he packed so many toys into his sack. I had stopped believing in Santy, as we called him, but pretended I did for a couple more years, so I would get a present. The last of these presents was a silver cap gun and cowboy hat that I wore when playing with Jimmy Quinn in and around Rourke's Moors. Jimmy was still firm in his belief that he was, in fact, Kid Cutler, a fast gun of the Old West, and I went along with him because he was a friend. And besides, he always had some of the latest comics, which he loaned me. However, I was becoming less interested in cowboys and rustlers; something inside me had changed. Instead I found myself drawn even more to the accordion and the music I heard on the radio. I was also playing more of my Aunt Maggie's records, even though I struggled to identify particular notes in their melodies. The inconvenience of winding up the gramophone and placing the needle on the record was tedious. Sometimes a tune might surprise me; it would be one I'd forgotten when suddenly there it was in a clearer pronunciation of sound. This usually produced in me a feeling of jubilation that had me going over the melody many times in my head before trying my luck with it on the accordion.

When the Christmas holidays were over it was back to school and before we knew it we were into another new year, 1960. This was the year that many Catholics in Ireland believed would signal the end of the world. I heard my mother talk of a secret message from the Virgin Mary, who was supposed to have given it to three little girls in an apparition at Fatima. It was believed that the end of the world was part of the message and somehow many people came up with the year 1960. At school Mr O'Connell reminded us that we had a new school calendar and spoke of how we could achieve great results if we studied hard. He also mentioned that our upcoming June examinations would be a priority and that now was the time to prepare, even though they were still several months away.

As the weeks went by we all settled into the demands of school, and I was also kept busy with home duties of gathering firewood and armfuls of turf, pulling hay for the cow and calf and the never-ending water hauling from Larry Farrell's well. Homework from school was always a perfect nuisance, the biggest problem being a lack of time. Despite everything, however, I continued to practise the music, inspired by sporadic visits from Bob Lynch, whose enthusiasm was very inspiring. He usually stopped by with news of Joe Delaney's visit to his house in Daingean. This meant I could cycle to the town for a session with Joe and hear him play some more music from O'Neill's book. Of course I didn't play a lot with Joe, because he had a considerable number of tunes that I'd yet to learn. Instead I would listen to him play most of his tunes from written music in Francis O'Neill's collection, which he liked to refer to as 'The Book'. I wasn't aware at the time that many of Joe's jigs and reels consisted of tunes that were the backbone of Ireland's traditional music. Sometimes Joe would suggest tunes, such as 'The College Grove' or 'The Widow's Daughter', and I would have to remind him that I didn't know them. 'Someday you will,' he'd say as he settled his jaw on the chin rest of his fiddle, 'someday you will.' And then he'd play a tune I remember as 'The Sligo Maid'.

Joe was a wonderful man who loved to talk about music as much as he liked to play it. He didn't have a high opinion of Turlough O'Carolan, the blind harper, saying he wasn't much of a harper but did have some sort of a knack for composition. He often played some of the harper's music and once I heard him say, 'Planoxtys, Planoxtys, plank, plank – what in God's name is a Planoxty?! Who in their right mind would make up such a word?' I was interested in its origin and asked Joe what it meant. 'It's a bastardised word,' he said, 'probably made up by some lunatic or other. It's what education does or doesn't do to some people.' With these words Joe began thumping the floor with his walking stick. It was time for tea and he was intent on reminding his sister-in-law. The tea was already in the making so we didn't have to wait very long. When it came Joe poured for both of us and said, 'Go ahead, eat some scones.' I didn't have to be told twice. After eating and drinking, Joe poured more tea from the pot. It was nicely balanced tea, not overly strong and just right in every way, as Joe would put it. The tea seemed to put Joe in a light mood so he began talking about musicians he once knew. Some of these were personalities of an eccentric nature, or characters of imaginative wit and humour. He told me a story about a fiddle player who composed great tunes but also worked on his farm for a living. One day while he was ploughing he was overcome with an idea for composing a new hornpipe. Without thinking of anything else he abandoned his two horses, still yoked to the plough in the field, and ran as fast as he could back to the house. Once inside he grabbed his fiddle and began probing at the outline of the hornpipe and shaping each bar around what he kept in his head. It took him almost half an hour to complete the tune, by which time he had forgotten about the ploughing and the two horses. He returned to find that the horses and plough were not where he'd left them. Instead they'd become impatient and had begun wandering in a zigzag pattern, dragging the plough behind them. The damage to the freshly ploughed field was minor in comparison to the adjacent side where his potatoes had been planted a fortnight earlier. It was a disappointing discovery, but he consoled himself later when he said, ''Twas a small price to pay for a good hornpipe.'

'So there you have it,' said Joe. 'I could tell you more stories but it's gettin' late, so what about finishin' up with a tune?'

46

Examinations

The national school exams were preceded by a groundwork of writing practice essays in both Irish and English. Mr O'Connell was overseeing us, with hints and subtle suggestions as to the kinds of stories we could use during our homework. We also had to memorise particular extracts from our catechism, and then there were mathematical problems – multiplication tables, and extra work with long division. Nearly all of us in class disliked the prospect of having to confront the inevitable 'sums' that would surely make or break our examinations. Many of my schoolmates were sceptical about doing well and this included myself. A few of the lads were talking about how they might be able to get some clues from their older brothers who had done exams in the past, but this was of little use to myself or Seamus Carr since we were two only sons in our families.

After I'd completed my usual evening routine with the water, hay and firewood I was sitting by the fire when my mother said, 'Paddy, your father and I are goin' to enrol you in the technical school in Tullamore. Some of your schoolmates are also going to be enrolled by their parents.' She added that my Aunt Mary was enrolling my first cousin Paddy and that she'd spoken to Mary already about Paddy and me cycling together each morning to keep each other company until we got used to the round trip to Tullamore. Finally she said, 'You can have my bike until we are able to buy you a proper one.'

My father said that it was six months before a final decision was needed and that I had plenty of time to think about it. His words were consoling because the idea had initially made me tense and nervous. My father said that he and my mother believed the technical school was the right thing for me because I'd have a chance to learn some sort of a trade. As I became older I realised how important this decision was for my parents and how concerned they were about my future. It was also a decision that thousands of families across the country were grappling with during the lead-up to the national school examinations.

My final months at national school seemed to pass without any particular incident except that Mr O'Connell kept prodding us about keeping our focus on the exams. I suppose he was hoping that some of his pupils would qualify for secondary school education. Secondary school could mean the first step towards the priesthood, or perhaps a scholarship to a big city university. None of this ever registered with me as something I wanted – due to the ever-present thoughts of music, cowboy comics and the Offaly senior footballers! It was that same year that the Offaly football team emerged as a formidable force, having won the Leinster senior football title for the first time.

On the day of our exams Mr O'Connell was in charge of overseeing the distribution of our exam papers as well as keeping watch on us, just in case we might cheat. We were all spaced apart as we waited for him to set his stopwatch, and then suddenly he yelled, 'Go!' It was the word that told us to open our envelopes that concealed the exam papers. When I read mine my heart sank a little. It was way too much for me. I felt that I'd be lucky to have an even chance with fifty per cent of it. Still, I decided to write something. As I think of it now, I am amused by the idea that the exam seemed so complex at that time, and would probably appear so simple to me now.

A couple of weeks later Mr O'Connell gave us our results. I wasn't surprised when I was told I had failed. There were several other boys who were expected to pass the test but had not done as well as he expected. Mr O'Connell was clearly disappointed but in the end was a good sport; when he said goodbye he wished us all the best of luck with whatever we did in the future. We were finished with national school! I still remember the wonderful feeling of exhilaration when we climbed the old stile that crested the outer wall of the school yard. Once outside, Willy Smith, Seán McCormack and I led a chorus of cheers and Indian war cries: 'Yip, Yip, Yippee, Yee, Yee, Yaa!'

47

Offaly Football

There was tremendous excitement throughout Offaly in early August when the senior footballers were scheduled to play against Down in the All-Ireland senior football semi-final. People in Offaly had heard about the Ulster champions from listening to the radio or reading newspapers, but other than that few people had seen the Down footballers in action.

Our local areas of Daingean, Croghan and Rhode were well represented by three of the greatest footballers ever to emerge from our part of Offaly. From Daingean we had right half forward Tommy Greene, who was elusive, speedy and had a knack for intercepting the ball and burying it in the back of the net. Mick Casey had a blacksmith's forge near Croghan and was referred to in the newspapers as the 'Iron Man'. He played in various positions as an attacking forward and his unselfish and accurate deliveries caused havoc. Paddy McCormac was one of the younger players on the team and played left full back. I still have an image of him storming out of the back line while under pressure from attacking forwards and kicking the ball to the centre of the field. He was to remain with the team until the early 1970s. His reputation was one of a fearless warrior and devoted footballer who served the spirit and honesty of the sport with dedication and pride. At one time he worked for the ESB near our house where he and other men were installing electricity in houses around our district. Sinking electricity poles was part of the procedure; and this had Paddy and other ESB men digging holes in the nearby fields and meadows. During dinner break Paddy and his fellow workers would use our kitchen for boiling water for tea. My mother told me that Paddy would run around the field opposite our house before the dinner break was over. She said it was a fitness effort that helped keep him in shape, and that he would leap over drains, ditches and barbed-wire fences. Word of how Paddy was training for the Offaly team had some people saying he was the reincarnation of Fionn MacCumhaill.

Work continued throughout that summer as men cut banks of turf, saved hay or worked at mowing meadows. The prevailing topic of discussion concerned the Offaly footballers and their chances of beating Down. I remember the wonderful atmosphere and its infectious spirit of hope for the fifteen men of the Offaly team. It was like the whole of the midlands was electrified. Everywhere I looked I saw green, white and orange flags and banners hanging from telegraph poles, trees, windows and cars. The big day was set for the third Sunday in August at 3.30 p.m. in Croke Park. On the night before the game we noticed extra traffic as cars passed by our house on their way to Dublin. The next morning for two hours before noon the sound had increased to an unabated growl, similar to a heavy-laden train. In our kitchen we had two batteries all charged up, ready for the broadcast on the radio.

Mícheál Ó hEithir came on at three o'clock sharp. 'Hello everyone and welcome to Croke Park.' He began by describing the overcast weather conditions and then spoke in awe of the massive crowd that packed every inch of the stadium. The next day's newspaper estimated that over 90,000 spectators attended the match and yet another said that there were at least another 10,000 people outside the gates because there was no seating or standing room available inside. Mícheál told his listeners that the Down team were running onto the field and the sound of their cheering supporters was deafening. He paused to let his radio audience hear the effect. Then after five minutes came the Offaly team, or as Mícheál said, 'And now on to the field come the men of the "Faithful County",' and another cloud-splitting roar came from the radio. I could hardly contain myself with excitement. I saw my father's hands shaking and when he tried to light a cigarette he was missing it with the lighted match. Then he gave up and waited until the game began. Mícheál was reading the names of the players of each team.

I sat close to the radio and in my imagination I pondered how each of the Offaly players would defend their back line, or how our midfielders might win the ball and put our forwards into action. I had the Offaly team lineup from the Sunday paper spread over the kitchen table in front of me and as I listened all kinds of doubts and anxieties came and went in my mind. Then Mícheál asked his listeners for attention while the Artane Boys' Band played our national anthem, 'Amhrán na bhFiann'. When the music was near its end the crowd let loose a gigantic roar of combined cheers that rattled the radio. Mícheál remained silent for a moment, waiting for the noise of the cheering crowd to subside, and when he finally spoke again his voice was forthright and clear. 'And the referee is looking at his watch,' he began, 'and now he is throwing in the ball and the game is on! The ball breaks away in the centre of the field and into the hands of Down's Kevin Mussen . . .' Mícheál was sounding ecstatic as the match began at a hectic pace. His voice had a hypnotic effect on all of us as we listened to his description of the back and forth play of the game. My mother was tip-toeing around the kitchen and when the referee blew the half-time whistle she began filling the kettle.

My memory of this particular game is of a Herculean struggle between two great football teams who had never played in an All-Ireland semi-final before. It was an unfortunate pairing in the sense that both teams deserved to win. It seems to me now that during that time I was experiencing my share of hero worship, which in turn influenced my estimation of some players. Mícheál's narration had an inspiring effect on many people and this was magnified by his flair for the dramatic, and his unerring memory for the names of all the players and their playing positions. All of it added much to my own romantic impression of what various players were doing, or how dangerous some individuals were once they had control of the ball. I believed that Down's full forward Brian Morgan was a particular menace who seemed to be everywhere, and whenever Mícheál mentioned James McCartan, Down's centre half forward, it gave me the jitters. McCartan was notorious for bulldozing into the square in front of the goalmouth where he would fall onto the grass and pretend he was injured and thus the referee would award him a penalty! We were being introduced to many players, whose talents ranged from place kicking to jumping high and catching the ball, or 'selling a dummy', which was how Mícheál described the art of side-stepping an opposing player.

Within minutes of the start of the second half Offaly's forwards began an onslaught that ended with a foul on Tommy Cullen. The referee blew for a free to Offaly. Har Donnelly was our very reliable place kicker and as expected he booted the 21-yard free over the bar. The rest of the game is a blur to me with its exciting finish and one or two points' difference between each side. Mícheál Ó hEithir was crowning every moment with language not unlike the praise poetry of ancient Irish bards. It was probably fitting that the game ended in a draw. The radio broadcast was an intense experience for my father and me. My mother was in a reflective mood, saying that we were lucky, but my father thought differently, insisting that Down were the lucky ones.

Vocational School

A few weeks later, in September, I began my first day at the vocational school in Tullamore. I had cycled the eleven miles from Daingean with a couple of other boys, including my cousin Paddy. It was a strenuous journey of fifty minutes, and with little knowledge of the road I was unable to anticipate the many small hills and turns that might give us a hint of distances or what part of the journey we were at. In school we were introduced to the various classrooms where we would begin our studies of Irish, English, science, electricity and magnetism, mechanical drawing, woodwork, and metalwork. We were also introduced to various teachers, whose attitudes appealed to me, that is until I got to know some of them. The dreary task of cycling home after school was a formidable one and would take a lot of getting used to. But somehow I persevered and continued with the other boys who also cycled long distances. As time moved along we banded into small groups of cyclists and settled into a routine that was accepted without complaint.

The replay between Offaly and Down was scheduled to be played in two weeks. My father travelled to Croke Park with Jimmy Mac and a couple of other men. He said it was a game he didn't want to miss. I suppose he saw it as a historic occasion, and added to his interest was the fact that Daingean's Peter Carey was scheduled to play at full forward. I would remain at home and listen again to Mícheál Ó hEithir's commentary. Radio batteries were once more charged in Joe Byrne's garage in Daingean. I picked them up on Saturday evening, and the following day Mícheál's voice came on at three o'clock. As usual he announced his sincere welcome to everyone throughout the Gaelic sports world.

Following the Artane Boys' Band and the national anthem, Mícheál told us the referee was tossing the coin to decide who would play left to right. Down won the toss. The referee threw in the ball and the game was on. Once again the match began at a dazzling pace with Mícheál yelling, '. . . there's a ding dong battle in the middle of the field . . . Seán Foran is surrounded by three Down men . . . he passes the ball back to Mick Brady . . . Brady delivers a long, relieving kick way down field . . . It's caught by Donie Hanlon, and now Offaly are on the attack!'

It proved to be another sizzling game and was rated afterwards by commentators as one of the greatest spectacles in Irish sport. Mícheál was in tremendous form with his rapid assessments and depictions of the players as the ball was kicked, punched, passed and soloed by Offaly's Johnny Egan or Down's Paddy Doherty. It can rightly be said that Offaly's half back line were a prized lot of courageous footballers – men like Tullamore's Phil O'Reilly, Mick Brady of Edenderry, and the ever-vigilant Seán Brereton. As the match progressed there were points for Down and more points for Offaly, each answering the other.

With my father at the game my mother was more talkative. Many times as we listened she repeated, 'They'll never do it, they'll never do it.' It wasn't something I wanted to hear and it peeved me to the point that when half-time came I was ready for a respite, perhaps as much as the footballers in Croke Park.

After five minutes of reviewing the first half Mícheál rested his voice. This allowed his listeners an opportunity to hear the Artane Boys' Band as they played the melody 'The Star of County Down', followed by a march as a tribute to the Faithful County of Offaly. I was to learn later that the tune was 'The Hurling Boys', a melody widely played in Offaly as a long dance during the 1860s.

My sisters had very little interest in any of the Gaelic football matches and instead were outside playing or strolling along the road, picking blackberries from the hedges. My mother had brewed a pot of tea and was pouring some into a mug when into the kitchen came the girls full of zest from adventure and fresh air. They were talking two at a time and the second half of the broadcast was about to begin. My problem was immediate. How could I get rid of them? Mícheál was already saying how the referee had ushered the captains of each team to the centre of the field for a goodwill shake of hands before throwing in the ball. I turned up the volume on the wireless. My mother saw my concern and came to my aid. 'Girls,' she said, 'why don't you all go outside and play some more, or maybe pick some flowers?' Moira asked why my mother wanted flowers and was told they were to be put beside the little lamp that was lit under the Child of Prague. 'Now, go on with ye,' ordered my mother. 'Paddy wants to hear Mícheál Ó hEithir.' I breathed a long sigh when the four of them were finally out the door. *A narrow escape* was what I was thinking when suddenly Mícheál lifted his voice and screamed, 'It's Peter Carey with the ball, he's thirty-five yards out, now he's twenty, he still has the ball, he's fourteen yards. Ooh – there's a terrific shemozzle in the parallelogram and in the middle of it all is Peter Carey! He's brought down! He's on the ground and the referee has blown the whistle. It's a fourteen-yard free for Offaly.' Mícheál was as excited as myself. 'It's Har Donnelly to take the free,' he continued. 'He steps up and is walking backwards, and now he walks gently up and taps the ball over the bar. And now Offaly are three points in the lead!'

After twenty more minutes Down's midfield were gaining control. This produced a series of passing movements intended to get the ball to James McCartan who was prowling around near the edge of the square. I couldn't help but be amazed at how Mícheál could keep up with such rapid movement of play and also keep his listeners informed so well about the circumstances that created so many opportunities for each team. Suddenly he raised his voice again. 'Jim McCartan has the ball. He's bursting his way through and pushes Greg Hughes. Johnny Egan is there . . . Paddy McCormack is blocking him . . . McCartan tries to break free . . . he's on the ground . . . he's on the ground . . . surrounded by Offaly players . . . the referee blows the whistle, it's a penalty, it's a penalty! The Offaly backs are protesting and the referee is shaking his head. Oh my, oh my,' Michael was saying. 'Oh dear!' He spoke with a clear, fervent tone as he continued, 'The Offaly supporters are booing the referee. I can see Willy Nolan pacing back and forth in the goalmouth. The ball is placed on the fourteen-yard line and Willy is left to face the great Paddy Doherty! Up he comes. He kicks. It's a goal! It's a goal! He sent Willy Nolan the wrong way! To my mind,' said Mícheál, 'it appeared that Jim McCartan over-carried the ball, but in the end 'twas the referee's decision.'

I was sick with disappointment when I heard what Mícheál said because he rarely said anything controversial on the radio. We were then two points in arrears with ten minutes left. Both teams scored a few more points, but the final score was Down 1-7, Offaly 1-5. The result came as a shock and I was in a state of despair for the rest of the evening. When my father came home he spoke of the game being a great one, but he was certain that the referee was no more than a blind donkey and that he might have to go into hiding for a couple of weeks.

Cycling to school was the best way to heal our emotions, which is what we did on our way to Tullamore the following morning. Nobody had suggested it, but somehow we all set a faster pace than usual with the help of the McEvoy brothers who were cycling two abreast and led the way. Directly behind them were Pat Pilkington and myself. There were twelve of us all told, pedalling as though we were possessed. We arrived at O'Connor Square in Tullamore in just under forty minutes, breaking our record of exactly forty minutes. My buttocks were sore as I climbed off my bicycle and it would be an hour before I'd cool off. Throughout the day my mind was racing back and forth and I couldn't concentrate on my studies. I suppose I was a discontented sports follower who couldn't understand how a referee could be so stupid when his decision meant so much to the outcome of such an important match. Later in the afternoon, when we were seated in English class, our teacher, Mr Kenny, had questions for us about the game. Several lads were anxious to voice their opinions and when I was asked what I thought I said that Offaly would have won the All-Ireland if they had won yesterday. 'How could they win it, Pat,' Mr Kenny asked, 'when it hasn't been played yet?' Before I could answer I was interrupted by laughter from some smart-alecks, including my first cousin. Not knowing what to say I became irritated by the sniggering and mystified by Mr Kenny's remark. Then it occurred to me that maybe it wasn't my day for predicting the future and so I didn't say any more.

My time at the technical school – vocational school – was a mixture of likes and dislikes. An example was our woodwork class. It appealed to me because I liked working with wood and I liked our teacher, Mr Kelly, who was from Derry in the North of Ireland. As we came to know him, his relaxed and laid-back personality helped us to respond to him. His was a gentle approach that inspired our interest and belief in what he wanted us to do. He had broad consideration for the fact that he was a fully developed adult who could guide us pupils who were trying to overcome shyness, self-doubts or a lack of self-confidence. Soon we were learning how to hold a hand saw and keep it straight while we sawed through pieces of softwood timber. Mr Kelly would walk among us checking to see how we were doing, stopping by and watching each of us and offering advice. In the coming months he introduced us to several small projects that had us working from plans and elevations that were neatly drawn on white paper. Our task was to read the measurements and apply them to blocks of wood that were to be planed or chiselled into shape. I found myself very much at ease with these projects and enjoyed the social benefit of getting to know the other woodworking boys. I was making friends with a few lads who sympathised with my disappointment over how Offaly had lost to Down. One lad was Danny Molloy from Rahan, who in a droll sort of way told me, 'We'll get them next year.' Danny looked like he knew what he was talking about and I think he may have instilled in me the belief that Offaly would in fact win their way back to Croke Park once the championship began again the following May.

Cycling to and from Tullamore continued to be a test of willpower, especially on windy days or when a night of black frost left a glossy shine on the surface of the road. A major concern were the dogs who dashed onto the road, running out through hedges or from under farmyard gates. There were at least three houses from where these animals were certain to bark their way onto the road. I always felt a small bit safer when accompanied by other lads from school, but on occasions when I cycled alone I was at the mercy of these vicious upstarts. These were supposedly house dogs that were intent on biting our legs or ankles as they snapped and barked uncontrollably. When seven or eight of us were together I would keep to the centre of the road and let the bigger boys take the brunt of the attacks. A few of them had boasted about what they had in store for the dogs and talked of well-directed kicks that would 'sort them out'. However, things didn't always happen as intended. One evening, when we were passing by a gateway, a contingent of five dogs, led by a big black Labrador, came charging onto the road. They apparently knew the sound of our bikes and it was as though they were waiting for us. The big dog was first and ran at the two front cyclists, almost knocking Ollie McEvoy over before he recovered and steadied himself. This caused Ollie to slow down and suddenly two terriers with their teeth peeled came at him and were snapping and biting at his left leg. One of the dogs managed somehow to grab the leg of Ollie's trousers and was tugging at it when his bigger brother slowed his bicycle alongside him and succeeded in booting both of the terriers away. Meanwhile the boys behind us were trying to ward off the big Labrador, whose tail was standing up, giving him the appearance of confidence and leadership. We had encountered this particular villain before and so it was obvious to us that he was indeed the leader of the pack. During these attacks the dogs would bark furiously, to the point of intimidating many of us, and so we began returning barks of our own as a way to ease our nerves. This helped us to release our frustration and heightened our lust for revenge. Many of us were cursing, others were shouting, and I saw Pat Pilkington landing a kick on the ribs of a snarling collie who backed away whimpering like a domestic lamb. Almost every evening we were ambushed by the usual assortment of barking hostiles, many of which were grey- or brown-haired terriers. Others were black and white sheepdogs or collies, and the black Labrador in the thick of it all, playing his role of chief mischief-maker.

After some weeks of being persecuted I hit upon a plan of my own, which was to cut a stout ashplant from one of the trees that grew near our house. As a matter of fact I cut three of them with my father's bush saw. Armed with the three ashplants I wasn't unduly concerned when I cycled alone to school the following morning. As I passed the gateway of the first house I was surprised by the stillness in the air, with no sight or sound of a dog. When I was well past the gate I dismounted and hid one of the ashplants under a hedge. I would pick it up in the evening on my way home and hopefully exact revenge on the black Labrador. I hid another ashplant the same way a few miles later and hid the third one about two miles from Tullamore.

That evening I was cycling home with my cousin Pat and when I told him about the ashplants he said I was overly cautious – until one of the dogs came out of nowhere and almost bit him as we passed the last house on our way into Daingean. The next day I had my chance with the ashplant when two of them rushed out of a hole in a fence. I swung and missed the lead dog but then tried again with a hard poking jab and caught one dog behind his right ear. It was a moment of triumph! I didn't wait to see the result of my action but did hear the terrier yelping and whimpering as though his paw had been trod upon. It was the sound of defeat and it gave me a deep sense of justice and a feeling of satisfaction that energised me during the rest of the journey home.

The following evening we were cycling home again and as we approached the same gate we spotted a stout-looking woman standing on the side of the road. She was holding a tall blackthorn stick in an upright position which reminded me of an old painting of Moses. There was little doubt in my mind; she was waiting for us! We didn't hear any sound from the dogs and as we cycled closer we saw the woman's face. It was red and flushed with anger. She began thumping the stick on the surface of the road. 'You crowd of rats,' she yelled, 'which one of you hurt my little dog? Stop, ye cowardly rats! Tell me, who hit my little dog Weeshie?'

We slowed down a little and someone said, 'We didn't do anything to yer dog.'

'It was you, wasn't it?' she said as she made a swipe with her stick and almost hit me. 'You sly louse, you,' she said to Johnny Dempsey as she swung the stick again, and this time she hit him on the small of his back. 'Now,' she went on, 'a little taste of yer own medicine!' We didn't delay any further, pedalling furiously until we were out of her reach. She had succeeded in frightening us with the long stick, and some of the names she called us bordered on poetry and religious fervour. 'You little fiend,' she shouted at Éamon Hickey, 'you miserable result of a happy moment!'

We never had any further dealings with her and were relieved when she kept her dogs locked up and out of sight as we passed by during the following months. We cycled the twenty-two-mile round trip to school five days a week for two years. I missed a day from time to time because of very rainy or windy weather and on one occasion cycled against a heavy gale-force wind and ended up an hour and a half late. It was an excruciating experience and when I finally arrived in school I saw that at least half of our class had stayed home. The next day some of the older boys began gloating and teasing those who were deterred by the storm, accusing them of being sissies, weaklings or old women. 'Isn't it great that those loud-mouth maggots have nothin' to badger us with?' my friend Danny Molloy confided in me. I was in total agreement.

49

The Meeting

Another Christmas came and I was glad of the rest from cycling to school. The holidays lasted for one and a half weeks and I was looking forward to spending more time practising the accordion. The demands of school had limited my time with the music. However, my single-row accordion continued to be a problem because of its limitations, which by this time were painfully obvious. I had no knowledge of keys or what key I played in except having heard Bob Lynch mention something about playing a tune in 'D' or 'G'. Bob seemed to understand how to recognise the keys he played in but was unable to explain where to find them on my single-row. In the meantime a branch of Comhaltas Ceoltóirí Éireann was scheduled to be formed at the courthouse in Daingean. Bob stopped by our house with news that the opening night would be the third Monday of January. He urged me to accompany him and also asked my father and mother to come along. In the end my mother stayed home, saying that my father and I should go on the condition that I get home no later than 10.30 p.m. because I would be cycling to school the next day.

When the time came Bob arrived early enough for a mug of tea, after which the three of us set off for the CCÉ meeting. Once inside the building we could hear a man speaking in Irish and as we walked into the hall he switched to English. Bob enquired of someone who the speaker was and a woman whispered, 'It's Paddy Duffy from Birr.' Paddy had a very fervent expression on his face as he continued talking of Comhaltas Ceoltóirí Éireann, its goals and its purpose. When he finished he said the rest of the evening was for playing a bit of music and that we should appoint someone to take charge of the session. It turned out later that when the music began in earnest a half dozen emcees got involved, each wanting to hear a singer or individual musician. In every sense of the word the whole affair was extraordinarily funny. Feet were tapping and girls were swaying their heads and someone was playing the spoons. Then tea was made, and sandwich trays passed around. A song was called for and a young woman obliged with 'The Banks of the Lee'. As soon as she finished, a box player began, with a banjo player joining him. Then a man from Geashill pulled out a tin whistle from his inside pocket. He looked a little unsure and seemed to hit and miss his notes, which were out of rhythm with the tune. Nevertheless nobody complained; it was the novelty of the occasion that mattered and besides everyone was having such a good time. After another song a woman asked for Ellen to play a tune.

'That's right,' said Bob to me and my father, 'she's a little topper.' I was curious and asked who she was. 'Ellen Flanagan,' he said. 'She's goin' to be a champion one of these days.'

Someone else said, 'Where is she?' and an older woman urged, 'Get her to play a couple.' I had never heard of Ellen or her box playing and when I saw her she was wearing a little green-coloured overcoat and she had black hair. She had a simple smile on her lips that looked a little like that of the Mona Lisa and I guessed she was thirteen years old. She removed her accordion from its box and lifted it onto her lap. It was a red Paolo Soprani that Bob said was a C#/D. She began with a jig called 'The Lark on the Strand'. It was gorgeous music and her playing had a strong and steady rhythm. She also had a very natural style and she fingered the keyboard with remarkable ease. As I listened I wanted to inhale the tune or swallow it. More tunes followed and as she continued playing my mind was in a swirl, especially when she moved on to a hornpipe known as 'The Flowing Tide'. She went on to play a few more and I wondered where she found or learned the tunes she played because I hadn't heard them before either on the radio or on my grandfather's gramophone.

On the way home Bob was in an excitable mood and as talkative as a sports commentator. He was ecstatic about Ellen's music and praised her over and over. He was truly impressed and I, of course, wasn't far behind him. My father remained very quiet and was happy to listen as Bob and I aired our opinions of the night's music. For weeks after I was imbued with the sound of Ellen's tunes. The memory of some of them stayed with me a long time, as portions of the melodies dodged in and out of my consciousness.

50

Likes and Dislikes

Despite the music and its plaguing lure I continued with the demands of school. Cycling to and from Tullamore each day was an adventure of sorts that bestowed on us unreliable weather, dogs waiting inside cosy nooks, or last-minute dashes as we tried to beat the clock on the steeple of Tullamore's Catholic church. While in school I tried to focus on a few of the projects presented to us. Woodwork and metalwork were interesting and even satisfying but my impression of some of the teachers perhaps merits a little mention here. For example, I have often wondered why Mr Walsh was so biased towards one group of pupils while ignoring the other. It was so obvious who his favourites were and how he included them in class discussions. Personally I felt totally isolated, almost to the point of non-existence. It's little wonder that I and other lads were bordering on the paranoid when we heard it said that Mick Hamill, our metalwork teacher, often gossiped to other teachers about his pupils. His selective criticism may have influenced particular teachers, who already had misgivings about us, in a personal or negative way. How can any potential students be guaranteed fair-minded attention in school when an adult behaves in a gruff and uncommunicative manner or smears the character of young teenagers who crave a word of kindness or a helping hand from their teacher?

It's quite remarkable and sad that Tullamore's vocational education board put in place a school system that shielded some of the most inept and unprofessional staff imaginable. Another example was our Irish teacher who didn't know or care about the concept of bilingual examples as a means of helping us develop the little Irish we knew. The same teacher often arrived late for class and with a few inaudible words would begin scribbling an essay across the entire blackboard. He would then walk out of the room, leaving his class to try to decipher his hasty handwriting. As my cousin Pat Pilkington remarked on one occasion, 'What are we supposed to do next? This is like bein' left in limbo!' Within minutes this so-called Irish teacher could be found sitting on a high stool in the Brewery Tap drinking the afternoon into nowhere. This was the sort of behaviour that we as pupils endured, and needless to say most of us failed the Irish exam when it came around.

After a year and seven months of various studies Mr Kenny informed us of the upcoming practical and theoretical exams. These were to be our final exams, which would more or less determine our prospects for the future. The majority of us in class were already set on becoming automobile mechanics, fitters, electricians or carpenters. As far as I was concerned I didn't know what I wanted to do, nor was I interested in any of these conventional trades.

It was 1961 and Offaly's senior footballers had beaten Carlow in the first round of the Leinster championship. My father and I had travelled to the match with Jimmy Mac, Tom Graham and Tommy Wright. It was a close game and very exciting. I can't help but remember an Offaly supporter who turned his back to the wind that was blowing in his direction from across the football field. It was half-time and the supporter was trying to light a cigarette. The fellow was of middle age and very chubby around his neck and jaw. The flesh on his face was trembling like jelly from the excitement of the game and the cigarette was trembling between his lips. Every time he struck a match his hands shook and each time he tried to light the cigarette he missed it. A friend who was standing beside him rescued the situation when he held the fellow's cupped hands together, shielding the lighted match from the wind while steadying his shaking hands. With one long pull the cigarette lit up and the man let go a cloud of blue smoke from his mouth. 'There's a man that follows the Offaly team everywhere,' said Jimmy.

'Well,' said my father, 'a more nervous man I've never seen.'

Several weeks later we were told our exams were to be at the beginning of June. This left us with two weeks to prepare some of our Irish and English essays and a list of possible questions that our teachers had given us. When the day came we were each given a desk, spaced at intervals throughout the classroom. The teacher in charge walked around and gave all of us an envelope. When I looked over its contents I was surprised at how difficult the questions were. In the end

I didn't do very well, in those subjects at least. Our results would be published in the *Offaly Independent* over the following weeks. In the meantime we were finished at the vocational school and released 'to make our way in the world', as Mr Kenny told us when he said goodbye.

Meanwhile, Offaly had won another round of the senior football championship and once again the county was alive with new hope and expectancy for the men who wore the green, white and orange. It was an exciting time waiting for the exam results and the notion that our footballers might get to the All-Ireland final, something I felt confident about.

After some six weeks of waiting, the exam results appeared in the paper. My name was listed among the winners, having passed three subjects: mechanical drawing, woodwork and metalwork. I had also passed a separate exam for machine drawing. In any case I had succeeded by a hair's breadth, which I suppose was something. My parents were glad, and hopeful about getting me started with an apprenticeship for some skilled trade. I wasn't particularly enthusiastic about any of it, but I had no choice other than to go with the flow.

51

A Gallant Friend

The summer proved to be a busy time with work on the bog, saving the hay and weeding potatoes and mangels. It was also a time when my father had secured a small grant for building a new family house that would be adjoined to the one-room slated building that was already joined to the back of our old thatched house. Meanwhile he became staunch friends with a young married man whose name was Liam Weir. They were working together at the local briquette factory and during dinner breaks they talked at length about the cost of building supplies and the labour involved in building our new home. Liam was very sympathetic to my father and agreed to take on the job of constructing our new house. I was told that I was to work with Liam as a sort of apprentice; in reality there weren't enough funds to pay Mr Weir a decent wage.

When we began we were in high spirits and in three weeks had made great progress. But very soon, when we came to fitting windows and door frames, I could tell that Liam was in dire straits financially. For some time he had to work elsewhere to support his family before finishing the work on our house. I feel there aren't enough words available to thank such a gallant man as Liam Weir of Ballinamere for how he helped my father. It has often been my intention to meet him now as an adult and express my gratitude for what he did. I still have great memories of working with him because it was my first real experience of such an undertaking and he taught me a lot about the building trade. My parents and sisters lived in the new house for many years. The house still stands in that very same place, in the townland known as Castlebarnagh. It was sold after my mother passed away, my father having gone before her a few years earlier.

My memory of when and how our house was built is still strong in my mind, perhaps as strong as my memory of a young man of tremendous character and integrity, a young man who befriended my father when they worked together in Mountlucas briquette factory.

52

The Interview

Sunday afternoons were often the highlight of my social entertainment, with many of the Gaelic sports championships being broadcast live on the radio. During that particular summer the Offaly senior footballers succeeded in winning their second Leinster title and were scheduled to play in the All-Ireland semi-final at Croke Park on the second Sunday in August. Their opponents this time were Roscommon, who had emerged as champions of Connacht.

In the meantime I was coaxed into filling out an application form in response to a series of Bord na Móna advertisements for apprentice fitters and electricians. In less than two weeks we received a reply by post, which my mother opened. When she read the letter she immediately sat down. 'Well, Paddy, aren't you the lucky lad.'

'What is it?'

'You have been called for an interview at Boora workshop next Monday, at twelve o'clock. You and five other lads.' I had never heard of Boora and had no idea where it was. My mother was bothered by the short notice – less than four days. She was thinking very fast and said, 'I'm going into town to see if Gilbert McCormack has time to drive us there.' In less than an hour she was ready with a change of clothes and was soon cycling the short journey to Daingean.

On her return she explained that Gilbert wasn't available but she had met Seán Lynch on the street and told him about our situation. Seán was immediately sympathetic and offered to help us out. My mother appeared to be very relieved to have found someone as decent and considerate. ''Twas a stroke of luck,' she said, removing her overcoat. When my father came home from work he was amazed at how fast things had happened since the arrival of the letter. As he finished his dinner he remarked that Seán Lynch was a reliable man. 'I hope you said we'd pay him something for his trouble.'

'What do you take me for?' said my mother. 'You must think I've a head like a silo.' My father lit a cigarette and looked at her. I thought he was going to laugh, but he didn't.

It was a twenty-three-mile drive and when we arrived in Boora we were half an hour early. After we got out of the car Seán excused himself and went for a stroll. I looked around and saw that the car park was crammed with cars, many of them Volkswagens. I had never seen so many cars parked in one area. My mother was keen for us to walk across to the main office and introduce ourselves. When we got there we sat down and waited.

In a short while a hatch window opened and a staff member told us where the interview room was. My mother remained seated and wished me luck before I walked the short distance to the workshop door. Once inside I was surprised by the flash of welders and men working on a huge machine. From a small clerk's office a young man saw me and pulled back a sliding glass hatch. 'You're here for the interview, aren't yeh?' he asked.

'Yes,' I said.

'Go inside the next door and sit down. There are two other lads already in there. Mr Usher will be with you in a few minutes.'

I went inside and sat on a vacant chair beside the two other lads. There were no introductions or pleasantries spoken. We sat in silence facing the window. The noonday sun was shining brightly outside on what was a fine August day.

All of a sudden the door opened and a man in his forties came in and sat behind a small desk. He was wearing a black beret, and had a solemn face, almost like a priest about to say Mass. 'I'm Peter Usher,' he said, 'and I'm goin' to ask you some questions, but first I want your names.' He had a list on a piece of paper that lay flat on the desk. He began talking about loyalty to the job and the work ethic of quality and quantity. The interview seemed to be more of a lecture than a test of intellectual awareness. I felt a little nervous as I answered a few questions. In response to one, 'Who does your father work for?' I said he was with the Turf Board since 1939. My answer seemed to impress Mr Usher, who lifted one eyebrow as a sign of respect. Much of what Mr Usher said is now a blur, but I do remember that the interview lasted twenty-five minutes.

On the way home my mother pummelled me with questions about how I had done. Seán was also curious but didn't press me and very soon my mother grew tired of my minute bits of information. In fact the interview had left me mentally jaded and I couldn't wait to get home.

My father was glad I had told the interviewer about his working record with the Turf Board. 'Good man, Pat. That should make him sit up. Come to think of it, me and my brother Martin cycled to Clonsast bog in 1939. That was when they were openin' up the bog and we were workin' at diggin' drains. It was the first time we worked for Bord na Móna.'

'Uncle Martin,' I said, 'didn't he play the melodeon?'

'Indeed and he did,' said my father. 'Poor Martin, he died in the Mater Hospital in Dublin. He was only nineteen. 'Twas meningitis that killed him. I was sitting beside the bed and I knew he was sufferin' a lot but I could do nothin' for him. He beat his head against the bedpost tryin' to ease the pain. He died shortly after that. It grieves me even now to think about it.'

My mother, who was mutilating a head of cabbage with her breadknife, was listening to my father as he spoke. 'Was Martin a good melodeon player?' she asked.

My father was surprised by the question. 'He was. I remember him on Saturday evenin's when he'd finished washin' and shavin' he'd sit on the hob by the fire and play for a couple of hours before goin' to bed.' My father was close to tears as he spoke.

The semi-final between Offaly and Roscommon proved to be another ding-dong battle, which was how Mícheál Ó hEithir described the game during his radio broadcast. In the end it was Offaly that won, thanks to some great scores from Daingean's Tommy Greene. Both teams played their hearts out but it was Tommy's contribution – two goals and two points – that swung the game in Offaly's favour.

Once again the people of Offaly were in a state of football fever with everyone itching for another crack at the footballers from the 'Mourne County' who on the following weekend beat Kerry in the other semi-final. It would be another historic showdown in which Offaly would face the current All-Ireland champions from County Down. It also meant that Offaly would play in their very first All-Ireland senior football final.

My father was anxious about how my interview had been evaluated by the Bord na Móna hierarchy in Boora. While he had no idea of what was what, he seemed resigned to the notion that I had an even chance. On the other hand my mother had settled into an attitude of keeping her fingers crossed, but underneath I believe she was hopeful of some supernatural intervention. 'A few prayers to the most attentive saint in heaven might do wonders,' a sympathetic neighbour had said. When he was asked who or what kind of saint he was thinking of, he said he'd find out from his missus. (It was almost a year before we saw him again.) This gave me the idea of asking my mother who the patron saint of musicians was. She said she didn't know. 'Anyway,' she added, 'who ever heard of a saint for musicians?' Later on I asked a few other people the same question but nobody knew of such a saint.

One day Mrs Behan stopped by on her way home from shopping. 'My God,' she cried, 'what will people be prayin' for next?' Her remarks didn't surprise me at all because I knew she hadn't a note in her head.

A week later, before the big game, a letter was delivered by Dan Kearns, the postman. Dan was an amiable sort. 'It looks like the letter you've been waitin' for, missus,' he said, handing it to my mother. 'It's from Dublin,' she said, looking at the postmark, and, blessing herself, she tore open the envelope. Having read it she looked at Dan and me. 'Jesus, Mary, and Joseph, our prayers have been answered!' she declared. She gave me the letter and as I read it I saw I was to begin a fitter's apprenticeship in Boora Engineering Works the following Monday morning, just five days away. That evening when my father came home we talked about the letter and the very short notice. 'That's the Monday after the match,' he said, 'it doesn't give us much time.' My parents were then faced with the dilemma of finding lodgings for me in Tullamore and working out how I would travel to Boora and back to Tullamore each morning and evening.

'Mary Kate,' said my father, 'Mary Kate. I'm goin' to Tullamore to have a chat with her. I'm sure she and Jimmy will have enough room for Paddy to stay with them until he gets used to the job.' My mother was restless but she had her own plan. 'I'm goin' to town to try and find Seán Lynch. He said to call on him if we needed someone to drive us anywhere. Maybe he wouldn't mind drivin' us to Boora again. And another thing we have to think of is how Paddy will go back and forth to his job each day. Surely to God there has to be someone from Tullamore that works in Boora, someone that drives there and back, but first of all I'll cycle to town and try and find Seán.' After a small amount of preparation she was ready, and on her way to Daingean.

As luck would have it, Seán was at home. After hearing the news, he said he'd be at our house at two o'clock the next day. In fact he pulled up at our gate at three o'clock; he was an hour late but we still had some time to spare. And so we began our second journey to Boora.

We arrived late in the afternoon and Seán parked his car in the car park. As we stepped out of the car we noticed a few fellows on their way to the car park. My mother quickly enquired from one of them about the availability of a seat in a car and if they knew of anyone with room enough for me. One of the men directed us to ask another fellow nearby, and my mother approached the man. 'Excuse me,' she said, 'I'm told you are Mr Doyle.'

'That's right, ma'am,' he replied.

'Someone said you might have room in your car and I'm wondering if you would mind carryin' my son Paddy to work. He's due to begin his apprenticeship here on Monday.'

'No problem,' said Mr Doyle.

'We will pay you whatever it is,' my mother told him.

Mr Doyle said he had other passengers and they paid him ten shillings each per week. My mother reached into her handbag and pulled out a red ten-shilling note. 'Take this, for the first week,' she said. 'I hear that Bord na Móna don't pay their workers' wages 'til the end of the first two weeks from when they begin workin'.'

On Saturday afternoon, the eve of the big game, my father cycled to Tullamore, continued through the town and all the way out to the Charleville Road and finally to Saint Colman's Terrace, where his first cousin, Mary Kate Maguire, lived at number 75. After a mug of tea he explained the circumstances of his visit, adding that there was little time for finding lodgings for me. Mary Kate agreed to take me in and when my father returned home he was visibly relieved and full of praise for his cousin. 'I knew she wouldn't let me down,' he kept saying. My mother quietly acknowledged how he felt, saying afterwards that Arthur Guinness has enough power to work wonders on the nature of a man overwhelmed by the 'gift of a good turn'.

The next day we were caught napping when we found our radio batteries unreliable and I had to cycle to Jimmy Quinn's house so I could listen to the broadcast of the Offaly–Down All-Ireland final. I remember that many people, including my father, had either gone to a neighbour's house or to a pub to hear Mícheál Ó hEithir's commentary on the game. While I listened to the broadcast I was burdened with a heavy sense of mixed feelings – nervous tension and befuddled thoughts about how I'd fare out in Boora. I tried to imagine my new lifestyle of rising early in the mornings and how I'd feel about living in Mary Kate's house, or if I'd feel at home there. I was also concerned about whether I'd be allowed to practise my accordion, or if the Maguires had a dislike for Irish traditional music. Then I heard Jimmy shout at me, 'Hey, Pat! It's half-time and Offaly are ahead!' My mind had wandered and I'd lost track of the game, but during the interval I started to feel positive about the outcome. Then I heard Jimmy and his mother saying how easy it was going to be for Offaly, who led Down by a couple of points.

However, when the match resumed Down went on the attack and countered with some quick scores that brought them to within a point. Fourteen minutes later Down went ahead after a goal by Brian Morgan. This was a major setback for the Offaly players, who began losing their momentum and were unable to recover their first-half display of clever catch-and-kick football. In the end they were outrun by Down's superior fitness. It was another heartbreaking defeat for the players, not to mention another huge disappointment for their devoted followers.

I cycled home as soon as the game was over with my mind set on what I needed to pack in my suitcase to get me through my first week away from home. I was already putting a list together of shirts, underwear and a couple of pairs of pants. Seán Lynch was to pick me up at ten o'clock and my mother said she would accompany us on the twelve-mile journey to Mary Kate's home. When I finished packing I had begun to eat a late supper when my Aunt Maggie stopped by. It was a surprise visit, a sort of send-off for me that she had planned. It was also something I never forgot. My mother was very emotional about my going away and I saw tears in her eyes. My father was in a practical mood, saying that one 'had to be cruel to be kind', and there was some reluctant agreement with what he said. Nevertheless my kindly aunt would still feel better if I remained at home. Just before Seán Lynch came she gave me a pound note as a parting gift and, of course, I didn't have the proper words to thank her. This memory has stayed in my mind for many, many years and if such a long-held memory is a true indication of my gratitude, then I have thanked my Aunt Maggie on behalf of everything that is me.

Soon afterwards we were on our way to Tullamore. I sat in the back seat with my accordion and suitcase. The entire journey took us half an hour on account of driving through the town, which was crammed with traffic that was still making its way home from 'the big game in Dublin'. Mary Kate's house was across the road from a surrounding wall that enclosed Charleville Castle and its landed estate. The wall ran along a stretch of road that began a mile southwest of Tullamore. A short distance on the opposite side of the wall was a small lane where we turned left into Saint Colman's Terrace. Another short distance brought us to the front gate of the Maguire home.

My mother went to the front door and used the heavy knocker. The door was opened almost immediately, revealing a dark silhouette that was Mary Kate. 'Well, hello Molly,' she said, 'come on in.' The three of us went inside to what was the sitting room and sat down. My mother was quick to say that she wasn't going to stay very long and that there was no need for tea. Mary Kate offered me cocoa and I said, 'Yes please.' Her husband Jimmy came from their bedroom and shook hands with me and said I was welcome and that I was to make myself at home. Mary Kate brought the cocoa and a few biscuits on a plate while my mother was apologising to Seán Lynch for neglecting the introductions. Jimmy was very casual about it all with his warm grin and kind words of welcome. I felt relieved by his sense of humour and later on he and I became good friends. A short time later we said our goodbyes and then I heard Seán's car pulling away. It was then I realised how alone I was and so I told Mary Kate and Jimmy I was tired and they showed me my room. Within minutes I was fast asleep.

It was 6.30 a.m. when I woke to the sound of Mary Kate's voice. 'Paddy, it's time to get up.' Minutes later I was washing the sleep from my eyes with cold water in the bathroom. There was no heated water, which meant that water was usually boiled for a bath or when Jimmy needed to shave. I had a quick breakfast of a boiled egg, tea and brown bread and butter. Mary Kate had my lunch packed in a tin box that I took with me. I ran the short distance to where I'd stand on the side of the main road and wait for Paddy Doyle's Volkswagen. As I waited I was serenaded by the cawing sound of crows calling each other through the wind in the trees. It was an eerie atmosphere of low-lying fog with the mysterious wall of the estate across the road from where I stood. After ten minutes I saw the Volkswagen break through the mist and pull up beside me. Paddy Doyle was already leaning across the passenger seat when he pushed the door open. 'Hello, young fella, get in,' he shouted. I sat in the front seat beside Paddy. 'You have the best seat in the car,' he said, 'not like the three shits in the back.'

'Now now, Paddy, control yourself,' said Gerry Ryan.

'Will you listen to him?' yelled Blackie Kennedy.

'You pair of jinnies don't get it,' said Paddy, who seemed to be enjoying himself. 'This young fellow here is my number one passenger, and don't you know why?' No one said anything. 'His mother approached me last week, and she paid me in advance. Now,' he said, 'what do you three fucks think of that?'

'Fair play to you, Paddy,' said Dessie O'Neill, 'you were always an auld charmer even if you are still full of it.'

The other two lads were giggling when Blackie let go a rasper of a Monday morning fart that had the effect of imposing a short interlude in the car, that is until Paddy recovered and shouted, 'Kennedy, yer a rotten maggot, there's a dead calf inside of yeh.' Paddy and the lads seemed to enjoy teasing each other while I listened in surprise and private wonder. Nevertheless I was totally amused by what they were saying, because in reality I would be travelling to and fro to work with a car load of comedians.

Before I knew it we had travelled past the Blue Ball crossroads and were then on our way through a brown bogland area that lay along each side of the road. Looking out from the car I saw where harvested peat lay in rows of long stockpiles all across a vast acreage as far as I could see. In a matter of minutes we passed through Leabeg and then turned left, off the road and onto a small sandy road that led to the workshop. I noticed that the building wasn't visible until we came to the car park. Paddy told me to follow him into the main workshop. After I checked in I was escorted to a small tea room by one of the office staff. There were six other new fellows in the room and like myself they were very shy and withdrawn.

We opened up to each other as the morning moved on and at ten o'clock we devoured sandwiches and mugs of tea. Near lunch time we were joined by another lad who seemed to know his way around. He explained that his father was a personnel manager and that he knew many of the senior fitters employed in the workshop. He was in a very talkative mood and appeared very sure of himself. At first I didn't know what to make of him except he was from Tullamore and his father was from Cork. During lunchtime another fellow came into the room and began filling his canteen with boiling water. When he saw us he smirked, saying, 'What have we got here?'

Someone said, 'Who are you?'

'Mull,' he replied, 'Mull. I'm from the "sparks" shop.'

'That's a good name for someone who forgot to wash the bog stuff out of his ears,' said the confident fellow.

Mull winked at the rest of us. 'Be careful of what you say to him, his auld man is a manager in the front office.'

The confident fellow blushed. 'Mull,' he said, 'that was below the belt.'

'All's fair in love and war,' countered Mull, who having filled his canteen was on his way out the door. When he was gone I asked who he was and the confident one said, 'That's Kevin Muldowney. He's a second-year apprentice electrician. By the way, I'm Peter Hogan,' he continued, 'some people call me Peadar.' He was looking at us like he expected us to say something and then he began to chuckle.

After lunch we were taken on a tour of the various workshop departments by a man who worked in the workshop office as a time-keeper. 'This is the Gearbox Department,' he said, 'and the man with the light brown coat is John Flynn. He's in charge here.' A short distance further on we were in the Locomotive Department, where we were introduced to an older man, the overseer of repairs, one Gerry Conroy, who was a very skinny individual in his early sixties. Gerry eyed us with a certain amount of suspicion, then turned away and went about his business.

As we left the Locomotive area a tall, green door was opened and we walked into an adjacent area. We were told it was the Harvester Shed. This was a huge place which accommodated three massive machines that had long jibs protruding out of the side of each vehicle. Looking upwards I saw a long crane that reached across from the near side to the far side of the building. Its span was probably eighty feet and it was located on rails at a height of about fifty feet. It could be rolled back and forth when a motor was operated by pushing a button on a box that was linked to the bottom of an electric cord attached to another motor on the crane. A huge chain with a heavy hook dangled from it and this was also manipulated by buttons on the same control box. The hook was used for lifting heavy machine parts.

Next we came to a corrugated sliding door, and stepping through it our escort warned us about the next floor level being lower than the door rail. 'This is where we repair the ridgers and millers,' the office man said. We continued walking until we came to what he called the Engine Department. The charge hand there was Johnny Owens, who was a stocky fellow in his thirties and wearing a black beret. He was standing beside a tractor engine and appeared to be in deep consultation with another man whom I later knew as Martin Coughlan. I could see that the emphasis there was on diesel engines and other related tasks that kept a large fleet of Massey Ferguson tractors in readiness for harvest duties.

Our tour party then moved across the shop floor to a small side door that opened to a very wide concrete yard on the outside of the building. While we were looking around, a runt of a little man, clad in another brown overcoat, came trotting over to where we were walking among a herd of tractors. 'This is Mossey Greene,' our tour guide said with a smile. 'He's in charge of the millers and ridgers.'

'Hello, young fellas,' said Mossey. 'One of you is starting with me tomorrow, it's young O'Brien as far as I know,' he went on. 'Is young O'Brien here?' he asked.

I raised my right hand. 'That's me.'

Mossey looked at me with a grin. 'Don't worry,' he said, 'we won't work you too hard.'

We strolled back to the front bay area where the tea room was located and we continued to follow our man, who finally told us who he was – Vincent Daly. He then showed us through a small door with a glass window and announced, 'This is the Electricity Shop,' which was another department just off the big bay area. It was a small cell of a place with a couple of short benches to work at. There were a couple of electricians at work and two apprentices cleaning batteries. Mick Callery was the eldest man there. He wore a hat that concealed the fact that he was bald and I later learned it was a sensitive issue with him. During the following months we became familiar with particular sensitivities or vulnerabilities of some of the workmen, and these so-called flaws gave some apprentices more than a little ammunition for laughter.

Near the Electricity or 'Sparks' Shop was the Lathe Shop. When we went inside, two operators were busy beside lathes that were revolving furiously, turning out long ringlets of skimmed metal, while a third fellow was working a drill press. A young second-year apprentice was operating a third lathe, skimming the welded edges of rollers that would later be used as wheels.

We departed the Lathe Shop and walked along the workshop floor until we came again to the tea room. Our tour guide, Vincent, said we should make some tea as a way to while away our time until five, our time to clock out. However, we were left in a state of limbo as to what was expected and most of us had no idea of where we were to begin our duties the next day.

That evening Paddy Doyle dropped me off at the top of Saint Colman's Terrace, which was where he would pick me up again the next morning. 'See you tomorrow,' he said as I got out. When I arrived at Mary Kate's I could smell the bacon and cabbage she had prepared. 'Get that into yeh,' she said as I sat down. She had some boiled potatoes laid out in a bowl and I set about peeling one. Looking at me across the table she said, 'I'm goin' to take a walk into O'Connor Square in Tullamore this evenin'. The Offaly football team are comin' home on the train from Dublin and there's a big crowd expected to welcome them.' When I said nothing she offered, 'Would you like to come along?', and when I replied, 'Yeah, I suppose so,' she smiled.

It was an hour later when we began the twenty-minute walk to O'Connor Square, arriving at 7.30 p.m. This was where the team and its supporters were scheduled to gather for the big welcoming. At the far end of the square in front of the vocational school a platform was ready, having been built on the back of a long lorry, with decorated railings on each side. Another long lorry was waiting at the train station and would carry the team from there to where a massive crowd waited in the square. We were standing on High Street, but when we tried to force our way through the crowd we couldn't make any progress with so many people jamming the entrance to the square. While we waited, more people thronged the street and soon we were swallowed by a deluge of Offaly supporters. Suddenly a mighty cheer erupted as the lorry was seen crawling down the hill in the middle of High Street. The side guards of the lorry were covered with the Offaly colours of green, white and orange. When it came to the levelled part of the street we could see most of the team. Many of them were waving at the crowd. Mary Kate was also waving and pulling at the sleeve of my coat. 'There's Phil Reilly and Paddy McCormack!' she shouted. I had already seen them and noticed how all of the team were wearing suits with white shirts and striped ties of blue, red, maroon and grey. Then I saw Tommy Greene and Mick Casey, who were heroes of mine. Everyone was in a fantastic mood, almost as though the county had won its first All-Ireland. The crowd were relentless in shouting and cheering, and some people were doing a little solo dancing. Then the lorry made a right turn into the square but stopped for five minutes. The local Guards had to intervene and help make way so the lorry could continue its crawl to the far end of the square. When it finally arrived the team changed lorries, a sound system was quickly tested, and John Dowling gave his welcome home speech on behalf of everyone in the Faithful County. Again the crowd went wild as John gave an eloquent appraisal of a great Offaly team that contributed so much to the game and achieved a remarkable first-time appearance in an All-Ireland football final. Other GAA leaders spoke of the great honour of it all. Another man gave three cheers to the Down team that overcame a heroic and gallant bunch of Offaly footballers to win their second All-Ireland final.

Mary Kate gave me a nudge with her hand; it was time to go home. As we were walking up High Street we saw a separate crowd of bystanders on each side of the towpath and some standing on the street. In the middle was a bare-knuckle fight between a fellow of about twenty-five and a lean, bald-headed man of perhaps fifty. They were circling each other like two roosters when the younger lad landed a nice one on the jaw of the older man, who was knocked out of his stride but steadied himself and made a rush at the younger man, who ducked out of the way just in time. Mary Kate pulled at my coat. 'Let's get past these eejits,' she said. When we came to the island at the top of High Street I looked back down the hill and saw the two fighters still swinging at each other. They were not finished. Mary Kate saw me and said, 'I wonder what all that is about?'

53

The First Day of Work

The next morning I waited again at the top of the lane. Paddy Doyle was ten minutes late but I didn't say anything. When I got into the car a heated argument was in full swing. Paddy was staring over the steering wheel as he drove. A mischievous grin flooded his face and I saw him looking into the rear-view mirror. 'What do you think, Pat?' he said to me. 'What do you think? The three fucks in the back think that Offaly deserved to lose.'

'Wait a minute,' cried Blackie. 'Come on, Paddy. We didn't say that.'

'Hey,' said Paddy, 'didn't I hear you say that Down had a great team? But I didn't hear you say that Offaly had a great team.'

'Aw, come on Paddy,' said Gerry, 'yer just pissed off because they lost.'

'Of course I'm fuckin' pissed off! We should have fuckin' won!'

'Paddy, Paddy,' yelled Dessie O'Neill, 'will you watch the fuckin' road! Jesus!'

Arriving at the workshop I was given a card and shown how to clock in to work and how to clock out each day. Lal Daly escorted me down to the very far end of the workshop to where Mossey Greene was in charge. When we got there Mossey was sitting in his small office, which was an upright wooden box with glass windows in front and on the right side. It was 6½ feet in height and each side was 3½ feet in width. The left side was open and served as a doorway. Its sliding door was already pulled back. Lal shouted, 'Hey, Mossey, I have a new young lad here. He's one of the new apprentices.'

Mossey stepped out of his box. 'Yes, yes,' he said, 'I've been expectin' him,' and then he looked me up and down. He was a small man, five foot five, with a round red face and black hair. His brown overcoat was too big for him and its sleeves came down over the knuckles of his hands. He eyed me like it was the first time he'd seen anyone in over a year. 'Aha,' he said to Lal. 'Okay, Mr Daly, you can leave him with me.'

'Young man,' he said, 'if you follow me I have the very man for you to work with.' We walked a short distance to where a man was bent over cutting the heads off bolts from the scraping blade of a ridger. He was using an acetylene/oxygen blowtorch and was wearing dark goggles as protection for his eyes. He was unaware of us until Mossey tapped him on the shoulder.

All at once he stood up, turned off the torch, and removed his goggles. 'Mossey, what can I do for you?' he said.

'Paddy, this young fella is startin' his apprenticeship today and I'm puttin' him with you for a few months.'

'What's yer name?' asked the man, who looked at me with a sheepish grin.

'Paddy,' I said.

'The same name as meself,' said the man.

'This is Paddy Murphy,' Mossey interjected.

'And yer last name, young man?' asked Murphy.

'O'Brien,' said I.

'All right,' said Mossey, 'I want you to watch Mr Murphy, watch everything he does. He's your senior fitter, and whatever job-related task he asks you to do you will do it, won't you?'

'Yes,' I replied, and then Mossey walked back to his box.

Paddy seemed to relax after Mossey's departure. Lighting a cigarette, he said, 'Well how're ya, Paudgeen?' Before I answered he added, 'Don't mind that little bollocks. He thinks he's the bee's knees. A well-directed kick in the hole is what he needs!'

Hearing Paddy speak relaxed me but at the same time I was dumbfounded and didn't know what to say. He was a friendly sort, a man of good nature, and his off-hand manner did a lot to settle me into my new surroundings. As we got to know each other we shared a lot of questions and answers. He later told me that Mossey was from County Cavan and that he wouldn't 'spend Christmas'. It later transpired that this was a prime case of the pot calling the kettle black. I would later learn that small-minded backbiting was a typical trait among many who worked together in an enclosed environment. However, at that time it entertained and amused me greatly. Paddy was a great man at coaxing conversation and before the day ended I had talked about the music and told him that I played the single-row accordion. He was curious about this and asked what kind of music I played. When I told him it was Irish traditional, he said, 'It's an awful pity you weren't around when Francie Brereton worked here.' Paddy went on about him being a great tradesman, a wonderful box player and devoted musician. 'He used to lodge in Bill Coughlan's house in Cloghan. When you see Bill you should ask him about Francie.'

It was a very inspirational moment when I heard about Francie. My curiosity was awakened and I had several questions for Paddy. What kind of accordion did he play? Did he have many tunes? But Paddy didn't know anything more, so I gave up.

After a few days it became clear to me that I wasn't expected to do much work, if any. Each day I stood around watching Paddy as he went about cutting warped steel rods, bolts, or tie bars that needed replacing. After one o'clock dinner break I usually felt refreshed, until one late afternoon when I felt a sense of tiredness, and my feet were sore from standing on the concrete floor. It was the beginning of many repeated instances of what the workshop floor meant to many beginners in Boora. After every half-hour or so Paddy would quench his torch and smoke half a cigarette while he had me posted as a lookout in case Mossey caught him off guard. On one of these occasions while he blew a blast of blue smoke from his mouth one of the side doors suddenly opened and shut with a loud clanging noise. Paddy quickly dropped his fag and was about to pull his goggles over his eyes when he saw the fella that came through the door. 'In the name of Jaysus,' he yelled, 'where the fuck did you spring from?'

'Stop cursin' in front of the young lad,' said the fella, who explained, 'I'm finished over in Drinagh for this year anyway.'

'So now yer back in the workshop for the winter?'

'Yeah,' said the fella.

'Well,' Paddy continued, 'we have a new musician here; that should keep you and yer banjo busy.'

The fella looked at me enquiringly and then turned to Paddy. 'Is this him?'

'Young Paddy O'Brien, who else?' replied Paddy, who was looking at me with a grin on his face like he was presenting me proudly at an auction. I was immediately curious about the banjo player and I asked him his name.

'Seamus Egan,' said he. 'And what do you play?'

'The accordion,' I said eagerly.

'Paddy O'Brien, Paddy O'Brien,' repeated Seamus, 'isn't there another Paddy O'Brien who plays somethin'?' Seamus was thinking before he spoke again. 'Yeah, he's from Tipperary, I hear he's a genius on the box.' We started to talk about the music and musicians of note but were interrupted a few minutes later by the wailing sound of the workshop siren, its noise drowning us out, but at least it was time to quit for the day.

Paddy Doyle's Volkswagen was usually alive with wit and humour, and Paddy was a formidable fellow at teasing or getting someone's dander up. Dessie O'Neill was a laid-back and quiet sort of lad. Sometimes his eyes were closed during the journey, giving the impression that he was asleep. I found out later that his eyes were prone to being sore from the flash of welders, or from working at long-term welding jobs. 'Aren't you the sly auld fox,' began Paddy one evening when some of us were half asleep. 'Gold diggin', isn't that what we call it?'

'Who's gold diggin'?' enquired Blackie Kennedy.

'Didn't you hear about sleepin' beauty back there?' said Paddy, 'and he dancin' with an auld one twice his age.'

'Where was this?' Gerry Ryan spoke up.

'At the Marquee, where Dickie Rock was playin' Sunday night.'

'Jaysus,' said Blackie, 'what's the harm in that?'

'But,' said Paddy, 'the same woman is known to be connected to an old moneyed family. Fair play to yeh, Dessie, I like a fella who values an opportunity.'

I looked back at Dessie and saw him opening his eyes. 'Mandrake,' he shouted, 'shut the fuck up.' Paddy's nickname, Mandrake, came from the name of a magician featured in a comic strip in the *Irish Independent* newspaper.

'It's the money yer after, isn't it?' Paddy roared. 'Have you no—'

'Mandrake,' shouted Dessie again, 'you shit-stirring weasel.'

'Jaysus, Dessie, we thought you were asleep, we were just havin' a joke amongst ourselves, sorry.' Paddy's voice had taken on a tone of concern but Dessie wasn't impressed.

Raising his own voice, he yelled, 'Be the holy Jaysus, will you listen to him now? It's in the confession box he should be.'

Paddy was a genius at garnering sympathy and with the aid of his dark eyes, wide open as they were like large pools of pity, he would withdraw momentarily into his own world of quiet approval. In a short while I noticed he was once again staring into the rear-view mirror, and with an expression of innocent wonder he began warming the three lads into another topic. The Volkswagen was pulling to a stop at the top of the lane and as I got out I wondered who was next and what kind of angle he had in mind for either Blackie or Gerry.

Mary Kate was sitting close to the range when I entered the kitchen; she was finishing a cigarette. My dinner was ready and when she put it on the table I began eating while she sat waiting to hear how my day went. She was a fair-haired woman in her early fifties, with sharp blue eyes and fair skin. Her face held the grim look of someone who knew what she wanted. She wore a light blue cardigan and dark grey skirt, covered by a large white apron. On that particular evening it occurred to me she was trying to size me up or perhaps she was curious about getting to know me. Both of us were at a disadvantage of not knowing much about each other and conversation was slow in coming. In the beginning I offered bits of news or small talk of Paddy Doyle's teasing habits in the car. 'I'm not surprised,' she said. 'I knew Paddy when he worked in Sault's factory. He was a great character and always full of devilment.'

After dinner I excused myself and went to my room for a rest. When I lay on my bed my thoughts turned to Francie Brereton and the music. Apparently Francie had quit working in Boora just a couple of weeks before I started my time there. As I thought about it more I became mindful of the bad luck of missing such a golden opportunity – an opportunity that was gone like a feather in the wind. In an effort to heal my disappointment I jumped up from the bed and reached for my little Hohner accordion and began playing 'The Cook in the Kitchen'. Playing this tune turned into a long practice session that included many different jigs and reels. It was dark inside the room when I realised I'd been at the accordion for a little over two hours and had forgotten to turn on the electric switch. This developed into a habit of mine, almost like a continuation of when I practised so often in the dark room at my home in Castlebarnagh.

At Boora I eventually settled into the everyday routine of standing beside Paddy Murphy. This became a solitary bore of waiting and watching, and my feet continued to ache in reaction to the hard cement floor. After some three months Paddy allowed me to use his cutting torch. At first he had me practise on some scrap metal. Then he showed me how to cut the heads off steel bolts that would free old, worn swamp shoes (wooden tracks) from their caterpillar holdings. I made good progress at this and after an hour my use of the torch gave me a great sense of achievement and confidence.

When winter came, Mossey's Ridger Department was a pretty cold place, with draughty wind currents drifting across the workshop from the constant opening and shutting of its side doors. Fitters and older apprentices would clap their hands crossways on each shoulder to keep themselves warm.

There were a number of men who worked as fitter's helpers who often moved from one work situation to another. This depended on the circumstances of manual labour, where lifting a heavy sprocket into place was too much for one man or pulling swamp shoes into position and linking them together, another strenuous task. On one occasion, while Paddy stood by waiting for a helper he left me in charge of a three-foot sprocket which he had balanced upright on the floor. My job was to hold it in place and not let it fall on the floor. The sprocket was a heavy object, its weight in the region of a hundred and twenty pounds. While I was holding it Mossey came for a visit and began chatting with Paddy. Paddy offered Mossey a cigarette and, turning towards me, said that I should watch the sprocket and not let it tip over. I realised what he said was for Mossey's benefit and not mine and it had the effect of breaking my concentration. While they were chatting I somehow lost control of the sprocket and its weight knocked me off balance. I tried desperately to hold on to it but it was too heavy and it fell. There was a very deep thud followed by a long ringing sound as it hit the floor.

Mossey jumped. 'Jesus!' he screamed. The heavy sprocket had missed his legs by inches, and when Paddy turned towards me his face had turned white. Mossey looked at the sprocket and then at me. At first he didn't know what happened, or what to say. I could see he was very shaken.

'You bold brat,' he crowed. 'Remember, this will be written down in your first-quarter report.' Then he turned and retreated quickly along the workshop floor and back to the sanctuary of his little box.

'Serves him right,' said Paddy, who had recovered his composure and was now loving every minute of it. 'Wait 'til the lads hear about this.' I was feeling terrible about what happened and despite what Paddy said to me I felt disoriented and guilty.

A couple of weeks later I was moved to the Gearbox Department for six months. Here I became familiar with the company of John Flynn, Éamon Fleming and a third-year apprentice, Kevin Coffey. Our foreman, John Flynn, wasted little time in giving me the task of washing small rollers and journal bearings in a tray of diesel oil. He presented me with a small, narrow paint brush with which to remove dirty grease from within the bearings. Very soon I was making friends and as I got to know Éamon Fleming I learned of his ability as a footballer with his home club, Clara. He was also a member of Offaly's senior football team as a full forward and as a substitute during the famous semi-final against Down in 1960. He was a quiet and thoughtful man, six feet tall, a man of solid integrity and a tradesman who contributed greatly as a fitter. He also had a sympathetic sensibility for apprentices and encouraged us with subtle words and gestures of even-handedness and guidance.

The Gearbox Department had two workbenches with small wooden pallets on the floor for standing on. My work often entailed filing and scraping splines to be fitted into differential gearboxes and sprockets. My standing position was very convenient as a vantage point because it was in an open area where I could see various workers walking back and forth from the store hatch. This kind of going and coming was a common part of a day's work in Boora and very often groups of three or four fellows would stand at the hatch, waiting for service or while being helped by the store attendants. Among the many items ordered at the hatch were armfuls of cotton rags which were used by everyone for drying or cleaning our hands. Like everything else, a requisition was required and had to be written and signed by a foreman or a charge hand. There was a story about a fitter in the Locomotive Department who faked a requisition and gave it to his apprentice who went to the hatch door and waited. When the store attendant, Johnny Fox, came asking for the requisition the young lad handed it to Johnny who read it and walked away with a grin on his face, and little wonder. Written on the piece of paper were the words 'one long stand'. Fox disappeared and left the apprentice standing for half an hour at the hatch. When Fox returned the lad was still waiting. He said, 'What kind of fuckin' lame brain are you? Don't you know what a long stand is?' Johnny was a sporting kind of fellow and could be very funny. He loved to impress the younger apprentices with stories about how he lured some girls into his web and how easy it was for the girls to fall under his spell. One of his opening lines was that he was a businessman who owned a stable of prized stallions. While talking to him at the hatch I was surprised when he said, 'I hear you play the accordion.' I asked him how he knew but before he could answer, a dark-complexioned man of about forty came up beside me. 'Hello Bill,' said Johnny.

Bill looked at me and said, 'You're one of the new young lads, God bless ya.' Johnny looked at me and said, 'This is Bill Coughlan.' This came as a surprise and I asked, 'Is it true you knew Francie Brereton?'

'Indeed, and I did,' answered Bill. After Johnny introduced us Bill and I began talking and Bill had great stories about Francie and the music. Listening to Bill fired my imagination, inspired my tenacity for playing and motivated me into buying a new Paolo Soprani accordion at a time when I had very limited wages.

My travels to and from work with Paddy and the lads was more often than not a time of hilarious banter between him and the lads in the back seat. Gerry Ryan would try to counter Paddy's slagging by referring to himself as 'brainy' and 'salubrious' and saying that Paddy didn't merit an answer from a fella of such high intelligence as he. It was, of course, a ploy Gerry used to try and rattle Paddy, and in return Paddy would launch into an exaggerated laugh that prompted a nervous Dessie to roar, 'Watch the fuckin' road.' The truth is we never knew for sure if Paddy was ever rattled, or if he was just bluffing. In reality it was the stuff of friendship and I learned something new each day. Paddy's Volkswagen was my first university, a seat of learning for words and ways that loosened my own humour and developing wit. It was a listening experience that bolstered my confidence and liberated me from some of my inhibitions.

After eight months I was still working in John Flynn's Gearbox Department and had served almost a year of my apprenticeship. Meanwhile word had gotten around that I was a musician, which gave some of my workmates ammunition for some teasing. The first upstart was Gerry Ryan, who stole up behind me and speaking directly into my left ear made a suggestion that I would soon be sucking up to 'Ould Tray', our nickname for Andy Freer, who was a senior foreman in the department next to ours and a producer of variety shows in the Foresters' Hall in Tullamore. 'Don't worry,' said Gerry, 'you're next on the list, he'll be jawin' into yer ear in no time and yer ear will be yellow from you know what.'

During the same year the workforce in Boora was being supplemented with additional fitters, many of whom had served their apprenticeships as garage mechanics in Tullamore. I was intrigued when told that one of them was Tom Nolan and that he played the pipes and was also an ex-member of the Ballinamere Céilí Band. Furthermore, from talking with Seamus Egan I learned that Tom played a practice set of uilleann pipes. A week later, while standing at my workbench I noticed a dark-haired fellow working inside the adjacent area, which was the Loco Department. Having asked Kevin Coffey who the man was, Kevin said he thought it was the piper from Tullamore. Without delay I went over to where the fellow knelt beside a small engine. He was busy with a ratchet.

'Hello,' I said mildly, 'I hear you play the pipes.'

Tom looked up at me cautiously. 'Ah, a bit.' Tom was twenty-five years old and seemed to be a shy sort. It was several weeks before he opened up to me but in a short time it became clear that he had a deep passion for traditional music.

Gerry was spot on when he teased me about the senior foreman, and as he had said, one day I was approached by Andy, who out of nowhere was suddenly standing beside me. As he spoke from the side of his mouth I felt him breathing into my left ear. It was as though he used one's ear as a microphone each time he spoke to someone and I still remember what he said to me. 'I hear you play the accordion. Maybe you wouldn't mind playin' a few tunes for me. I'm puttin' on a bit of a concert in a couple of months and a few of the lads from here are with me as well.' Andy had a way of softening his voice, coupled with a low droning tone that was intended to imply confidentiality. It was his way of coaxing fellows on the job to do something that was a major inconvenience. As I listened I was overcome by Andy's authority and persuasiveness, and before I knew it I was outfoxed and defenceless.

My meek answer was a nervous, 'Yes, I'll give it a go,' even though I had never played at a concert in my life! After Andy disappeared into the next department I was stricken with butterflies in my stomach, because even though I knew the concert wasn't scheduled for at least another two months, the prospect of playing in front of a crowd of people gave me the willies.

The Forge was a small square building beside the car park. Its dark interior contained a red-hot furnace with a large bellows for pumping air under its fire. Two to three men worked together in continuous movement, heating, hammering, re-shaping and bending all kinds of steel brackets, angle irons, tie bars and more. Most of the steel repair work belonged to ridgers, harvesters and several other machines that were used on the bogs. My first visit there was to pick up a small drive shaft. The Forge entrance had a sliding door that was pulled open, allowing a long, wide channel iron girder to stick out through the doorway. When I walked inside I saw Bill Coughlan fitting a steel plate to its other end by using heavy rivets with his muscle-powered hammer. When he saw me he stopped working and asked, 'How're ya getting' on with the music?' I told him I was learning a couple of jigs and that I was hoping to buy a new Paolo Soprani accordion when I got my second-year raise.

He seemed to know I wanted news about Francie Brereton. 'You know,' he said, 'Brereton was a lodger in my house for a year or so. He was a fuckin' slave to the music, that's what he was. Ya know, after he ate his dinner in the evenin's he would go to his room and practise on the box for hours. He was indeed a very serious musician. I remember him playin' in the All-Ireland accordion competition one year, but he was placed second. It was a big disappointment.' Bill grinned when he told me that Francie swore he'd never play again in a competition. The experience was nerve-racking and it caused him to miss a couple of notes. Bill was looking at the ground. 'Only for that he would have won it. "Farewell to Éireann", that's the reel he played.' Bill seemed almost angry as he continued, 'Why in the name of fuck he played such a hard fuckin' tune in a competition is beyond me. Do you know it?' I told him I knew bits of it, but not all of it. Bill was in a passionate mood and was just warming to his story. 'It's a fucker of a reel and there's a jump in it from the top of the keys to the bottom ones, and Brereton could do it! Oh God, he was a mighty tulip and totally dedicated. And another thing about him . . . ' Bill lowered his voice to explain . . . 'he was a very tasty tradesman and a terrific welder.' Before saying I'd better go, Bill told me he hadn't forgotten about the photos. These were a couple of old black and white pictures of Francie and a flute player, taken at a Fleadh Cheoil when he played in a duet competition with P.J. Maloney, also from Tipperary.

After Christmas 1963 I was told to begin a spell in the Lathe Department for what turned out to be another six months. My job there was either bench work or using a drilling machine. I was amazed at the many sizes of drill bits available and the various adjustments the drilling table could accommodate. The bench work was of a tedious nature that involved the use of an assortment of files. The files were of various sizes: some were flat, some round, square or triangular. It was the kind of work that exhausted my spiritual energy and deadened my mental capacity for creative development and limited the novelty of discovery. In those days I didn't know how to discern or even understand how I felt, but later as I came to know other young apprentices I found that all of us shared a common complaint: boredom.

At weekends I would take the eleven o'clock Saturday morning bus from High Street in Tullamore to Daingean. My family were always happy to see me and were anxious to know how I was doing in Boora, or if I had met anyone strange or unusual. I told them that I had met some eccentric people but had yet to figure out which end of them was up. I tried to add some spice to small pieces of news but generally I lacked any energy for gossip-style reporting. My mother revelled in the role of inquisitor until finally she became frustrated with my inability to entertain. In other words she had come up against a genuine teenager. My return to Tullamore was on the 9 p.m. Sunday bus. It was a matter of routine to walk with my accordion and suitcase from the bus stop to Mary Kate and Jimmy's house. It usually took me twenty-five minutes to finish my weekend return journey from Castlebarnagh.

The idea of buying a new Paolo Soprani box was gathering momentum in my mind, especially since I had seen some on display in the window of Kilroy's furniture store on High Street. The notion of paying for it through a hire purchase agreement meant I'd have it paid for in a couple of years. But my purchase would depend on how Mary Kate responded to the idea. I was supposed to give her an extra pound and ten shillings for my lodging when I received my annual raise, but I desperately wanted to put that money towards the new accordion. I was extremely nervous when I asked Mary Kate about it, saying I would pay all that I owed her after my next raise in the months ahead. When she agreed to this I was moved beyond words, but being a young fellow I wasn't able to convey to her the depth of my gratitude and appreciation. In the end I was never able to truly thank her for her help and consideration, and fate decreed that I never had the opportunity. This is something I've very much regretted. One evening some time later Mary Kate told me during dinner that she and Jimmy were emigrating to Australia and that she was beginning to put in motion preparations for what would be a huge change in their lives. She said her daughter Alice would also be going with them when the time was right, which she said would be in another year. She added that this would give me enough time to organise my own arrangements for new lodgings in Tullamore and that there was no hurry.

After purchasing my new accordion I withdrew more and more to my bedroom where I would practise for two to three hours during the evenings. It was some time later, when talking to another box player, that I learned that my C/C# box wasn't tuned for playing along with other concert-pitch instruments such as the fiddle, flute or banjo. It was a disadvantage that no musician wanted to accommodate or deal with, and it irritated me to the point of exasperation. After further thought I decided that I'd visit Kilroy's on High Street and talk to one of the salesmen about the possibility of trading it for a B/C box.

Each morning as I waited at the top of the lane, the never-ending chorus of crows cawing and flying from tree to tree played games with my imagination, inspired in part by memories of Alfred Hitchcock movies. I have always regarded crows' calls to each other as a lonely, forlorn sound of anxiety when accompanied by wind, rain or morning fog. It was just such a morning when Paddy and the lads pulled up and once again I limbered into the front seat. Paddy was in his usual element as he opened up and began ribbing me about being 'Tray's little yes man.' He had heard from Andy that I was to play in his variety show. 'Hey lads,' Paddy started, 'did ye hear about our prized passenger here in the front?'

'Mandrake,' yelled Dessie O'Neill, 'aren't you a right feckin' hypocrite.'

'What did I do?' exclaimed an incredulous Paddy.

'What did you not do?' Dessie continued, still shouting. 'Didn't you sing and dance in Freer's show for the past two years?' The other two lads began cheering and laughing and Paddy fell silent. Dessie had saved me.

My work in the Lathe Shop was a continuous routine of very simple work duties, and all the while, unknown to anyone, I was piecing together tune selections or lilting and learning them in my mind. It was a very private type of exercise and I lived it each day. One of the young turners, standing on a wooden pallet in front of his lathe, was a third-year apprentice whom we knew as Mickey Foy. As well as being an exceptional turner he had an amazing capacity for joking and taking the mickey out of anyone and everyone who came under the spell of his wit. Mickey was also drawn to traditional music and with this understanding he was someone I relied on as a supporter and confidant and with him I became more vocal in my quest for musical information. I still remember how he coaxed and persuaded me to play a solo at a small fundraising concert in his home village of Killeigh.

When the night came I was already frightened out of my wits sitting in the back seat of a car driven by Joe Lee as we made our way to the concert. Joe's girlfriend Dolores Plunkett did all she could to console and encourage me but none of it had any effect. When I finally sat on a chair and the curtain opened I was shocked by the sight of a sea of faces that came right up to the edge of the stage, all waiting in anticipation. And then I started to play and the tunes lifted my spirits and a sense of calm came over me; before I knew it I had played three selections. As I departed from the stage I could hear a loud commotion of yells, clapping, whistling and feet banging the floor. It was the first time I played solo in public, thanks to the persuasive powers of Mickey Foy and Dolores Plunkett.

Over a period of several months a musical understanding developed between Tom Nolan, Seamus Egan and myself. As we became friends, both of them were very generous with their music and contributed greatly to my repertoire. They also provided me with extra knowledge of the tune titles and this in turn impressed upon me a mental image of the sound of each tune. Throughout my life as a musician these images, along with the tune titles, were of tremendous benefit when I needed to memorise a tune. It's difficult for some people to understand why so many different jigs, reels, etc. come alive in my memory from the mere mention of their names. This phenomenon is the result of practice and an acute instinct for the sound of particular music, which in my case is Irish traditional music. It has been extraordinarily useful throughout my career when rehearsing with bands, recording, or suggesting music at sessions when a particular repertoire is more appropriate for flutes or other instruments. For example, if one were to say the names Seamus Egan or Tom Nolan to me I could immediately remember many of the tunes we played together over forty years ago.

The Harvester Bay was situated halfway down a long block of buildings that made up Boora Engineering Works. I knew I was due to do several months of my apprenticeship there and so I wasn't surprised when Andy Freer came to me one afternoon and said I was being moved there and that I was to bring my toolbox and follow him. The foreman in charge was a quiet-spoken County Roscommon man by the name of Bernie Jennings. Andy introduced me to Bernie, who nodded his head slightly before taking a final pull on a Players cigarette. At first he didn't say anything, preferring to listen instead as Andy talked about some minor job-related issue that had nothing to do with Bernie. When Andy was on his way out of the door Bernie threw the tiny cigarette butt onto the floor and with a simple movement of his right foot crushed it under the heel of his shoe. 'Wait here,' he said, and then he disappeared between two of the huge harvesters that were in for repairs. He soon returned and told me he had a man for me to work along with. 'Come on over,' he said and I followed him, and then he pointed to the man, whose name was Bill Kinsella.

And so began another long stint of standing around, watching and waiting while Bill continued his work of removing a drive shaft that was connected to a small conveyor belt. Bill was a kindly sort of person in his late forties, a man of mild manner and modest character. After a couple of weeks he settled into giving me small chores of unscrewing old nuts and replacing them, or trips to the store hatch for orders that included the usual old linen or cotton rags. In time I relished the Harvester Bay for all its great hiding places among the three huge harvesting machines.

It was during this time that I fell under the spell of a six-part hornpipe that was coming and going in my head and I was really drawn to specific parts of its melody even though I really didn't have all of it figured out. I'd heard it played on the radio some weeks earlier by box musician Tony MacMahon from Clare. To help me feel my way through what I knew of the tune I whistled it over and over, hoping that more of it might come to mind. Years later I've thought of Bill Kinsella's persecution complex or perhaps his patience as I whistled various parts of the tune. Of course poor Bill had no feeling for Irish traditional music and as far as he was concerned I was a mixed-up young fellow. I don't believe the tune of 'The Drunken Sailor' hornpipe was ever so well attended to as I whistled it over and over, until Bill politely told me he had had enough and that he was sorry he had to tell me to stop! I stood beside him in disbelief and said nothing for a while. After I recovered from the shock I went for a short walk as a way to escape the boredom of standing around. When I returned, Bill put me to work and everything was fine, that is until I forgot myself and drifted into another round of the 'Sailor'. If there's any redemption between Bill and me, I might whisper a message into the wind and remind him that I was his own private blackbird whether he liked it or not.

It wasn't long before I became known as a whistling menace, at least to some fellows who knew nothing of Irish traditional music and whose serious life irritated me. In later years I was to conclude that the lives of many Irish men were long-drawn-out affairs of insecurity fostered by a conventional lifestyle of marriage, work, religion and the pub. On the other hand my whistling may also have been a symptom of an escape mechanism: perhaps I desperately needed to free my restless soul. As it was, I felt locked inside a struggling world of melodic thought that found little relief, that is until I bought my first reel-to-reel tape recorder.

The weekends were always something I looked forward to and I would board the CIÉ bus on High Street and be home in Castlebarnagh by noon on Saturday. During one trip I noticed an uncomfortable feeling of dizziness with a slight headache just as I walked down the Mill Road. My limbs were aching with a dragging sensation of heaviness. Arriving home I described how I felt to my mother, who concluded that I had the flu and that I should go to bed as soon as possible. That Saturday night I had to be content with trying to listen to Seán Ó Murchú's *Céilí House* from where I lay in bed, behind the wall of the kitchen fire. Four days later my condition had barely improved. I'd have to stay laid up for a few more days. In the meantime I spoke with my parents about the Maguire family departing for Australia and that I would have to find new lodgings in Tullamore. My mother insisted that she was going to Tullamore to speak with a Mrs Elliot, a woman who already had some Bord na Móna lodgers, including Kevin Muldowney, who worked with me in Boora. My mother reached a quick decision and next day she took the bus to Tullamore and called on Mrs Elliot. The two women agreed that I would begin lodging there as soon as I recovered from the flu. The agreement was concluded when my mother prepaid the woman the sum of three pounds and ten shillings to cover the cost of my first week.

I recovered from the flu near the end of my second week in bed. I was still a little weak in my legs but began gaining strength after the first day of walking around. The next Sunday night I travelled back to Tullamore. This time I had a shorter walk – less than half a mile – from the bus stop to Mrs Elliot's, which was a welcome relief. Arriving at Mrs Elliot's I introduced and excused myself and went straight to bed.

The next morning I was back in the Harvester Shed. Bill Kinsella wasn't around and I was waiting with nothing to do when Bernie, the foreman, came from behind me and asked me about my health and if I was up for a little bit of work. After a few exchanges of small talk he had me follow him to another machine and put me alongside a senior fitter, Willy Creavan from the nearby town of Kilcormac. Willy was in the midst of a huge welding project, the repair of a chassis on which the main gearbox of a ditcher machine was mounted. Willy was a happy-go-lucky fellow of perhaps twenty-seven years. He also came up the ranks as a Bord na Móna apprentice and with this in mind I felt an unspoken bond with him. Soon enough he kept me busy with some welding or cutting new steel plates.

After ten o'clock tea break I noticed that Bill Coughlan – who was known as 'the farrier' – was working on the opposite side of the shed on a third machine, another harvester. I assumed he was finished with his work at the forge, and I was delighted at the prospect of some more chats with Bill regarding Francie Brereton. After a couple of days I found an opportunity and so I approached Bill, who was busy with a sledge. I asked him the question that was nagging me: was there any chance Francie Brereton might come back to Boora?

'Oh, Jesus God, no,' chuckled Bill, 'he couldn't wait to get out of here.' Bill was in an excitable mood with glints in his eyes and little squirts of saliva squeezing out of his front teeth. I didn't know until later, when a neighbour of his told me, that Bill's home team of Cloghan were scheduled to play Daingean in the Offaly county minor football final in a couple of weeks. It never occurred to me that Bill was keen to talk football, given that his son Johnny was on the Cloghan team.

In any case I kept intervening with more questions about the music, and in particular a reel I was curious about. 'Did you say "Dr Gilbert's Fancy"?' Bill's face lit up, and he spat on the floor. 'By God, I remember Brereton playin' it,' he said. He used to practise it over and over in his room, my missus heard him one evenin' cursin' the tune and tellin' it that he'd best it yet and he used to play another favourite of his after it, one called "Bunker Hill".' I was having a fine time with Bill when I happened to see through an opening in the machine that our foreman Bernie was heading in our direction. Bill raised his voice at once, shouting at me to run over to the store hatch and get him a crowbar. This was a ploy to give Bernie the impression that we were immersed in our work. Furthermore he shouted after me, 'I'll be over in a minute. Wait 'til I get a requisition from the foreman.' This was how Bill covered for me when I might have had some explaining to do as to why I was away from my usual work place.

My stay at Mrs Elliot's lasted only a week, when she announced she was cutting back on keeping lodgers at her home. She told us she had alternative accommodation with a neighbour and friend of hers, and that we could begin lodging with a Mrs Doran, at Charleville Parade, a short distance from her house. It would be a convenient place and close to the railway station, and the railway bridge would be my waiting spot where Paddy Doyle would pick me up for work in the mornings.

The following weekend I walked from Mrs Elliot's to Mrs Doran's and hit the iron knocker three times. The door was opened by a bespectacled thirteen-year-old. After I said who I was, she invited me inside and shouted, 'Mother, come here,' then she withdrew to the sitting room. I sat down and waited. Moments later Mrs Doran came downstairs and looked at me before shaking my hand. She still had her reading glasses on and a little make-up, and I saw a small hint of a smile. She directed me to my bedroom saying she hoped it would be comfortable enough. When I told her about practising my accordion she responded that her daughter Hillary was a student of the piano. 'What kind of music does she play?' I enquired, and she told me it was Beethoven and Mozart and that she was presently practising 'The Maiden's Prayer'.

Through the wall of the bedroom (as though she sensed we were talking about her) came the sound of the piano from the sitting room. 'That's Hillary,' she said. 'You met her when she answered the door. Well, anyway, I think it's time for some tea, and what did you say your name was? I've forgotten already.'

'Paddy,' said I, 'Paddy O'Brien.'

On Monday morning I waited on the brow of the railway bridge. Paddy Doyle was twenty minutes late, which wasn't too much of a surprise. We finally arrived at the car park in Boora and as we stepped out we saw an assembly of men gathered beside the Forge. Our shop steward was standing amid a large circle of men and was speaking to them. 'It's Paddy Healy,' someone said.

'We're on strike,' yelled Blackie Kennedy.

Dessie O'Neill was excited. 'By God you're right, and it's about time.'

Paddy Doyle continued walking past everyone, saying, 'See you later.'

Curious, I asked Dessie where Paddy was going. 'To work,' said Dessie, 'he belongs to a different union.'

The strike was provoked by poor heating conditions throughout the workshop. Within a few hours, however, it was called off following an agreement between the manager and our shop stewards. The terms of the agreement were accepted by the workers, who voted to return to work. Our personnel manager had promised our shop stewards the installation of oil heaters in the workshops on the following day. The strike had lasted only four hours. It was a small disappointment to many of us apprentices who longed for a day off with no fingers pointed at us.

54

The Banagher Group

Despite my outer persona, my inner self could be equated with a live music box. A constant flurry of tunes were bouncing in my head, note patterns from pieces of separate melodies, or the first few bars of a variety of jigs or reels, some of which came from listening to Tom Nolan when he was in one of his whistling moods. Alongside all of it, my relationship with Seamus Egan became easier and more relaxed and I came to know him as a friendly sort. On occasions he would lilt some tunes even though he'd complain that he wasn't much of a lilter. He also did a bit of whistling, which was a small improvement. A few of his favourites were jigs – 'The Bride's Favourite', 'Tatter Jack Walsh' – and a reel called 'The Girl That Broke My Heart'.

It's without speculation now, and of course I didn't realise it then, that both Tom and Seamus were in sympathy with my addiction to the music, especially Tom, who often initiated opportunities for me to join him and Seamus on what he called 'musical safaris'. I remember his first invitation when he said, 'We're goin' to a session next week!'

This was something new and it mystified me. 'Where are we goin'?' I asked.

'To a secret session,' he said, 'and it's next Thursday night. You can walk up to my house, it's only a few hundred yards, and don't forget to bring yer accordion!'

I was puzzled and asked him again, 'What's a session?'

He looked at me with his dark, steady stare. 'Don't tell me you don't know what a session is.'

I didn't know and with quiet resignation I said nothing, but deep in my mind I was thinking, 'You sly auld fox, Nolan. You love havin' me over a barrel. You know somethin' that I don't and it makes you feel powerful. Fuck ya!'

Over the next few days I bumped into him again and try as I might at asking him about the session, he still remained silent. It wasn't until late Thursday afternoon that he confessed where the session was.

'Banagher,' he said. 'My uncle Jim wants us to play in a Scóraíocht competition with his branch of Comhaltas.' He also mentioned that Seamus too would be there, along with other local musicians. As he spoke I felt a new sense of excitement and enthusiasm, and the notion of playing with other musicians spurred an instinctive prelude in my mind, which was how I would prepare the music we needed. I hardly heard any more of what Tom was saying.

We arrived in Banagher at nine o'clock that evening and stopped at Mr and Mrs Jim Nolan's house on Banagher Street. After we had tea, all four of us drove to a hall on the main street where a dozen people were waiting. Seamus had already arrived with his banjo, along with a wooden flute player, Joe Cashin. There were also several others I didn't know. After some discussion it was decided that the name of our competition entry would be 'Finnegan's Wake'. Other considerations were debated and I heard someone mention the Kelly brothers, Eddie and Martin, who played the fiddle and button accordion. Jim Nolan offered to drive across the River Shannon to Eyrecourt in Galway and talk to the two musicians about playing with us. Joe Cashin had another suggestion; that someone should ask Billy Burke to play the role of Tim Finnegan. Billy was a popular choice and Joe was asked to approach Billy, since he knew him as a neighbour. As for Tim Finnegan, I had no idea who this character was and knew nothing of James Joyce or any of his writings. As far as I was concerned my interest was in music and the prospect of playing with other musicians and so I went along with the wishes and judgements of everyone there.

After some back and forth comments from several individuals regarding dances, attire and some stage dialogue, we the musicians were free to do some practice. Having grouped in a small circle, Tom and I, with Seamus and Joe Cashin, began playing some jigs and reels as a way of checking out what we could play together. We practised in this way for an hour and then we noticed the time – it was getting late. On our way back to Tullamore, Tom and I began to memorise and compare more tunes that came to mind, so we could build a group repertoire. Slowly but surely we pieced together enough selections for an entire hour if needed.

One's memory is an important factor, especially for me because I automatically assumed the role of lead musician. This was an accepted choice because the accordion is the loudest instrument in a group of fiddlers, flutes, banjo and pipes. It also meant I would have to discipline my memory to remember each tune and the transitions from one into the other. Once I played the first note the entire group joined in – pipes, fiddles, banjo and flute. I could hear it all in my head as Tom drove and then I noticed we were turning left at Blue Ball village. We were nearing the end of our drive, with only six miles to Tullamore.

That weekend I went home again to Castlebarnagh. It was six weeks since I had last visited my family. When I stepped off the bus in Daingean it was raining steadily and I still had a mile to walk. I had little patience for waiting out the rain so I began walking with my suitcase in one hand and the accordion in the other. I had gone past the turn at the back road when a car pulled up beside me. It was Danny Hanlon, a neighbour. His timing was a godsend. In a matter of minutes he dropped me off at our house where I began drying myself beside the fire. My family were delighted to see me and as usual were interested in whatever news I might have. As usual, though, I wasn't very forthcoming with details, which irritated my mother and sisters. But I made up for it in bits and pieces over the next couple of days. I told everyone about my new musical situation with the Banagher group, and that the first round of the Scóraíocht competition was scheduled to be held in Edenderry in a couple of weeks. They were touched that it was to be presented on their side of the county. That evening I went to the small room where I slept and went to work on the tunes that Tom and I had selected. After a few minutes my father opened the door. 'Pat, why don't you come into the kitchen? It's warmer here.' I went along with his suggestion and found a chair beside the kitchen fire and began playing. In the meantime I saw that my father was preparing to go to Daingean for his Saturday night pint. Before putting on his topcoat he started to dance on the kitchen floor. My mother looked at him with astonishment and my sisters were cheering him on. My eldest sister Moira, was about to say something when a sudden hiccup made her shake on her chair. It reminded me of a small whiskey bottle that popped when a cork was pulled from its neck – it was a funny moment. I stopped playing and my father reached for his topcoat. 'Before I go,' he said, 'would you play me "The Lark in the Morning?"'

Without saying a word I started the tune and as I played it I saw him put down his coat, and once more he danced back and forth around the floor. My mother was sitting on the edge of her chair with her hand over her mouth. 'Indeed aren't you the light-hearted man!'

'No other way to be, woman! That's what keeps me goin'.'

It was late on Sunday evening when I disembarked from the bus in Tullamore. I walked the short distance up High Street and down the small hill to Charleville Parade. I had my own key and let myself in to Mrs Doran's house. Someone shouted, 'Is that Paddy?' to which I answered by walking into the sitting room where all of the family were watching *Star Trek* on television – except Hillary, who was sitting at the far end of the room deeply engrossed in a book. After a few exchanges with everyone I asked Hillary what she was reading and she said it was a book of poetry by Patrick Kavanagh. Now and then she would smirk at what she was reading and I became a little curious. I was about to ask her another question when Mrs Doran announced that she was about to make a pot of tea and asked me if I'd like a cup. I happily said I would. When told to take a seat I proceeded to squeeze between her eldest daughter Geraldine and the near end of the couch. It was a tight squeeze.

The next morning I waited again for my ride to work. We had a new means of transport, with one J.J. Conroy who drove a black Ford Anglia. Like Paddy Doyle, he was nearly always late. Paddy himself hadn't been to work for several weeks and the word was he'd taken ill and was laid up in bed. However, the fun in our new car resumed with more persistent teasing and wisecracking, Gerry Ryan and Dessie O'Neill taking sides against Peter Hogan, who was adept at giving back as much as he got. J.J. usually played devil's advocate and would set up Peter by prodding and goading him into explaining what he'd been up to over the weekend. Rumours, true or false, were used to push Peter up against the ropes but he was always able to turn the tables in his favour. All of this foolology was met with laughter or roars of approval and shouts became sneers and jeers as voices tried to drown out other voices. It was pandemonium, and the hilarity of it was infectious and often lasted until we reached our destination. I suppose it was a sort of relief mechanism that allowed us to say what we liked within the confines of our knowledge of each other. It was also a challenge for me as I tried hard to keep up with the wit and humour of it all. In another way it was as though we were experimenting in a drama school for teenagers.

It was early springtime when I was chosen for another stint in the Gearbox Department. When I got there Éamon Fleming was fitting a gearbox with new seals and shims. When he finished he turned to me and said, 'Fonsie, I want you to come with me on an excursion.' Éamon always called me by that name. It came from Vincent O'Brien and his brother, Fonsie – the two of them were famous racehorse trainers at the time.

I'd no idea what he meant except it was a mystery quest and I liked the idea of the unknown. Éamon was a man who never dallied around with small talk, preferring instead to cut through to the task at hand. He told me to bring along some clean rags and a long screwdriver. When he said, 'Let's go' I followed him out of the workshop and we walked for a while until we came to an area known as The Field. This was a place where the harvester machines were parked in long rows with their jibs facing each other. They would remain there throughout the winter where they were singled out for repairs. Éamon's job was to inspect particular gearboxes that were reported to be vibrating or making grinding sounds, which in itself might be a symptom of worn bearings, loose gears or broken gear teeth. Éamon put me to work unscrewing a score of nuts with the use of a small ratchet that helped alleviate the repetitive nature of the work. This being done, we lifted the cover of the main gearbox of the machine. He was a very considerate sort of character and as a senior fitter he worked quietly, not saying very much, and he rarely looked in my direction when speaking to me. And yet he inspired confidence and I felt as an equal to him as a human being. Working with him was very encouraging because I believed he understood what it was like to be a young self-doubting apprentice.

As the day wore on we were closing the cover on the gearbox when Éamon said, 'I hear you and Nolan and Seamus Egan are stirring up the natives down in Banagher. I'd like to know what all of ye are up to.' There was a hint of good humour on his face so I obliged him with details of our rehearsals and the competition in Edenderry. I explained what the Scóraíocht competition meant in terms of its half-hour presentation and what our lineup consisted of. When I'd finished, Éamon said nothing. Instead he began walking along between several harvesters while I followed him until he found the number of another machine. Then as we began work on the second gearbox he said, 'Well, Fonsie, good luck on Sunday night.'

It was Thursday, and while standing at the store hatch waiting for an order of quarter-inch nuts Tom Nolan seemed to appear out of nowhere. Speaking directly into my right ear he said, 'Be at my house at eight o'clock this evening.' That was the time we would leave for Banagher for the final rehearsal.

That evening as I sat at the table, Mrs Doran came into the dining room carrying my dinner on a tray. A couple of her lodgers were also sitting at the table and a lot of chitchat was going around. Meanwhile Mrs Doran was taking a break and as she sat on her couch smoking a cigarette she casually said to me, 'Paddy, I see where you and a group from Banagher are playing in Edenderry on Sunday night!'

The other lads stared at me and one of them said to Mrs Doran, 'Where did you see it?'

'Oh,' she said, ''twas in this weekend's *Offaly Independent*.'

'Aha,' said Jimmy Gonoude, and repeating himself added, 'Aha, our Paddy has a secret life playing music with a crowd of hayseeds beside the River Shannon. So that's where you go on Thursday nights.'

'Now, Jimmy,' said Mrs Doran, 'a fellow must amuse himself, and besides it must be nice playing music with other people.' Hillary had pushed her head just inside the door and heard us talking. 'Oh mother!', she snorted as she slammed the door and withdrew to the sitting room.

I walked the short walk to Tom Nolan's in less than five minutes and when I knocked I could hear him playing his pipes inside. 'You're early,' he said when he opened the door. 'I was just warming up the pipes.' I was glad to hear this because it meant he was truly committed to the music and besides it motivated me and gave me an extra sense of purpose. During the journey to Banagher he asked me to lilt the beginning of a few reels. Again I'd no problem remembering any of them providing Tom had their titles or reminded me of who had played them. Arriving in the town we drove directly to the hall, where we noticed the Kelly brothers and Joe Cashin had just arrived. The rest of our crew were already there, sitting around or standing in small groups chatting.

Tom's uncle Jim gave an introduction and thanked everyone for coming. Teresa Hough was asked to sing a song of her choice, which

I recognised as 'Eileen Aroon'. Her voice suggested a calm, contented tone in perfect tune with herself. When she finished, Joe Cashin turned towards her and shouted, 'Good girleen,' then turning to Tom and me said, 'Now that's somethin' for the cuckoos to think about.' Martin and Eddie Kelly were opening their fiddle and accordion cases – they were itching to play. Seamus Egan was busy trying to tune his banjo. 'Paddy,' he said, 'give me an A.' Tom had his pipes already strapped on and was also trying to tune up. Soon he was pumping the bellows under his right arm and looking at me. 'Give me a D.' It was an order, not a request.

After a few further delays with tuning and the usual suggestions for what we were to play, we began a selection of slip jigs, leading off with 'Hardiman the Fiddler'. When we finished I noticed Eddie Kelly was repositioning his spectacles. Apparently while he played they'd slid down his nose, almost falling onto the bridge of his fiddle. 'It was touch and go there for a while,' he said chuckling. 'Anyway, no harm done.' Then I heard a voice, 'Have we any reels we might know together?' It was Seamus. 'We have a nest of them, here's a few we can play,' Tom responded. He had their names ready and said, 'The first is "Sheehan's".' And so we began playing together, two accordions, one fiddle, flute, pipes and banjo. We finished with a short stop that shocked the hall into silence. As Joe Cashin lowered his flute he spat on the floor. 'Bejaysus,' he said, 'I don't know about the rest of ye, but that sounded pretty good to me and a nice lilt to it as well.' Eddie Kelly was enjoying a thinly disguised giggle that left many of us on the edge of laughter. He said with his pronounced Galway accent, ''Twould charm the birds out of the ivy.' Tom was amused at Eddie's wit and when I looked I saw him bow his head gently, a small indication of approval. To me it was a sign of us pulling together socially as well as musically.

We played the relevant selections to be used in the competition but it was only part of what was required for the overall production. We still needed to either use an emcee or make up some dialogue between us, so as to give some continuity to the theme of the presentation. As it was we had music, singing by Teresa and Peter Nolan and also some dancing by some local girls. Meanwhile the ever-vigilant Emily Horan was quietly writing notes with ideas of what format might work.

Our theme of 'Finnegan's Wake' was simple and direct, but none of us had any experience in drama, or writing a script. We were amateurs, as amateurs usually were.

We gathered in a circle when Jim Nolan asked us for some order – he had something to say. 'Listen,' he began, 'we should make arrangements for how we should travel to Edenderry. Anyone with a car should carry three or four people. I have room for two as well as Peter and my wife.' It was decided that I'd travel with Tom, and Seamus would hook up with us in Tullamore. It was almost a foregone conclusion that we were ready for Sunday night, but as we prepared to leave the hall we heard a voice somewhere behind us. 'Wait, wait. What about me?' It was Billy Burke.

Jim Nolan was clearly embarrassed. 'Billy, where were you? I didn't know you were here. I'm sorry, I didn't.'

'Don't worry, Jim,' said Billy, 'I was lyin' on the floor between the benches, practisin'.'

'Practisin' what?' said Jim.

'I was practisin' bein' Tim Finnegan and after a while I fell asleep.'

'Fair play to you Billy,' Jim chuckled, 'fair play.' Billy was a character, and very funny. I heard someone say he had great wit and should have been a comedian.

Tom and I stopped at his uncle Jim's house on our way home, on Banagher Street. Jim's wife Peggy made tea and ham sandwiches. A few other people joined us and soon the conversation became lively. Everyone seemed to be in a spirit of jest, especially when Billy Burke's name was mentioned and why he'd fallen asleep on the floor. It was almost midnight when we started out for Tullamore – a twenty-five-mile drive, much of it over bumps and small hillocks as we drove over the irregular bog road with its poor foundation underneath. It was one o'clock when Tom dropped me at Mrs Doran's door. I was worn out and went to bed almost immediately. When morning came I stayed on in bed and didn't rise until 11.30 a.m.

55

The Scóraíocht

A few days later it was Sunday and as arranged Tom picked me up at six o'clock that evening. Seamus was with him, having driven from his home in Lumcloon to meet us. The weather was damp and cold and it was raining when we drove through Daingean. Seamus was in the back seat and was talking about how unreliable the weather was. 'Lads,' he said, 'this is one miserable dog shite of a night. We must be feckin' mad to be doin' this at all.'

'Doin' what?' I asked.

'Drivin' to the far side of a one-horse town on a night like this.'

'Don't worry, Seamus,' said Tom, 'we're not the first to do it and we won't be the last.' Very little was said after that. We continued on and as we came within a couple of miles of Edenderry we could see the streetlights of the town in the distance. When we were within the 30 mph speed limit, Tom slowed the car. We were passing the local police station when all of a sudden he said, 'Now look at that, it's stopped raining!'

I turned to Seamus. 'Maybe it means good luck for us.'

Seamus's mood seemed to improve as we made our way down the long hill and when we came to the centre of the town he said, 'Paudgeen, you might be right, maybe it is a good sign.'

We found a spot for parking near the side of the hall. We retrieved our instruments from the trunk, crossed the street and climbed a number of steps to the front door of the hall. People were already queueing for some early seats. We made our way along the side of the queue and inside the door a man ushered us to another door at the far end of the hall. Inside we saw the Edenderry group preparing for their positions on stage. They were listed as number one on the schedule. We found a corner behind a partition near the rear wall and left our instruments there. Then we went back outside to the front area and found some empty seats near the back of the hall. People were now filing in to whatever seats were available and the hall was full when the curtain parted on one side of the stage. A well-spoken young man dressed in a light grey suit and blue tie stepped forward and reached for a long stand with a microphone clipped on its top bracket. I recognised him as Paddy Duffy, secretary of Birr's branch of Comhaltas. He began his introduction with greetings to everyone in Irish and continued in English, saying how fortunate we were because a wonderful lineup of talented people were about to grace the stage. 'It's my pleasure,' he said, 'to introduce the first group to perform, so ladies and gentlemen, please put your hands together and give a warm welcome to the Edenderry Comhaltas group!'

Almost immediately the audience erupted with a loud burst of applause as the curtains swept open from centre stage, each parting drape moving slowly to the opposite side. As it did so a rousing sound of music muted the audience and an upbeat blast of reels was played by the full force of accordions, fiddles, a whistle and wooden flute, galvanised by superb piano accompaniment. I noticed that the music of the whistle player could be heard above the overall sound, and despite being outgunned it came through specifically on high notes, giving out mischievous music of fine quality. The total selection amounted to 'The Corner House Reel' and 'The Glenallen'. The theme of this presentation seemed to be 'A Kitchen Session Scene', with no dialogue. All music, song and dance performances came on, one after the other, with no intros. A fiddle performance by a young solo musician captured the heartstrings of many in the audience and this was reflected by a young lady who yelled, 'More power to yeh, Dennis!' I recognised the tunes as two of Ed Reavy's reels which I was trying to learn. When the fiddler was finished he was greeted with instant applause and was immediately followed by an unaccompanied *sean nós* male singer who sang a ballad in English. Next came a hard-shoe jig dancer, a young girl wearing a blue and white uniform. Hers was a riveting exhibition of heel and toe tapping as she danced from side to side, turning and moving with poise and perfect rhythm, then bowing with her right foot forward at the end of her dance. The whistle player then proceeded with a slow air, the well-known 'Slievenamon'. At the end of the air the crowd around the hall erupted again with someone shouting, 'Me life on you Joe!' and yet another, 'Fair play to you, Joe Smollen!'

Seamus gave me a prod with his elbow. 'We're up against it with the home crowd. If Edenderry lose it'll be wigs on the green.'

'Seamus,' I said, 'don't worry, people here are the same as people in Banagher or Cloghan, or anywhere else. Look,' I continued, 'I think they're goin' to play the last selection. Tell Tom we'd better make a move towards the back of the stage. We're on next.'

The group on stage commenced their final selection, starting with a reel called 'The Boys of Ballisodare', as we moved quietly to the side steps that led to the back of the platform. Then onto the stage came a group of casually dressed dancers who were ready and waiting when the musicians changed to a second reel. The entire combination of music and dance was a dynamic parting shot and one that could influence the adjudicator in allotting a point or two in favour of the home performers. And then it was over and as the group vacated the stage the huge crowd went wild with tumultuous applause, stamping feet, whistling and good-natured cheers.

Back on stage Paddy Duffy announced the first intermission. This would give us enough time to move into our positions behind the curtain. As I was sitting near the back of the stage I saw Billy Burke and Tom Corrigan carrying a table and placing it with one end facing the curtain, which was where Billy's naked feet would face the audience. Many of the crew were already seated as Joe Hoary and Eddie Kelly began tuning their fiddles together. Tom was busy with his pipes, trying to tune to my accordion, when I saw Billy Burke again in his bare feet and wearing just his pants and undershirt. Someone was helping him onto the table, where he settled himself before lying on his back. Emily Horan was ready with a small cushion, and lifting Billy's head she placed the cushion underneath. 'Will that be all right for yeh, Billy?'

'Grand, ma'am,' said Billy, 'but the sooner we get started the better.'

'Wait a minute,' said Emily, 'the girls are comin' with the candles.' Then she took out a small packet of flour and began rubbing it on Billy's face. It was supposed to make him look lifeless, or, as she put it, 'as dead as a doornail'. While she rubbed the flour on Billy's neck she moved the palm of her hand upwards and accidentally applied too much on his nose, which set Billy into a fit of sneezing. Martin Kelly was nearby holding a white sheet to be draped over Billy and the table. He saw Billy's predicament and pulled from his inside pocket a tiny bottle of whiskey. 'Here Billy, take a mouthful of the craythur.'

Billy was coughing when he grasped the bottle and swallowed a little, but after another swallow he relaxed and settled back onto the cushion. The white sheet was then draped over him and his hands were crossed outside it on top of his chest. More flour was rubbed on his hands and feet where they were sticking out from underneath the sheet. The sight of Billy with two lighted candles at each side of his head and the sheet draped across him was very effective, and proved to be a very convincing display of what a corpse might look like at an old Irish wake.

Suddenly the curtain moved and Paddy Duffy stuck his head through. In a hushed voice he asked, 'Are ye right? I'm goin' to introduce you. Are ye ready?' We were, and as soon as Paddy urged the audience to applaud and welcome us we began with the tune 'Finnegan's Wake'. As we played it the curtain began to open and the crowd started to clap to its rhythm. I saw then that the musicians with me were smiling and looking pleased with the sound from the hall and this gave us a feeling of acceptance and spurred us on as the curtain flew open. At the end of 'Finnegan's Wake' we immediately launched into a couple of lively reels. When our selection ended we waited for the applause to die and then one of us shouted (I think it was Mr Corrigan), 'God bless him! He was a great sport when he was alive.'

Another of us added, 'He was the life of the party.'

And still another, 'He had a heart of gold and was very independent.'

Emily Horan yelled, 'Will someone for God's sake sing a song for poor auld Tim because he was a great man, for . . .' Her voice faded when she saw Peter Nolan standing near the front area where 'Tim's' feet pointed upwards. Peter began to sing. His song was the same song I sang in school, the same old Fenian song called 'Down Erin's Lovely Lee'. He sang it with a clear voice and his phrasing of the melody captured the song's story. It was the first time I ever heard him or his style of *sean nós* singing in English. It also occurred to me that his performance would greatly bolster our presentation. Peter ended with a simple nod of his head to the 'corpse' and then to the audience and a great surge of applause filled the hall. Indeed the audience was in a jubilant mood, and was wonderful to perform to.

Our agenda continued with another round of tunes that consisted of a selection of slip jigs. As we played on, a man in our cast stood up from his seat and began limping his way to centre stage. He had a crooked ashplant that he leaned his hand on and wore an old battered farm hat. His brown topcoat was hanging open and swayed back and forth as he eased into a slow canter of a dance. He hit his boots a few slaps against the floor and used the ashplant to balance himself. He was the most elderly member of our group and as he mixed his steps with the music he also belted the floor a few times with his stick. Withdrawing backwards, he removed his hat and waved it at everyone before returning to his seat. The crowd went wild and were cheering him on as he sat among us; they wanted more of him. However, the noise subsided when Jamesie Burke shouted, 'Begod Tim, what did you think of that? Come on, tell me.'

'Stop it,' cried Emily Horan. 'Don't you know a dead corpse when you see one?'

Jamesie ignored her. 'Where's Teresa? Is she here?'

'Where's Teresa?' someone yelled. 'She's sittin' right beside ya.'

'Let's have a song then,' Jamesie shouted. 'Yes, yes, a love song for Tim before he crosses over into the unknown!'

Teresa was laughing at everyone as she walked lightly forward and stood close to the lone microphone. She was looking very attractive, wearing a beautiful dark-coloured dress with a large white and red flower print and a shiny wide black belt around her waist. The audience fell silent as she started to sing, an Irish song of love known to us as 'Eileen Aroon'. Her interpretation was smooth in its delivery and her soft tone of voice seemed to cradle the song and offer it as a gift to everyone. We all loved her for how she sang and when she finished she bowed to the audience very slowly and they in return treated her to a long and appreciative round of applause.

Finally, when everyone settled down, Eddie Kelly came forward with his fiddle and began a solo, a selection of two of his favourite reels, 'Paddy Fahy's' and one of his own compositions. Playing with confidence and dexterity, his music probed our senses – not overly fast and a wonderful choice of reinterpreted note structures. He had his own style but it also reflected the fiddle music of east County Galway. His was a valuable performance, defining as it did his solo ability in contrast to our group playing. More applause followed Eddie's rendition and then we were near the end of our presentation. We were given a signal to begin our last selection and so we launched into a set of double jigs. Another signal was given to our dancers, who were to oblige us with a figure of a set. Responding to the rhythm of the music the set dance included the battering of their feet that put me in mind of bodhrán beaters when out with the wren on Saint Stephen's Day. It was energetic stuff, the stuff of body and soul in harmony with tempo and rhythm. The set dancing seemed to instil a sense of adventure within the audience, whose reaction at the end was another burst of energy that carried my mind away. Then suddenly Mrs Corrigan shouted at us, 'This is the best wake I've ever attended. Where's the whiskey? Who's hiding the bottle?'

Tom Flynn was standing across the way on the far side of the corpse. Reaching underneath the table he lifted a bottle of whiskey and as he tried to pass it over to the woman he pretended to lose his footing. The resulting effort caused him to slip and spill some of the whiskey on top of Tim. Tim could take no more and slowly hoisted himself up from the table. Someone yelled, 'He's alive. He's back from the dead.' Tim was sitting upright in a bewildered state as we musicians charged once again into the tune of 'Finnegan's Wake'. In addition to the tune people on and offstage were clapping their hands along with the sound of the music. We kept at it until the curtain closed and without a word we departed the stage, leaving it ready for the next group.

Paddy Duffy announced the second intermission, reminding people that the Birr branch of Comhaltas were next on the programme and would be ready in fifteen minutes.

Some of our group members had left the hall and went to Larkin's Hotel across the street for a drink. A few others decided to drive home to Banagher and take advantage of less traffic before the pubs closed. The rest of us found a few remaining seats where we sat and waited for the next group of performers. Then I decided to go outside for a short walk. I wanted to clear my head with some fresh air. In a couple of minutes I was walking along the main street with my hands in my pockets and my head hanging downwards. Thoughts of how I missed some buttons when playing on stage addled me, or perhaps irritated me. Still, I believed we all did fairly well. In any event the competition would be determined later by four adjudicators. While I was thinking about it all I'd forgotten about the length of my walk and looking at my watch I realised that the Birr group were already on stage.

By the time I returned the hall was dark, with the lights off, and I had difficulty finding a seat. The Birr group were at least ten minutes into their presentation and a solo dancer was in action, putting on a wonderful display of footwork. He was dancing to the music of

B/C box player John Bowe and John was playing a double jig called 'The Trip to the Cottage'. At that time John was nineteen years old and had won the senior All-Ireland two-row accordion championship the year before at the Fleadh Cheoil in Mullingar in 1963. He was the youngest senior box champion ever, having turned eighteen a couple of weeks prior to the competition. The solo dance finished with a resounding applause from the audience, who to my mind were clearly impressed by the man who was the solo dancer. Nevertheless it gave me an opportunity to move to the back of the hall where I saw Tom and Seamus standing with their arms folded. When I got there Seamus whispered, 'Paudgeen, where were yeh? We thought you were kidnapped by the Banshee!' I said, 'No, nothin' like that. I just went outside for a walk and met a young one outside the door. She showered me with praise and said I was better than the rest of ye.' I was enjoying my big lie to Seamus and waited for his reaction.

He looked at Tom and said, 'Did yeh hear that? Paddy's a fast mover. He's been prowlin' around outside chasin' the girls.' Tom was making a chuckling noise when someone in the back row began shushing us to keep it down. I moved quickly away in case any more was said and walked around trying to find a side seat near the front area. John Bowe began again, this time playing a set of two reels, 'The Shaskeen' and 'Mary O'Neill's Fancy'. I stood and listened to every note, marvelling at the accuracy of his playing and its solid rhythm. He played the tunes with remarkable energy and his style impressed me to the point that I wanted to do cartwheels around the hall.

I was thinking, 'Oh God, what wonderful tunes,' and I wanted to know them because of how they touched me and, besides, I'd never heard any of them before. I think everyone in the hall was struck by the power and delivery of John's music and when he finished he was greeted with a frenzy of applause that was accompanied by piercing shrieks from young ladies who travelled all the way from Birr in support of their heroes.

The adjudicators were busy. I could see the movement of their pens as they totted up the number of points allotted to each of the three groups of contestants. The rules allowed points to be given to each category: 25 each for dancing, singing, music and presentation, which amounted to 100 points. No one group would reach the top of the spectrum and most would do as well as 19 to 22 points in each category. This would allow each adjudicator room to use their point system to the best advantage for everyone. There was a delay of twenty minutes before we saw the four men walking down the aisle on their way to the stage. The curtain was again pulled aside as three of the men sat on chairs while the fourth introduced each of the judges before apologising for the delay; he then appraised each group's contribution to the evening. I can't remember everything he said, but he made many positive remarks about each group's musicianship and how it accommodated the overall production. Wasting little time, he continued briefly, and then announced the points given to each group's presentation. We were surprised to hear that our group was in the lead, ahead of the other contestants by two points. The next judge came to the microphone and seemed to be trying to find his notes among a cluster of papers. He pulled out the page he wanted and spoke of the great time he had had listening to the musicians from each group. He wasn't very critical of anyone, saying instead that we all deserved to win, but in the end he gave an extra point to the Birr group who went ahead for their combined musical performances. Shortly after that the singing judge stepped forward to the mic and began his summation. We knew him as Seamus Duffy, a very fine singer from County Mayo who had won a major competition for singing on Radio Éireann's popular programme *Fleadh Cheoil an Radio*. He spoke with enthusiasm about each of the singers with each group, defining their merits or special appeal. He seemed to be equally happy with each performance and spoke of how close each singer was to the other. The standings at this stage showed a tie between Birr and Edenderry, with our group going ahead again by two points. Peter and Teresa had emerged as our most solid contribution, which was no big surprise to us. The fourth judge finished the night with remarks concerning both solo and group dancing. His remarks were minimal and to the point. He seemed particularly impressed with Birr's solo dancing. He ended the night by calling out the third, second and first places: Edenderry third, Birr second, and Banagher first place! We had won!

There was a lovely sense of peace and calm in Tom's car as we drove back to Tullamore. The journey seemed shorter compared to our earlier journey. Tom didn't say very much and Seamus was a little surprised by the result. I was very heartened and remember saying how reliable Billy Burke was for lying so still and so quiet during all the shenanigans. Seamus saw the humour in what I said and remarked that Billy was ideal for the job. 'Just imagine – if he'd moved or coughed or farted, we would have lost.'

'And another thing,' said Tom, 'we were lucky he didn't begin another sneezin' fit, especially since there was still a lot of flour left on his face, the same flour that caused him to sneeze behind the curtain with two minutes left before goin' on.' The rest of our travel continued with little conversation. I suppose we were tired and quietly happy. Tomorrow we would begin the week again in Boora, but at least we would have good news to tell our workmates.

At work the next day I was busy washing roller bearings when John Flynn approached me. 'Pat, congratulations. I heard you and the lads won the competition in Edenderry.'

'Yeah,' I said, ''twas a close call.'

Éamon Fleming was nearby and heard John speak. 'What was that?' he asked.

John looked surprised. 'Didn't you hear about the Banagher group that Paddy plays with? They won the competition last night in Edenderry.'

Éamon had forgotten about it, or maybe his thoughts were somewhere else, but in any case he said to me, 'Fonsie, not bad goin'.' Throughout the day news of our victory spread to all departments in the workshop. Word of mouth is, indeed, the best form of advertising.

56

Winning and Losing

The following year we competed again in the Scóraíocht and again won the Offaly championship. This time our presentation had a new theme, 'The Night at the Fair'. We also had two new fiddlers who were middle-aged men. One was Syl Donellan, who was Seamus's uncle. The other was Mickey Doorley, who had a habit of not wearing shirt collars and used suspenders to hold his trousers up. Both of them were easy-going and gentle individuals who showed me a lot with their kind nature and humble dispositions. I suspect they have long gone to their spiritual reward, as have so many others who played the music with me during my younger years. Another newcomer was a young teenager I later knew as Frank Cassidy, who played the penny whistle. Frank was a fair-haired lad and his speciality was playing slow airs. He was of a private disposition and later proved to be a very capable musician. A number of years later he would emigrate to Canada.

Once again our rehearsals began with the introduction of new ideas and the playing of new selections of tunes. By this time we had lost the musicianship of the Kelly brothers, which was a disappointment, but the inclusion of Syl and Mickey resolved our situation. On the night of the competition we succeeded in winning our way through to the next round, but were later informed that no further competitions were scheduled for that year.

The following year, 1966, was an exciting one that saw us win our way to the Leinster final with a new presentation entitled 'The Tinker's Wedding'. At this time I felt we had become more experienced, and this led us to experiment with the use of small animals on stage. We had already used a goat during a previous production, the success of which prompted a few other ideas. As we prepared for the Leinster showdown one of our women actors was keen to use a hen and was, in fact, including the hen in rehearsals. The idea was to acclimatise her to the sound of our rehearsal, so the old bird would get used to the overall commotion, especially the rousing sound of set dancing and music.

We also had a handyman build a wooden imitation structure that would look similar to the front of a traveller's caravan with a rounded roof, painted green. There were three short steps that led to its half door, which was painted red. Inside the doorway we had Teresa Hough, in the role of a Gypsy woman, leaning on the half door in readiness for her turn to sing. Two wooden shafts were leaning downward from the frame of the 'caravan' and resting on the stage floor. Emily Horan was in charge of the hen and was teaching her to roost on one of the shafts throughout the half-hour. The success of this was helped by the hen herself because she was old and less fussy than a younger bird. Another advantage was her indifference to being surrounded by strangers – she wasn't a shy bird. In fact we noticed she had a tendency to cooperate more willingly when our group burst into a bunch of reels.

The competition was scheduled to take place in the Marion Hall in Birr, which could accommodate four to five hundred people. Four county winners from Leinster were competing: Wexford, Offaly, Westmeath and Dublin. During the weeks that led up to the event there was great enthusiasm among many in southwest Offaly. The prospect of the competition had touched the imagination of the people in the area.

It was on a Sunday night in February 1967 when Tom, his fiancée and I drove from Tullamore to Birr. When we arrived I noticed the hall was full of supporters of our group and many others who had travelled in solidarity with their heroes from Dublin, Wexford and Westmeath. I saw several young people sitting on a ledge that lined the bottom of a row of skylights on the roof of one side of the hall. It was a vantage point from where they could watch developments on stage, but nevertheless a reckless one.

Tom and I wasted no time in moving to the back of the stage, where we met Seamus. Both of them began tuning their instruments to my accordion. As we did so the Wexford group were also busy tuning up while others were carrying bales of straw onto the stage. They were in a festive mood and light-heartedly joking with each other. Tom was uncomfortable about our tuning and suggested we should do it later.

Instead we hung around and watched the Wexford men and women prepare. Some were wearing long dresses and dungarees and the men had their sleeves rolled up. Straw hats and old caps were passed around and a young lad climbed onto the stage carrying a couple of pitchforks, which he stuck into the bales of straw. I was amazed at the preparation and thought that went into their production. I told Tom and Seamus that we were up against it and that it would be no walkover. Having nothing to do but wait, we went outside to the hall and were lucky to find some seats near the middle aisle area.

Once again Paddy Duffy was master of ceremonies. As was his way, he held small paper cards in his left hand as he tried to adjust the microphone stand for height and reach. With his fine speaking voice and cordial manner Paddy brought an element of sophistication to his introductions, making him an ideal presenter. After a few short sentences in Irish he welcomed the first presentation, which was 'The Day of the Thrashing', to be performed by the Bunclody Comhaltas group from County Wexford.

They opened with a round of jigs that were joined by intermittent displays of solo and group dancing. This was followed by a variety of solo and trio instrumentals that were introduced with an assortment of simple dialogue that served as a means of linking each performance to the other. At one point the stage lighting became very dim, which was a signal to Gerry Forde and Tim Flood to begin their duet of fiddle and banjo in a slow air. I'd heard them before on Seán Ó Murchú's *Céilí House*. Theirs was a lovely exhibition of duet music and their playing of the air was sentimental and had a gentle confidence and control. I wondered if the banjo player was the same Tim Flood who played midfield with the great Wexford senior hurling team that defeated Cork in the All-Ireland final of 1956. Later I was told he was indeed the same man. When the duet ended there was a fantastic reaction from the audience, whom I felt were touched by the wonderful playing of the air. Bunclody's overall performance gave me an insight into the entertainment value of presenting a cultural scene on stage. The visual impact of golden straw bales, used for seating, added a pleasing texture and background to an array of colourful hats, cravats, dresses and dungarees. Their entire production had a life and energy of its own and it was great fun.

Our group was next 'for slaughter' as we often said. I've already written about our production of 'Finnegan's Wake' but in this our latest effort we had to make some personnel changes. One was a surprise talent who fitted into our routine with exceptional ease as *fear an tí*, or group patriarch. I can't go any further without describing Mickey Carroll, a short, stocky, red-faced man in his late fifties. Mickey worked as a clerk at the old power station in Lumcloon. He was a man of quiet temperament and yet when with us on stage he became a different character, almost as though he had undergone a personality change. With an old walking stick in his hand, he introduced our various performances and made up his own dialogue as he went along, thus helping our transitions from one piece to another. His presence seemed to relax everyone, and despite the pressure of competition I think we always looked forward to another night on stage with Mickey.

As our performance continued, everything we had practised fell into line and our presentation of music, song and dance was once again greeted with wonderful appreciation and enthusiasm. I do remember, with affection, our little red hen roosting comfortably on the shaft of the caravan, and how unconcerned and well-behaved she was, especially during the loud applause of the audience. Our half-hour on stage went along like a dream, as if time itself carried us along. And then we were finished and the curtain quickly closed to deafening applause from the audience. Paddy Duffy wasted little time and within a minute was again in front of the microphone announcing another fifteen-minute intermission, along with reminders of upcoming events, including a bingo game. Twenty minutes later the curtain flew open again and this time a rousing rendition of reels came from the Booterstown group from Dublin. All of them sat in a long straight line of boys and girls playing timber flutes, whistles, one fiddle, a teenage girl playing a harp, and two lads playing bodhrán and bones. I didn't know many of them but I loved the pure melodic sound of their music – fantastic tunes and several of them were new to me. Many of their selections came from the playing of County Clare musicians along with other styles of tunes from Seán Ó Riada's Ceoltóirí Chualann, which was a small folk orchestra based in Dublin. The freshness of it all was extraordinary for its influential impact on me. I was later to learn that an assortment of their tunes were of a local or regional style of music from the west of Ireland. The theme of their presentation was 'An Seisiún' or, translated into English, 'The Session'. It was straightforward or perhaps simple, in its idea, which was an honest rendition of music, song and dance with special emphasis on the use of the Irish language. I don't believe anyone in the hall, especially the audience or adjudicators, fully appreciated what this younger generation of musicians represented. In later years historians were able to speak of the great folk revival that began in the USA during the mid-1960s, the impact of which resonated in Ireland as well as other European countries. It was a time when a number of groups and organisations became involved in what became a growing revival of Irish traditional music, song and dance. Its influence caught the attention of a younger generation of people and I dare say that the young group of musicians performing in the Scóraíocht competition were the result of a renaissance among Irish traditional musicians in Dublin. Many years later it occurred to me that we were listening to a rebirth of songs in Irish, old slow airs and dialogue presented in our native language.

A teenage singer with her harp accompaniment gave me cause for more reflection, along with honest flute and whistle tunes from three girls whom I later knew as Proinsias Ní Dhorchaigh (flute) and the Bergin sisters, Antoinette (harp), Mary (whistle and flute) and their eldest sister Martha (whistle). The lone fiddler, Antóin Mac Gabhann from County Cavan, I had met on a brief visit to Dublin and also at the County Fleadh Cheoil in Delvin, County Westmeath. His music was vibrant and energetic and meshed well as a duet with Jimmy McGreevy's box playing. Jimmy was from Castlerea in County Roscommon and was one of several country lads who were new members of the Garda, the police, in Dublin. He played a grey model Paolo Soprani B/C accordion and its exquisite tone intrigued me, especially when he played a particular set of reels. His selection highlighted his formidable and stylish box playing ability, which to my mind was worthy of national attention.

The group's finale was a mixed selection of west Clare and Donegal reels that prompted a figure of a set that brought a group of dancers with battering feet to centre stage. As the music continued, the audience were treated to a swinging exhibition of graceful body movements inspired by the group interpretation of a Clare set. The visual impact of the set spoke its own language of rhythm, beat and tempo, all of it in harmony with wonderful music. As a dance presentation we were witnessing a natural outgrowth of the spirit of a music that was largely ignored in Ireland, and now through the medium of a new generation of musicians it was making a return visit to the people of Ireland. It was hearty stuff with great energy and many members of the audience were hard pressed to retain their seats. In the beginning the curtains were trembling a little and then they swayed as they moved from each side of the stage. It was a momentary journey before they finally closed again in the centre. We were sorry not to hear and see more of Booterstown's presentation.

Another interval was announced and Paddy informed everyone that the last competitors were a group from Rathconrath in County Westmeath. It was another twenty minutes before he came back to the mic and this time he appealed for what he called 'a little bit of quietness' before he introduced the next group. Without further delay the curtain flew open again to the music of fiddles, accordions, whistles and a banjo. It was a fusillade of jigs with unified participation from everyone: hands clapping, bodies swaying, musicians giving it all they had; and then the dancers – a swarm of them came on and their dancing was in a wild and loose peasant style. Straw hats and straw dresses glittered in the light as six of them, with feet lifting and kicking and pounding the floor, glided around the stage – it was a mummers' dance. The theme of this presentation was 'The Harvest Is In'. A noted banjo player sat on a barrel and when the dancing was over he began playing a solo of two hornpipes. I had heard of him by reputation as 'The Whistling Postman'. While he played, some of the group members shouted their appreciation, 'Good Man, Billy!', 'Fair play to ya!', and a woman wearing a long dress was yelling loudly, 'Billy, Billy, I want to marry ya!' He looked as though he was struggling but as far as I could tell he never missed a note. A song followed Billy's solo, a song of lost love sung by a young lady who wore a purple shawl. When she finished there were a couple of seconds that hung in the air before massive applause engulfed the hall and I felt the floor vibrating under my feet.

When the audience simmered down I saw a box player move to another seat, a tiny little stool. He wore a cap and a narrow scarf around his neck. When he had settled himself on the stool he pulled two straps over his shoulders and with his legs crossed he began playing a reel called 'The Bag of Potatoes'. His playing was precise and had good lift to its rhythm. I noticed how he kept watching the bellows of his box as he played, and it gave me the idea of doing the same when I practised. He changed into a second reel, which was 'The

Swallow's Tail'; I thought it was a nice key change. This was followed by another thunderous round of applause for the box player, whose name was Frank Gavigan and who was also a past All-Ireland senior accordion champion from the early 1950s. Next came a solo dancer – she began walking from near the side stage entrance. Arriving in the middle of a circle of other performers she stood to attention as a fiddle played 'The Harvest Home'. After a short introduction she stepped forward and began a hard-shoe exhibition of the hornpipe. It was a no-nonsense hit-the-floor dance and the sound of her steel-tipped shoes tapped out each bar of the tune with distinct precision – each step a crisp heel-to-toe exercise that paraded the hornpipe with athletic grandeur. When she bowed to the audience the sound of applause allowed the fiddler to shift into a reel called 'The Wind that Shakes the Barley'. Playing with wild abandon and encouraged by the accompaniment of a spoons player, he shifted into another reel called 'Lord McDonald's', which was a signal for the other musicians to join him. In a matter of seconds eight country-style dancers came forward and began a social-style portrayal of a house dance. The audience began warming to the energy and brashness of the dancers, while they in turn were delivering shouts of glee and pleasure in response to the music. It seemed that everyone in the hall was clapping their hands or tapping their feet when the curtain started to move again, grudgingly at first, then closing slowly from each side, depriving us of a wonderful spectacle of revelry and gaiety. It was the end of the competition and the clock said it was almost midnight!

Fifteen minutes would pass before the three adjudicators walked up the steps leading to the stage. Everyone in the audience waited in silence as the first gentleman stepped forward to the microphone. He was a man in his early thirties and wore a light grey suit with a cherry red tie. When he spoke, his voice was clear and direct. I soon realised he was the one in charge of the music and his job was to give us an insight into how he rated each group of musicians or individual players. Much of what he said centred on specific tunes, how they were played or the effect of the music when played for dancing. He didn't have much hard criticism for any group or individual players, and if anything his remarks were very encouraging. When he totalled the number of points given to each contestant a difference of only one point separated us from the Bunclody group, who were now in first place.

I cannot continue without telling you that I later became familiar with this particular adjudicator who also adjudicated button accordion competitions. I remember his fair-minded remarks being of vital importance to young musicians who played in competitions at various Fleadh Cheoils. Very often his closing summations were insightful and very encouraging to many of us who were to compete again in the future. I'm writing now from my memory of Michael Hynes of Connemara, native Irish speaker, musician, and the last man to adjudicate my playing in a competition, the Oireachtas that took place in Gweedore, County Donegal during the autumn of 1976. It was also the last competition I took part in. Afterwards I met Michael Hynes in a hotel lobby and he said, 'Paddy, I've often heard you play better and I didn't give it to you.' His words rang true because even though I had won, I knew he was right.

The singing from each group could be classified as old style in the Irish and English language, otherwise referred to as *sean nós*. Our second adjudicator was well known for his own singing ability. I recognised him as Seamus Duffy of County Mayo, whom I've written about earlier. He spoke well of each individual singer with his usual enthusiasm and said it was difficult to pick a winner because all the competitors were excellent in their own right. Our two singers, Teresa Haugh and Peter Nolan, were given special mention with well-chosen words of admiration and respect. I thought I sensed an element of unease in his disposition because having to decide between each singer wasn't something that appealed to Seamus's sense of goodwill. He spoke highly of the young teenager who sang and played the harp with the Booterstown group and marvelled at her song in Irish. In mentioning the girl who sang for Rathconrath he praised her unique style, which reminded him of another great singer, Ann Mulqueen of Carrick-on-Suir. In fact he acknowledged everyone with comments of profound appreciation, but in the end he favoured Bunclody because their singer, Paddy Berry, gave an outstanding performance with his rendition of 'Ballyshannon Lane'. He referred to Mr Berry as having sensitive phrasing and solid delivery but failed to mention anything about his choice of song.

Group and solo dancing were included in the overall assessment of presentation and this was adjudicated by a third judge. As he began his remarks I noticed he was wearing a Roman collar, which meant he was a Catholic priest. He opened his remarks by saying how he was in awe of all our creativity and that he was rightfully amused at some of our inventiveness, which, he said, 'bordered on ingenuity'. He went down a list of each of us, praising various dances with equal acclaim and saying how impressed he was with Rathconrath's presentation and its theme. He had little to say of Booterstown's theme of 'The Session' and didn't make any comments regarding their Irish dialogue or that they were part of an Irish revivalist movement in Dublin. He went on to speak of our Banagher group. Again he was full of praise, except for what he claimed was one doubtful aspect of our presentation. He said that it was hardly possible to include a hen on stage and have her roost quietly on a wooden object for a whole half-hour of music, song and dance. He added that he'd have to deduct two points because he believed our little red hen was glued to her wooden roost for the duration of our programme. It was difficult to believe what he was saying – I was astonished! Some of the audience groaned and grumbled. We had been placed second by this imperious man of the cloth all because of his narrow-minded speculation. We had lost the competition and with it an opportunity to take part in the All-Ireland final. The Wexford group had won and Rathconrath's group were placed third. I went around to the back of the stage to retrieve my accordion and saw Tom and Seamus talking together. When I asked them what they thought of the outcome they looked at me like men who had been stung by a parade of wasps. Seamus began to speak but Tom beat him to it.

'It's hard to believe,' he said. 'It was stolen from us. We didn't lose it. It was stolen from us by a priest, a *priest* of all people. A thick-headed, ignorant jackass!' Tom was very upset, as were we all. Most members of our group collected together before travelling home. It was as if we all wanted an answer or an opinion, something that would clarify the reason why a priest could be such a downright cheat or moron. 'He's no moron,' said Tom Flynn, 'and I'll tell ye why. He's the producer of the Roscrea group that won the Munster Scóraíocht. If we won here tonight his group would have had to compete against us in the All-Ireland final.' When we heard this it added further fuel to our disappointment, which was already one of outrage and deep-seated anger. Before we departed, one of our people confronted the priest and spoke on behalf of many of us. 'Father,' he said, 'yer a very lucky man to be wearin' a collar.'

57

The First Pint

Mrs Doran tried to rouse me out of bed on Monday morning following our loss in the competition. Fifteen minutes later she again knocked on the door but I pretended to be asleep and she went away. After another fifteen minutes she was at the door again. 'J.J. Conroy's car is outside,' she shouted. 'He's waitin' for you. What will I tell him?' From out of the blankets I yelled, 'Tell him I'm sick.' After that I fell asleep.

It was almost noon when I woke and immediately washed and dressed. During lunch I told Mrs Doran about the competition and how the priest had deprived us of the laurels of victory. After she heard my story she rose from her chair, and before going upstairs said in a low voice, 'Those people have too much power.' Then she continued up the stairs. It was time for her early-afternoon nap.

After lunch I went back to my bedroom and tried out some ideas with my accordion, but after a couple of minutes I felt my urge for music had disappeared. Instead I put on my jacket and overcoat and went for a stroll along Charleville Parade. A short while later I stopped at the top of the town and for a minute I looked down the hill of High Street. I felt very alone and in a reflective mood. I was amused at the idea of so much traffic going downhill on one side while other traffic was driving uphill. Everyone was going about their business, perhaps repeating a routine of work-related duties. It occurred to me that our lives are so full of repetition that it squeezes aside much of our personal freedom and so, I wondered, what is the meaning of it all? It was a time in my life when I was beginning to ask questions and I craved at least a few answers. Meanwhile I continued my stroll down High Street and when I came to William Street I turned right at Hayes's Hotel. After walking another two hundred yards I found myself outside the door of Joe Lee's public house. Before entering

I felt a momentary sensation or nervous desire, followed by a kind of calm intent. One could say I was prompted by a careful sense of adventure. In other words I saw myself as a prime candidate for a pint of Guinness! In fact I might try two of them. Inside I saw at least a dozen customers sitting around the bar counter. I stood at the bar near the door before climbing onto one of Joe's new bar stools. I perched there for a while until I was finally spotted by a young bartender. Five minutes later a pint was pushed in front of me. It looked like a good one, fresh and nicely settled, and for me it was my first pint and the beginning of my drinking career. I pushed a pound note in front of the bartender and when he returned with my change I enquired of him if Joe was around.

'He's upstairs,' he replied, 'let me give him a buzz on the "whispering wires".'

Within minutes Joe came down from his apartment above the bar. He was a fellow who stood six feet tall, with black hair combed backwards. There was an aristocratic pallor and shape to his face that made him look younger than his twenty-six years. Like me he played a B/C Paolo Soprani accordion and was totally immersed in the sound of various styles of box players, the music they played and where they came from. Joe inherited the bar from his old uncle John and immediately set about remodelling its interior. With creative taste and design the result was an upgraded lounge bar on one side, with a new general bar area on the opposite side. The seating accommodation of both areas was cosy and comfortable, with the lounge bar especially suitable for women who relished a quiet getaway from the bustle of home. Joe had invited me to 'come down' to his bar shortly after he opened it for business in 1963. At that time I was extremely shy of being seen carrying my accordion in the town and I suppose I was overly self-conscious as a country lad who was also socially backward. Now, four years later, I'm sitting on a bar stool and I'm reaching for my first pint of Guinness.

I lifted it and swallowed deeply, enjoying its satisfying flavour and its coolness. I had broken the ice. I became a frequent customer at Joe's and we soon became good friends. Our conversation was initially one of questions and answers in relation to the music. Joe was very up-to-date about new musicians and at that time had bought an assortment of accordions. Often he would have one or two nearby and if the bar wasn't busy he would play one for a while before letting me have a go, or as he said, 'try it out'. Then after I played a bit he would ask me what I thought of the instrument – a second opinion would help him reconsider what he already knew. Unfortunately having little experience of accordions other than my own I could offer him little more than to say, 'It's a nice one,' or 'It has a nice tone.'

In the meantime my drinking experience with the pint had gone well and later when I went to the 'men's' I found myself steady and clear-headed. Satisfaction might be a better word to describe my feeling. When I returned to the high stool I finished the pint and ordered a second one. When it came I waited a short while before putting it to my mouth. God, it was even better than the first! I drank it slowly, which was the way most elderly men were drinking in those days, nice and easy, and relaxed. I was finished in a little under an hour. The bar was beginning to fill up with men who had finished their day's work. It was time for me to leave the premises and so I said, 'See you later,' to Joe, who was adjusting his TV.

Outside I began walking back towards Hayes's Hotel. The afternoon had been grey and dismal a couple of hours earlier but now the sun had emerged, making tall shadows along the sidewalk as I made my way up the hill on High Street.

The next morning I was up and about early and just as I finished breakfast I saw, through the front window, J.J. Conroy's car pulling up outside. I was astonished and said, 'I don't believe it!' to the other lads at the table. When I got into the car I was expecting a slagging from everyone on account of losing the competition and taking Monday off from work. But it was not so. In fact J.J. was in a conciliatory mood, saying he had heard about how well we did. He had also heard about the episode with the priest and the hen. Gerry Ryan added that the 'said adjudicator was a low-down fuck of a human being'.

'What could you expect from a Tipperary man?' J.J. replied, a dig at the priest but also at Gerry's home county.

'He's not from Tipperary,' said Gerry, 'he's from Kilkenny.' Peter Hogan sided with J.J. and told Gerry he was betraying Tipperary by crossing into the 'Norman' county, where the cats ate the weasels. It was the beginning of a rough and tumble argument that lasted all the way to Boora workshop.

We all clocked in a minute or two early instead of our usual five or ten minutes late. Paddy Healy stood near the doorway and seeing us he made the sign of the cross. And when I got to the Gearbox

Department Éamon Fleming led a chorus of applause, ten clapping hands from a small impromptu welcoming committee – Éamon, John Flynn, Hughie Ryan, Christie Buckley and Larry Kirwan. I hadn't expected such a sympathetic welcome from any of my workmates, and it was a good feeling. Later, while I was filing the splines of a drive shaft, Éamon drew my attention to the store hatch. 'Look,' he said, 'it's Tom Nolan. When you get a chance would you go over and tell him I know where he could find a good poultry instructor? Tell him that.' This was an example of Éamon's subtle way of teasing someone and the effect of it would soon be evident.

When I ambled over to Tom he had returned from the store and was busy fine-grinding an engine valve. 'How's it goin'?' I said. When he saw me he said nothing. I suppose he wasn't in a sociable mood but nevertheless I relayed the message from Éamon.

Tom stopped for a second and stared at me as though he was seeing me for the first time. Then came his reaction, which was a calculated reply with a devious twist of his lips that passed for a grin. He said, 'Tell Fleming that you and him should be tied to a bull's tail and scuttered to death!' I said nothing and when I returned to the workbench Éamon was still busy fitting the drive shaft that I had worked on earlier.

'Any news from Tom?' he asked, so I told him of Tom's reply. Éamon didn't react at first, nor did he bat an eyelid. He carried on with his work but I thought I heard a slight whinnying sound, similar to a foal finding its mother's tit. It was a typical Éamon Fleming grunt of satisfaction followed by a fraction of a subdued giggle. Without betraying anything I looked over at Tom in the distance and saw him staring at the two of us, watching and waiting for a reaction. However, Éamon kept his eyes on his work and showed no response to Tom's remark. As for Tom, I imagine it was a case of having to go back to the drawing board. I've told this story because it is one of those cat-and-mouse games of teasing humour that was part of life in Boora workshop in the 1960s. Much of it inspired my own sense of humour during my teenage years when I marvelled at the notion of adults matching wits with each other.

After being knocked out of the Scóraíocht competition the music with Tom and Seamus became a rarity. We didn't have anything to play or practise for. In my bedroom at Mrs Doran's I continued to practise nearly every evening and I also taped lots of new music from Ciarán

MacMathúna's radio programme. This helped me to build up my repertoire and develop my listening ability so I could define and interpret the music for future reference. All of this became a great learning experience at a time when I began to notice particular keys associated with Irish traditional music. The novelty and freshness of the music continued to be a powerful stimulant that sometimes transported me in my imagination to dimly lit pubs where veteran musicians sat and played, or enjoyed swapping stories with each other.

In Boora I was settling into my work routine with a better sense of commitment, and as I moved on in my apprenticeship I was expected to assume extra responsibilities. This was an incentive in itself and led to various work projects that I could handle by myself. One day while I was riveting and assembling aluminium cabs for housing harvester operators, a voice spoke from behind me. 'What are you doin'?' It was Tom.

'I've just finished rivetin' and I was about to stand back and admire it,' I replied.

Tom smiled. 'I was talkin' to Dan Cleary. He's lookin' for an accordion player for the band. Would you be interested?'

At first I didn't know what to say but then on impulse I told him, 'Yeah!'

'Well,' said Tom, 'if that's the case you can join the band on Friday night, they're playin' at a céilí in Rahan Hall – I'll tell Dan and they can pick you up outside Mrs Doran's.'

Before I said anything further, Tom was on his way, leaving me slightly confused but excited. Being asked to join the Ballinamere Céilí Band was a great honour, considering its reputation around Ireland. The band had done numerous radio broadcasts, recorded several records and played at céilís from Dublin to Cork, from Connemara to Ballisodare in Sligo, and just about every major town in the midlands.

I continued on with the riveting job even though my head was racing with thoughts of how I'd fit in with members of the band and concerns about my ability as a musician. I should have asked Tom for some time to think about it or maybe I didn't hear him when he said, 'Let me know later on.'

The next day Tom was again walking by on his way to the store hatch when he stopped at where I was working. 'Do you still want to play with the band on Friday night?' he asked. I quickly said yeah. My mind was made up!

58

The First Céilí

At seven o'clock on Friday evening a minivan pulled up in front of Mrs Doran's; it was the transport hired by the band. I was ready and within minutes I was in the back seat waiting for the driver, who had gone to a nearby shop for cigarettes. There was another man in the front seat whose name was Peter Kilroe. I had never met him before so when the driver returned he said, 'This is Peter.' I assumed it was the same man who was a founding member of the band. Then the driver lit his cigarette and said, 'Are yez right, lads?' And we were on our way.

After twenty minutes we arrived at Dan Cleary's house in Ballinamere. Dan had heard the sound of the van as we approached and was already carrying a small sound board from his doorway when we pulled over. Peter and the driver helped Dan with the sound equipment and had it loaded into the back of the van within minutes. After a few words with Dan the driver sat in again and so we began the seven miles to the village of Rahan. However, Dan didn't travel with us and this was a huge disappointment for me. Later on I heard that he thought I might be nervous and he wanted to ease me into the band without undue pressure. It was his way of allowing me to relax as much as possible on my first outing. It would also help me get a sense of how the band presented their selections and how they worked with each other.

The other band members were already in the hall when we arrived and one fellow was busy setting up chairs on stage while another was testing his bass fiddle, pulling on its thick gut strings, their sound vibrating around the small hall.

I was standing near the stage when one fellow walked up to me and in a conciliatory tone said, 'How are ya doin'? I'm Mick Lynam.' I was about to say something when he continued, 'You're very welcome,

we haven't had a second box player in ages.' Then he said I shouldn't
worry if the band played anything I didn't know and that I should sit
in and enjoy myself. Mick played a three-row Shan Marino accordion
and was a very good musician, a man of twenty-eight years and of
calm personality, and his words were very reassuring and encouraging to me.

The task of unloading the gear from the van was made easy with
all of us helping out. One by one each piece of equipment was carried
inside and assembled on stage. We clipped four microphones onto
small brackets on top of four stands and each mic was plugged into a
sound board by means of four single cords. Other cords were plugged
into speakers and monitors and one larger cord came from the sound
board and was linked to an extension cord that was plugged into an
output at the back wall of the stage. Chairs were placed in front of three
mic stands for two accordions and flute/sax, while Seán Monaghan
and Seán Conlon preferred to stand behind as they played banjo and
bass fiddle. We spent a few minutes tuning our instruments before
Mick Lynam led off with a selection of jigs that I thankfully was able
to play. I remember the satisfaction of playing this first selection and
the sensation of remembering the tune changes into the second and
third jig. It was a great pick-me-up and so I wanted more of it!

About this time I noticed that people were trickling into the hall
and very soon we began playing in earnest. Mick told me the band
were going to try some waltzes. Some of these I didn't know, still I
was glad the music had the effect of encouraging a few couples onto
the floor. However, it was still early and a lot of people were yet to
arrive, which meant we had a chance to play some reel and jig selections along with a few waltzes.

It was almost ten o'clock before we could rely on enough people
for Mick to announce the next dance as the 'The Haymakers' Jig'. In
the meantime the hall was beginning to fill with young girls and fellows and a number of older couples of veteran dancing skills. Most
of the fellows were wearing their Sunday suits or a variety of casual
attire, while the ladies wore dresses or skirts with blouses. Very few
were wearing slacks or jeans, a fashion that hadn't caught on in country areas at that time. Finally, Mick spoke into the mic again. 'For
your very next dance, ladies and gentlemen, please take the floor for
"The Haymakers' Jig".' Four lines of dancers were already waiting,
one line facing the other, and then we began with what was to be

a long selection of jigs. The dance lasted at least ten minutes before Mick exchanged glances with the rest of us; it was time to stop! I had played some of the tunes and had had a fine time listening to others that I later had Mick record on tape for me.

After a short break we began again with a slow waltz, giving people time to catch their breaths before playing again for another céilí dance. Mick led the band with a round of waltzes that brought almost everyone to the floor. It was a reassuring scene and it had the effect of prompting Seán Monaghan to break into his version of 'The Wild Rover', a popular song of that time. When the dance concluded I saw Mick pull a handkerchief from his pocket and wipe his forehead. After a small break he leaned forward to the mic; it was time to introduce 'The Siege of Athlone'. The reaction was immediate, with a fresh flock of dancers skipping onto the floor with an eager dash, reminding me of racehorses released from a starting gate. And then almost as one they were hopping back and forth, united within the rhythm of the tunes. From where I sat I noticed some individuals whose style of dancing was either awkward, graceful or just plain funny. One fellow who caught my attention was a small man of fiftyish who was very lively on his feet but appeared to be impatient with other dancers, especially when we played 'The Waves of Tory' or 'The Haymakers' Jig'. He had a habit of nudging or pushing people as a reminder when their turn came for connecting with their partners. Waltzes were of little interest to him; at least I didn't see him on the floor at any time during our waltz selections.

At half past eleven we divided our band in two for a tea break and short rest. Seán Monaghan and I went down the side stairs of the stage and walked along the side of the hall until we came to a brown door that was a kitchen entrance. Inside, the tea was already poured, and waiting for us were two elderly women who were making ham, cheese and egg sandwiches. Sitting at a table we milked and sugared our tea and then waded into the sandwiches. The women enquired many times if the tea was all right and Seán, being very polite, was quick to settle any concerns. In contrast, I could only manage a mere 'thank you'. After a short while, as we were on our way back to the stage we were approached by the little dancer, who appeared out of nowhere and had probably waited for us to emerge from the kitchen. 'Excuse me, lads,' he said, 'I wonder if you would mind playin' "The Stack of Barley"?'

Seán looked at him without a blink and said, 'I've never heard of it.'

The little fellow was astonished. 'I can't believe you don't know "The Stack of Barley". It's played at céilís everywhere!'

'Not by us,' said a straight-faced Seán, who began walking away. I followed him to the stage and as I sat on my chair I looked towards the floor and saw the little man standing there. He hadn't moved and was watching us with a very curious expression on his face.

When the other band members went on their tea break Seán and I played a couple of waltz selections. By this time the floor was packed with couples, many of them having arrived after the pubs had closed. I could see the little dancer sitting alone on a seat beside the wall. Seán also saw him and when we finished the waltz selection he leaned down and said to me, 'Do you know "The Stack of Barley"?'

'Yeah, I do.'

'Good, let's play it now.'

'But,' I said, 'I thought you didn't know it.'

'Ah I was just teasing the little fella, I wanted to see how he'd react.' The two of us then launched into the tune and this time I saw the little man standing, looking in our direction. All of a sudden he made the sign of the cross before he turned around. It looked like he had blessed us. And so without further ado he began skipping lightly along the side of the floor, a routine of his or perhaps a prelude before finding a partner. It turned out he had already spotted her among a group of other girls near the end of the hall and with a small diddle of a dance he took her hand and she followed him to the middle of the floor. As we played on I was amazed to see an exhibition of dancing perfection, the pair moving as one within the confined rhythm of the music. It was an exhibition of body and spirit and it seemed as if they were oblivious to everyone in the hall. We played the 'Stack' over and over several times until I began to tire, but the couple were having such a great time I persevered. When we finally finished the tune I noticed they were the last pair to leave the floor and before sitting down the little fellow turned towards us again and bowed very low and when he stood up he gave us a military style salute. I turned around on my seat and saw Seán laughing and he too was making military salutes, returning the compliment to the little man and his woman.

Shortly afterwards I saw them leave their seats and walk together slowly towards the exit door. In the meantime our other band members had returned from their tea break and after Mick had strapped on his accordion he announced another 'Haymakers' Jig'. As usual, we played the first part of the first jig once over as an introduction, then stopped and waited for everyone to line up for the dance. While we waited I happened to notice our dancing couple just inside the door, where they were helping each other find the sleeves of their overcoats. After the short pause we began playing the first jig again and when we changed into the second tune I looked towards the door once more but saw no sign of the little man and his woman; they had disappeared into the night. I remember that I felt disappointed or a small sense of loss, as though they were old friends I'd never see again. I never found out who they were or what their names were, on that night when I played at my first céilí with the Ballinamere Céilí Band.

I played with the band for two years. It was two years of music, band practices, céilís far and near, the formation of friendships, the purchasing of a new sound system, and wonderful encouraging support from my fellow box player Mick Lynam.

The second céilí we played was in a bigger hall in the town of Ballyfarnan in south County Roscommon. Dan Cleary was with us on that occasion and as we all played together the sound of his fiddle gave our music a better sense of balance and tone. Dan sat on my right-hand side, which was where he preferred to be, with Mick sitting on my left. Peter Kilroe sat on Dan's right and the two Seáns stood behind us, which meant that we were six as a group. The céilí in Ballyfarnan was a rousing success and appeared to attract a lot of interest in the area. There was extra demand for reel selections from local set-dancing groups who wanted as much céilí dancing as possible. It was a hectic night! In between each dance we played a waltz selection that brought us a welcome relief. About halfway through the dance we were told that tea was ready. This was a break that I always looked forward to; it would refresh us and restore our energy. The céilí ended at one o'clock after we played our national anthem; it was the usual way we ended a night's entertainment. Meanwhile we still had to disassemble our sound equipment and load it into the van and then drive back to Ballinamere where we unloaded the equipment once again. By the time the van delivered me to Mrs Doran's I was dog tired. It was almost 4 a.m. when I hit the sack. Getting up in the morning after only three hours' sleep didn't appeal to my sense of justice and before I fell asleep I toyed with the notion of taking the next day off.

As a céilí band we were in pretty decent demand, sometimes playing at céilís almost every week, or sometimes two or three times a week. We were also meeting at Dan's house for practice sessions as often as possible and I would also visit Dan's on occasions outside the regular practice times for more music making. Dan was always ready for playing and was also a multi-instrumentalist, proficient at the uilleann pipes, whistle, piano accordion, piano, bass fiddle, etc. His interest in the music was based on a profound belief that Irish traditional music was a special kind of art form that should be fostered and taught to younger people in schools and colleges. I found him to be very sincere and considerate, a soft-spoken man of great humility and a man whose fiddle music was of a jolly nature. I always felt when hearing him play that his music was a very happy music, with uplifting rhythm and lovely sense of melody. His appetite for playing and learning new tunes inspired me greatly, and after several months we had developed a substantial repertoire of jigs and reels that we played in our spare time.

59

A Surprise Result

After my apprenticeship was completed I continued working in Boora workshop for another two and a half years. During the same time I was experiencing some extreme difficulty with low energy that caused me to miss numerous days at work. (It was a very troublesome problem that plagued me for many years until it was diagnosed during a doctor's visit in Minnesota in 1994. It turned out to be a rare heart condition referred to as HCM or hypertrophic cardiomyopathy.) In the meantime I carried on in competition with the Banagher Comhaltas group, and the same year, 1967, Tom, Seamus and I entered our names for the senior trio competition at the Offaly County Fleadh held in Banagher.

It was on a Saturday afternoon in May that we met in Hough's pub where we did a practice session for about forty minutes. The competition was scheduled for 3 p.m., which gave us enough time to pack our instruments and walk across the street to the town hall. As we made our way along the footpath the first drops of rain began falling and would later develop into a lingering drizzle throughout the rest of the weekend. The sky was dark and overcast as we entered the hall.

As competitions go it was a long-drawn-out process with eleven trios competing. Our participation may have been regarded as a little odd given the fact that our instrumental makeup of uilleann pipes, tenor banjo and two-row button accordion was an unusual combination as a trio. It was a couple of hours before the final trio finished the last of four tunes that were allocated for each act. Soon after, an old adjudicator came onto the stage and gave a summation of the various performances. He began by thanking everyone for what he called a fine exhibition of musicianship and added that he regretted having to single out winners or losers. 'There are no losers here today,' he said, 'because you are all winners in your own right.' However, he said that he must comply with what he was asked to do as an adjudicator. And so he went on to briefly mention the strengths and weaknesses of each trio. We were surprised by what he had to say about our performance. 'This combination of uilleann pipes, banjo and accordion,' he said, 'is not something one hears every day.' He continued that we were well balanced and well rehearsed, but that the highlight was how well we played the slow air. 'Now,' he said, 'a slow air is a delicate thing to play for one or for two musicians playing together, but today it was accomplished by – my goodness! – three musicians playing as one!' His voice lifted a little when he shouted to the audience, 'A brave endeavour! Indeed a very brave endeavour! When all is said and done,' he concluded, 'I've no hesitation in awarding these three fellows first place in the competition.' We had won!

And yet somehow we were a little bewildered, as most musicians are after winning at a Fleadh Cheoil competition. As a matter of fact we were almost stuck for words – except for Seamus. 'Lads,' he said, 'maybe we're better than we thought or maybe we were just lucky.'

After supper we met again in Hough's pub. This gave us enough time for a short rehearsal that lasted much longer when a few of our group arrived late. The first to join us were fiddlers Mickey Doorley and Cyl Donlon. Then came Teresa Hough, who began accompanying us on the piano. Its rousing rhythm was refreshing and seemed to galvanise us together and as we played our first selection our two flute players came through the door. While they made their way among us Joe Cashin found a stool and handed it to Johnny Coughlan who was behind him. An empty chair was waiting for Joe, who when seated began blowing into his flute while Johnny was busy assembling his. I could smell a strong odour of soup and porter coming from both of them, especially when they began playing. Looking across the way I saw that Tom was squeezing his mouth as though he was trying to push his lips upward in an attempt at shielding his nostrils from the smell. A tittering fever came over me and I lost my way in the tune and so we all stopped playing. Then someone mentioned another selection, but before we began, Cashin issued a mild warning. 'No fuck-ups this time.' He never knew that he had indirectly caused us to lose our concentration. It was after we had played for nearly an hour that one of us noticed the time – it was almost eight o'clock! We put away our instruments quickly and headed down the street to the hall. When we got there the sound equipment was already set up, and within minutes we found some chairs and positioned ourselves on the stage. The céilí was a typical Fleadh Cheoil céilí with lots of people and a great variety of dances inspired by several dancing groups from Birr and other parts of Offaly, Galway and north Tipperary. I was so preoccupied with the music and watching the obvious enjoyment of the dancers that when a short break was announced I hardly believed we had played for a little over an hour. Even though my appetite for playing was insatiable, I relished some time out from playing, and leaving the stage I walked down into the hall for a short stroll. I hadn't gone far when I heard a voice shouting from behind – it was Johnny MacNamara, who was walking towards me. He had a wide grin on his face. 'Not a bad céilí.'

John was a box player from Dublin whom I knew from meeting him at music sessions during other Fleadh Cheoil events. We had become friends and shared an interest in the older styles of traditional music, especially the music from County Clare. 'Not a bad turnout either,' he said, before reminding me to turn up the sound system.

'It's turned up as far as we can get it,' I replied, and I was about to explain more when he turned aside and shouted, 'Hello Tommy, Tommy, com'ere!'

The fellow he was shouting at turned and began walking towards us. As he came closer he looked like a well-built eighteen-year-old with dark eyes peering from under a grey tweed cap. He also wore a grey tweed jacket, pink shirt and black pants. Johnny was clearly excited and said to me, 'This is Tommy Peoples – he's the young Donegal fiddler I was telling you about.'

Tommy appeared slightly irritated at having to ask me who I was and when I told him he said, 'Yer playin' here at the dance?'

I said I was, and asked him if he'd like to play with us for a while. 'I would, he said, 'except I don't have the fiddle with me.' It was the first time I met Tommy, and little did I know that we would play many a tune together in the not-too-distant future. The end of the céilí capped off the closing hours of the Fleadh. I suppose the Fleadh was officially over when the last of its revellers were herded out of the pubs onto the streets. Some diehard musicians tried to extend their love of session playing on the sidewalks; there were box players sitting on window sills, while fiddlers, bodhrán players and others were content with playing standing up. However, after half an hour of session fever they were grossly interrupted and forced to abandon their merry-making when a nagging drizzle of rain became a serious downpour.

60

The Drimnagh Session

Some months earlier I had visited Dublin to meet with a group of musicians for what turned out to be a memorable music session. The session was held at Johnny MacNamara's home in Drimnagh and when he wrote telling me who he expected to be there I didn't need any persuading. With his promise of great music plus a chance to hear other musicians I had no problem in answering John's letter with one of my own that ended with: 'I'm really looking forward to it.'

He had also written of another enticement that got my attention, which was James Keane's name and a promise that he would also be at the session. James was an exceptional box player who played with the famous Castle Céilí Band along with his brother Seán, who played the fiddle. I was familiar with James's playing and had often heard him on the radio with piano accompanist Bridie Lafferty, who was also expected to be at the session. As luck would have it I had just bought my first car, an old Ford Anglia that was in good condition and sold to me by my friend J.J. Conroy. But I had never driven to Dublin and the prospect of how I'd navigate the journey daunted me a little.

Armed with a small map and a few written directions from Johnny, I set out for the capital late on Saturday afternoon. On the first leg of the journey I drove to Edenderry and straight on to Prosperous and then somehow as I travelled southwards I found the Naas Road. Turning left I drove eastwards until I came to what was then known as 'the dual carriageway'. This was a drive of seventeen miles until I came to the Long Mile Road where I proceeded to drive southeast. There wasn't a lot of traffic in those days and at the end of the Long Mile I stopped at the first traffic lights. It was 6.30 p.m. I was early. When the lights turned green I made a left into Drimnagh and with a couple more turns I was at Johnny's house.

Within a minute I was knocking at his door. It was opened by Johnny's father, and when I told him who I was he took his pipe out of his mouth and said, 'Yer as welcome as the flowers of May.' Inside I was introduced to Johnny's sister Marie and his mother, who was drying her hands before she took my hand and shook it. She and her daughter had just finished making sandwiches in preparation for the evening's entertainment. After shaking hands with everyone I was invited into the sitting room and Marie asked me if I'd like a cup of tea. It was exactly what I craved and I told her she was a gifted mind-reader. She giggled shyly and turned away in the direction of the kitchen.

After I had some tea and sandwiches we sat and talked for a while until the doorbell rang. The door was already left open and this allowed Johnny's dad to yell a hearty, 'Come on in.' When they heard his voice they came inside, one by one. There were at least a dozen young musicians, who politely introduced themselves and eventually found some chairs in the living room. A few minutes later came a young County Cavan fiddle player who was introduced to me as Tony Smith. When everyone was seated, Johnny lifted his voice and said that tea would be along in a while, but in the meantime everyone was busy tuning their instruments.

When they started to play, it was a wonderful sound of flutes, whistles and Tony's fiddle – and Jesus, they were playing tunes I didn't know. I was in heaven! One of the first tunes that caught my attention was a jig called 'The Exile's Return'. I remember how the fiddle joined in as the tune progressed. Then Johnny lifted his box and began fingering and squeezing and playing along – my God, he also knew it! The effect was instantaneous as everyone united in music that filled the room with what I felt was the most melodic tune I had ever heard. I wasn't sure what was happening when some of the musicians began dropping out of the jig, but my instinct told me it was being tapered to a finish. But not so – a lone whistler beckoned the jig forward with her lovely lonesome solo. As she continued, the room was magnified by another instrument that suddenly gave the tune another meaning. It was the accompaniment of a set of bones played by a young fellow who was sitting on the floor. As he played he was swaying his head from side to side and with his eyes closed he was clicking two short rib bones together in his right hand. I also saw that he was twisting and flexing his wrists while he moved his arm up and down to the rhythm of the music. I had never heard anything like it. There was something primitive in the essence of its sound and I was almost hypnotised by its tempo and beat. I wondered how he was producing such a neat clicking rhythm and the fact that he never missed a beat was amazing. It played games with my imagination and I found myself wandering amid the depths of a huge rainforest in South America. And then the playing stopped very abruptly along with the last beat of the bones. There was a finality to it that was exciting, adventurous and even mesmerising. What vision or imagination was responsible for its conception was a thought that became a question. I would have to ask someone. 'We learned it from a recording of Seán Ó Riada and Ceoltóirí Chualann,' replied Tony Smith, when I asked him where they got the tune and the idea of using bones for accompaniment.

Another musician, who played whistle and flute, was Mick Allen, a friendly young man who seemed to have an insatiable appetite for playing and appeared exceptionally confident and contented. He was indecisive about which instrument he wanted to use during the next round of tunes, but finally settled on the flute. The session was heating up with everyone playing except myself, for even though I had my accordion ready, the tunes were unknown to me. Nevertheless, I was satisfied and got a great charge out of hearing many new jigs and reels, and the fact that Johnny was taping the entire session was an added bonus because I knew he'd make a copy for me later.

After playing for what seemed like an hour we were pleasantly surprised when Bridie Lafferty walked into the room, and everyone stopped playing. Her presence was a great boost to everyone and we immediately felt drawn to her personality and sense of humour. She had a wonderful, gutsy laugh that usually became a nagging cough due to a problem with emphysema. She took a seat near the piano and began rummaging through her handbag until she found a packet of cigarettes. She was wearing dark glasses and a costume of a light beige colour that was tastefully set off with two pearl necklaces. She was a very polite sort of woman and when she said, 'Keep playin',' and 'Don't fuss over me,' her Dublin accent had a warmth and kindness that suggested hospitality and friendship. After lighting her cigarette she again reached into her handbag and brought forth a tiny bottle of Babycham. Then she reached again into her handbag and retrieved a small glass and began pouring. Before she drank she lifted her glass, and raising it she wished us all good health before taking a sip. Johnny asked her about playing and in a gentle show of respect he ushered her to a seat in front of the piano, but before she sat she asked someone to pass her an ashtray. Then she lit another cigarette and chuckled a little. 'God, ye're all so patient and quiet, I could have sworn I heard a cricket in the grate.' Somebody shouted about playing 'The Dublin Reel' and Bridie turned towards the piano and tapped out two chords and the music erupted once more. Bridie's accompaniment and the combined sound of all the other musicians had the effect of engulfing our surroundings and this in turn was taking us on a musical hayride as reel after reel hit the walls of the little room. During a break for tea John introduced me to several young ladies whom he mentioned as the 'Booterstown crowd'. These were the Bergin sisters, Martha, Mary and Antoinette. I would guess that Antoinette was perhaps fourteen and she was already adept at playing the harp. Her two sisters were playing whistles, and Mary also played a concert flute that she switched with the whistle from time to time, depending on the choice of tune. Another talented girl who sat beside me was Proinsias Ní Dhorchaigh, her instrument being the wooden flute. During a quieter moment she played a reel that she had composed; it was, as she later said, her first effort at composing. I was drawn to her tune and I wanted to know it but somehow it wasn't recorded on John's reel-to-reel.

All of these young girls and their companions were a great inspiration to me. Their enthusiasm and uncanny taste for old west Clare tunes was delightful and a valuable introduction to my own sense of what gave Irish traditional music its true nature and value. Nowadays I remember that particular night at Johnny MacNamara's home as perhaps a turning point in my life and one that would lead me to become more involved with the music.

Over the next couple of years I drove to various Fleadh Cheoil events and met the Booterstown crowd at several street sessions. Whenever we played together I was struck by their humility and encouragement, especially if I played something they hadn't heard before. They brought real musical spirit to these occasions and I have always remembered them for it.

As their playing continued I was hearing more and more of what I felt was a feast of new tunes, many of them from recordings of Seán Ó Riada's Ceoltóirí Chualann or from radio broadcasts of the great Castle Céilí Band from Dublin with whom Bridie played piano accompaniment. It was almost midnight when a very tall young man walked casually into the room; it was the box player James Keane. James wasted little time in taking out his nine-coupler Paolo Soprani accordion. He had been playing earlier in the evening at Mick McCarthy's pub, The Embankment in Tallaght, after which he drove, Fangio-style, a distance of nine miles to the session. When he began playing I was dazzled by the power and energy of his music. His natural ability and fingering prowess was obvious and he had an abundance of reels that not everyone knew, but also had enough for the rest of us to chime in. Then I remembered that Johnny said he was taping the whole session and that he'd make a copy of the tapes for me. With this in mind, I can't thank Johnny MacNamara enough for all his help and generosity.

The Drimnagh session was the first music session I attended outside Offaly and the first one I played at in Dublin. The experience is one I still cherish because it introduced me to the Dublin music scene with its many young musicians of my own age. It probably inspired my thinking of moving to the city, but that was a matter of when and how because as fate would have it I didn't reach a decision until a couple of years later.

The following morning I said goodbye to the MacNamara family after they treated me to a breakfast of tea, bacon, sausage, eggs and brown bread. I found my way out of Drimnagh and drove west on the Long Mile Road and settled into a ninety-minute journey to Tullamore. It was a bright Sunday afternoon as I continued along the Naas Road. I could still hear a mixture of sounds from the night before and a surge of mixed emotions came and went as I courted my memory of 'The Exile's Jig'.

Finally I arrived in Tullamore, drove west to Church Street and parked my car alongside the towpath. Just across the street was Joe Lee's pub where I intended to have a couple of pints of Celebration beer. It was a new brand of beer that I'd grown fond of and I had plenty of time to have a few before driving to Mrs Doran's for a quiet supper. That was during the autumn of 1967.

Meanwhile I continued working in Boora for another two and a half years, during which time I played dozens of céilís with Dan Cleary, Peter Kilroe and the other members of the Ballinamere Céilí Band. Some of our bookings involved long hours of travel that brought us

to County Cork, Connemara, Sligo, Roscommon, Tipperary and the
Irish Club in Parnell Square in Dublin.

I played with the Banagher Scóraíocht group for one more competition, which we won. As always, the experience of playing with
other musicians was a challenge because of having to figure out the
extent of their repertoires so we could build together a separate group
repertoire. Another important consideration of a more delicate nature
involved the inclusion of particular tunes that would accommodate
Tom's uilleann pipes. My memories of the competitions are full of
victories and defeats but they were always a good experience for me
during my younger years. There were also a few disappointments
from a few mean-spirited individuals from within our group. This
was another learning experience that helped me understand that neg-
ativity comes in many guises and that it's always at the expense of
something. In our case it was the music and the joy that came with it.
In the beginning it was a social message that I was slow to learn, in
part because of my addiction to the music and my complete trust in
all of my companions.

I still remember myself as a young teenage apprentice fitter in
Boora workshop and the many co-workers whose kind consideration
was of enormous help to me.

And then there are those musicians, especially Tom and Seamus,
who taught me many of the old jigs and reels that were the foundation of my repertoire, and many other players in Offaly whose
friendship and music motivated my own humble efforts. I've cher-
ished the memory of them all and have never forgotten the great
times we shared.